PEACE
AND
DISARMAMENT

PEACE

AND

DISARMAMENT

Naval Rivalry & Arms Control
1922–1933

RICHARD W. FANNING

THE UNIVERSITY PRESS OF KENTUCKY

Copyright © 1995 by The University Press of Kentucky

Scholarly publisher for the Commonwealth,
serving Bellarmine College, Berea College, Centre
College of Kentucky, Eastern Kentucky University,
The Filson Club, Georgetown College, Kentucky
Historical Society, Kentucky State University,
Morehead State University, Murray State University,
Northern Kentucky University, Transylvania University,
University of Kentucky, University of Louisville,
and Western Kentucky University.

Editorial and Sales Offices: Lexington, Kentucky 40508-4008

Library of Congress Cataloging-in-Publication Data

Fanning, Richard W.
    Peace and disarmament : naval rivalry and arms control, 1922-1933
/ Richard W. Fanning.
        p.   cm.
    Includes bibiographical references and index.
    ISBN 0-8131-1878-6 (acid-free paper) :
    1. Arms control—History. 2. Navies—History. 3. Sea-power—
History. I. Title.
JX1974.F29   1994
327.1′74—dc20   94-18444

To Sue

CONTENTS

Illustrations follow page 82

ACKNOWLEDGMENTS

I am indebted to Indiana University, Western Washington University, the Herbert Hoover Presidential Library, and the National Endowment for the Humanities for providing financial support for this study

I am also beholden to the librarians and archivists at Indiana University, Bloomington; the University of Washington, Seattle; Northwestern University; Haverford College; the Swarthmore College Peace Collection; The Manuscript Division of the Library of Congress; the Military and Diplomatic Sections of the National Archives; the Naval Historical Center at the Washington Navy Yard (especially the director of the Operational Archives, Dean Allard); the Herbert Hoover Presidential Library (especially Dwight Miller and Shirley Sondergaard); the Hoover Institution on War, Revolution, and Peace at Stanford University; the Public Record Office in London; and the British Library.

Praeger Publishers generously granted me permission to quote from a previous article of mine: "The Coolidge Conference of 1927: Disarmament in Dissarray," in B.J.C. McKercher, ed., *Arms Limitation and Disarmament: Restraints on War, 1899-1939* (1992).

Special thanks also go to John C. Reilly, Jr., of the Ships' History Division of the Naval Historical Center, Thomas C. Hone, and Marc Epstein for taking the time to discuss my work and make useful suggestions. Brian McKercher kindly permitted me to read manuscript chapters from his study on Esme Howard and shared his wide knowledge of interwar politics. David M. Pletcher and John Lovell read early drafts of this manuscript and offered insightful comments. Robert H. Ferrell encouraged me to undertake this study, read countless drafts, and offered penetrating criticism. I always marvel at his energy, knowledge, and commitment to the profession. For this and his continuing guidance and support, I give him many thanks.

I am most grateful to my family for their love, support, and good humor during this project, especially my wife, Suzanne Raymond.

INTRODUCTION

This study is a history of American naval arms control following the Washington Naval Conference of 1921-22. It describes the efforts of American leaders—political, military, and social—as well as those of their contemporaries in the two other postwar great naval powers, Britain and Japan, to come to agreement on naval limitation between 1922 and the mid-1930s. I particularly focus on the years 1927-30, a time when political leaders, statesmen, naval officers, and various civilian pressure groups in the major naval powers considered developing new limits on their navies. Americans were particularly interested in naval arms limitation after the signing of the Washington treaties, as they already had a small army and the nation's location meant that only the sea power of other nations could pose a threat to its security, especially in the Philippine Islands. Memories of the recent world war and a fixation on balancing national budgets also encouraged limitation. Eventually, these years saw the convening of two subsequent naval conferences including the United States, Britain, and Japan, one in Geneva in 1927, the other in London in 1930.

By analyzing what went wrong at Geneva in 1927, in contrast to the treaty-producing conferences that preceded and followed it, one may understand more about how the arms-control process of these years functioned and why some conferences fared well and others did not. Geneva stands as an integral event in the history of interwar naval arms control—or disarmament, as it was commonly, if inaccurately, known. Diplomats and navy personnel attending the conference tried to extend naval arms restrictions and, though they failed, ironically helped prepare the way for agreements reached at London three years later. As the depression deepened after the London Conference of 1930, more and more countries lost interest in disarmament, though new attempts were made periodically until 1936.

This study differs from other accounts of disarmament after 1922 in that it uses a variety of British, American, and Japanese sources and is really a comparative history of forces and personalities involved with naval disarmament in the United States, Britain, and Japan, relying to some extent on a bureaucratic-politics model.[1] I examine the activity of politicians and diplomats and their legislatures and departments. These people included Republican leaders in the United States who considered themselves pragmatists in international affairs, in contrast to the idealism of Woodrow Wilson's world vision. An example of their pragmatic approach was their insistence on developing a professional foreign service, similar to the well-organized British Foreign Office. In London, Labour and Conservative leaders ran hot or cold for disarmament, depending on their attitude and standing in Parliament. These politicians had to deal with forceful Admiralty officials who oversaw the world's most mighty navy. In Tokyo, finally, leaders of newly formed party regimes favored disarmament through the 1920s but had to pay increasing attention both to the civil war in China, which threatened Japanese interests, and to the views of the military.

But perhaps more important, I move beyond the narrow confines of the strictly bureaucratic model to examine the cultural underpinnings of the disarmament movement, especially the effect of public opinion on policymaking in these three societies. Although Realist scholars have generally downplayed the importance of public opinion on foreign policy decision-making, recent American and European scholarship emphasizing the importance of domestic factors in foreign policy suggests that public opinion, including that of interest and social protest groups, does indeed matter.[2] I therefore employ a controlled comparable-cases approach—necessary because polling data did not become available until the mid-1930s—to examine the internal elements of nongovernmental groups as well as the political domestic structures that permitted them to participate in disarmament deliberations.[3] In so doing, the interplay between pressure groups that supported or opposed arms control and those that sought to influence other citizens, legislators, and leaders of their governments is highlighted. Opinion toward the disarmament question was perhaps most divided in the United States where the debate involved a great number of people, including a number of thriving peace societies. Opinions ranged from the sentiment of the indomitable former suffragist leader Carrie Chapman Catt, who declared that she regarded any further obstacle to disarmament as a "tangled ball of yarn, which we may pull out in order if we get ahold of the right end," to that of Captain Dudley Knox of the Naval Historical Center, who attacked the "arm chair pacifists" who opposed naval building.[4] Views varied widely in Britain and Japan as well, though for different reasons.

Historians of interwar arms control have lately focused on Britain's role: Whitehall's bureaucratic infighting over disarmament, strategy, and naval architecture and technological changes.[5] This study also traces, if briefly, the strategic and design arguments that naval men of Britain and the other naval powers put before their leaders. Naval plans and premises cannot be overlooked because they often formed the positions powers took at the various arms control conferences. These arguments were often ill-understood by politicians, yet to gain domestic goals and achieve international accord political leaders had not only to interpret the technical reports, then accept, reject, or modify them, but also to defend them against domestic critics and before other powers with competing testimony from their experts. Small wonder that confusion arose from time to time.

Ultimately, this study raises important questions about why the United States and the other naval powers undertook extension of the Washington system of arms control. How did politicians, military leaders, and other interest groups affect this process? Which individuals or groups were most important? Was naval arms control wise, particularly between 1927 and 1930? And, most important to the contemporary reader, what lessons, if any, does the experience of the interwar period hold for those interested in arms control in the nuclear era?

1
THE POLITICS OF
DISARMAMENT

The idea of disarmament, that nations might limit their arms and thereby make themselves more secure than if they possessed more armaments, flourished in the decade after the First World War. The Treaty of Versailles had endorsed the idea of collective security—nations banded together in an international League of Nations to maintain peace in the world and put forward the idea of further disarmament. The country that believed most in disarmament was the United States (even though it had not joined the League), and there seemed good reason for such strong belief: in 1921-22, the Washington Naval Conference had slowed the race to build capital ships—battleships and carriers—and defined international positions in the Far East. Everything pointed toward more such successes. Wearied by world war and a sharp postwar depression, Americans ardently desired "normalcy" and were eager to proceed with disarmament. President Calvin Coolidge was reducing the national debt and hoped to allay the arms race. For Europe, the Dawes Plan of 1924 had established a schedule for payment of German reparations and encouraged Europe's leaders to believe that the Continent was settling down, that the economic troubles that followed the world war were coming to an end. The year 1925 saw the conclusion of the Locarno Accords, an Anglo-French-German-Italian guarantee of the Franco-German border. Similarly, peace seemed virtually established in the Far East, although the simmering Chinese civil war might flare up. Even in Japan the hostile reaction to the United States Immigration Act of 1924 excluding Japanese from American citizenship did not extinguish interest in naval disarmament. Japanese public opinion favored a strong navy, but continuing budget problems required economy.

VERSAILLES AND DISARMAMENT

The fourth of Woodrow Wilson's Fourteen Points of 1918 concerned arms control—nations coming together to limit their armaments. But translating this into policy at the Paris Peace Conference after the war proved difficult, not least because the president himself was unwilling to make significant reductions in the American navy, which he believed a necessary support to his pet project, the League of Nations, also under discussion at Paris. Another of Wilson's heralded Fourteen Points complicated matters: point two, dealing with freedom of the seas, a matter of great interest to the Americans, considering the recent British blockade, which had obstructed American shipping before American entrance into the war. The British at Paris were not interested in discussing this point, though they did bring it up occasionally to score debating points, for they rightly interpreted any British concessions in this area as meaning the end of the Royal Navy's hegemony in many parts of the world. Japan, the third major naval power, did not greatly value Wilson's outline for a new international order and worried about how any treaty might affect naval arms control in the Western Pacific, former German colonies in China, and a relaxation of trade barriers.[1]

References to arms limitation in the Treaty of Versailles and an informal arrangement regarding further disarmament between the British and the Americans emerged from the discussion at Paris. The Treaty of Versailles made two references to disarmament. Part Five of the treaty maintained that the arms reduction of Germany—the army and navy were limited and battleships over 10,000 tons were prohibited—was intended to set the stage for future international arms limitation. This meant that many European leaders, on the prodding of leaders in Berlin, would feel compelled to pursue disarmament during the 1920s and 1930s.[2] Article 8 of the League covenant, also established by the treaty, played on this theme as well, stating that international peace required armament reduction to the lowest level possible to ensure national defenses and that the new League would oversee plans for making such a reduction. These references to disarmament, which leaders would later point to as the basis of the disarmament campaigns of the interwar years, were only sketchily outlined and demonstrated the lack of consensus among nations about the wisdom and method of arms control. The French, for example, were prone to point out the troubling contradiction between the two parts of the treaty—that calling for limitation and that calling for reduction. Which was really meant by the treaty?[3]

After an abortive trip to Washington in December 1919 by Lord Grey of Fallodon, the former British foreign secretary, Lord Robert Cecil, the British secretary of state for foreign affairs, and President Wilson's adviser, Colonel Edward House, patched together a temporary understanding. The Americans would slow their arms building based on the large building plan of 1916 and the British would abandon their opposition to the inclusion of the Monroe Doctrine as a point of interest in the League of Nations covenant. Both men agreed that these measures would permit time for a later, more lasting, naval agreement. The question of limitation or reduction, in short, could wait.[4]

The Treaty of Versailles therefore set the stage for future disarmament talks. The British were interested in negotiations because they worried about the huge American naval building plan and the expense of protecting their worldwide empire given their weakened postwar economic condition. The Americans, less wholeheartedly, had also endorsed the idea of disarmament, hoping to reap savings and balance the national budget. Both nations knew that the new League would not require an international naval force, as that idea had been rejected in discussions. Finally, as the 1920s dawned, both nations sensed that somehow the system of collective security envisioned by the new League would probably at some point require disarmament. But, at least for the Americans, this did not mean immediate disarmament. President Wilson was more concerned with the ratification of the treaty, the future of the League, and the need for a strong American navy to back the League than he was about immediate disarmament. The Japanese prime minister, Hara Kei,* although concerned that the conference might restrain Japanese foreign policy in the Far East, accommodated himself to the new international system and began to think more in global terms, which included the issue of naval arms control. Nevertheless, Japan emerged from the experience of Versailles anxious about its role in the postwar world.[5]

THE WASHINGTON CONFERENCE

A principal reason for the Washington Naval Conference of 1921-22 was a common desire for economy on the part of the three major

---

* Asian names are used in traditional Asian order, surname first, unless they appear otherwise in works cited, in which case order follows the published source.

naval powers—the United States, Britain, and Japan. Navies formed a large part of national budgets—in postwar Japan the largest part, in the United States the largest single expenditure. The United States, to be sure, could afford a naval race, but the Japanese government, and even the British, after the huge expenses of the world war, could not. In the United States and, to a far lesser extent, in Britain, public opinion was negative toward the cost of munitions; similar sentiment existed in Japan.

The American government decided to extend invitations to a disarmament conference in 1921 because political conditions had changed since Woodrow Wilson's refusal in 1919 and 1920 to consider such a conference. The Republican victory in the presidential election of 1920 had replaced Wilson with Warren Harding of Ohio, who was less opposed to disarmament and who sought an issue that might bolster his position with members of his party. Senator William E. Borah of Idaho had sponsored a resolution calling for the American government to take the lead in sponsoring an international disarmament conference. The argument was even made that the advent of bombers, capable of destroying battleships at sea (as demonstrated by Billy Mitchell in 1921 with various naval targets including an old German battleship), might make battleship limitation possible.[6] In addition, Lord Lee of Fareham, the new British First Lord of the Admiralty, hinted to Washington that time was running out for a new conference, as the Anglo-Japanese alliance of 1902 was due for renewal soon and disarmament would be harder to achieve if a new alliance were agreed on by London and Tokyo.[7]

Whitehall in 1921 was more reluctant than Washington to proceed with a disarmament conference, a reversal of the American and British roles at Paris in 1919. British Prime Minister David Lloyd George was not deeply interested in disarmament and did not consider it until forced to by the convening of the Imperial Conference and the impending renewal of the alliance with Japan, a matter which many in the Cabinet opposed. A majority of the Cabinet ultimately overrode the prime minister's opposition and decided to postpone discussion of the alliance while engaging in parleys with Washington.[8]

Meanwhile Premier Hara had navigated through the Diet (the legislative body) an arms expansion program that included an ambitious naval building program. Tokyo was not initially much interested in a disarmament conference but came to change its opinion because Hara could not sooth American worries about Japan's new program by diplomacy alone; in addition, a public campaign by

Ozaki Yukio in the press and in the Diet persuaded more politicians to call for talks with Washington.[9] The Japanese also did not want to be left out of a disarmament conference if the Americans and the British were going to participate, as Japan's greatest potential threat in the Pacific after the war was the United States. The Japanese worried about America in part because the Anglo-Japanese alliance of 1902 would soon expire and, although the alliance had weakened over time, Japanese politicians did not want to abrogate it, leaving themselves more vulnerable to the U.S. Navy.[10] And it was certainly unclear if the alliance would be renewed. Finally, Hara hoped that a naval agreement might strengthen his cabinet's ties to the navy while reducing the power of the army to meddle in foreign affairs. He might use the conference to enhance civil control over the military because the Meiji constitution afforded the military the right to appeal directly to the throne, leaving the cabinet and premier and Diet in a weak position. Hara hoped that arms limitation and warmer personal relations with the admirals could provide the political leverage he desired.[11] At length, the Japanese decided to meet with the Americans and the British at Washington.

The American delegation to the conference that met beginning in November 1921 included political leaders and naval officers. Secretary of State Charles Evans Hughes led the delegation, assisted by naval advisers, including Theodore Roosevelt, Jr., the influential and colorful assistant secretary of the navy, Admiral Robert E. Coontz, commander in chief of the U.S. fleet, Rear Admirals William V. Pratt and William A. Moffett, and Captains Frank Schofield and Luke McNamee.

Taking advice from the navy's General Board, an advisory group of senior officers responsible for ship design and construction, the naval experts of the American delegation fashioned a plan that would leave the U.S. navy stronger than those of other nations. They hoped that the navy might complete the delayed schedule of ships set by the naval acts of 1916 and 1918 and achieve parity with Britain in capital-ship tonnage at a total of 820,000 tons. They also wanted to establish a 2-1 ratio for cruisers over Japan and a 10-10-5 ratio in other fleet categories for the United States, Britain, and Japan. They might accept a ban on construction of capital ships if the right tonnage ratios in that category were agreed upon. Believing that any limitation agreement should expire in 1928 (presumably at the end of the American building program), they held privately that it could extend six more years without harm to American security. Finally, they hoped to see the abrogation of the Anglo-Japanese alliance of 1902 and opposed any dismantling of fortifications in the western Pacific. Fortifications had helped check Japanese strength in the area, a source of concern since Japanese naval expenditures had increased from $85 million in 1917 to $245 million in 1921.[12]

But the strong-willed Hughes accepted only some of the advisers' arguments, preferring political agreements, especially on the Pacific islands and China. Faced with General Board intransigence, he came to rely on a special board of advisers, including Roosevelt, Coontz, and Pratt. Coontz and especially Pratt were less opposed to limitation than members of the board as they were Anglophiles and paid more attention to the Pacific than did many older officers on the board.[13] Hughes also had determined to maintain his department's control of the negotiation. During the conference, the secretaries of war and of the navy had invited Hughes to appoint a State Department representative to sit with the Joint Army and Navy Board, which had been established in 1903 to coordinate the two services. He declined, remarking that only the secretary or the undersecretary of state could vouch for questions of national policy and neither was available for the assignment. He later agreed to send a representative whenever matters "interwoven with the international policies of the United States" were under consideration.[14]

Negotiation at Washington had proceeded smoothly on the limitation of capital ships, even if conversations over other categories of vessels encountered trouble. Delegates agreed to tonnage limits on individual ships. Generally they used tonnage to measure strength because, as the American delegates noted, it provided the simplest way; gun caliber, age, speed, and armor were usually all related to tonnage. Moreover, battleship tonnage gave an indication of capacity in other ship categories, as ratios tied to battleships determined the numbers of cruisers, destroyers, and submarines, and, to a lesser extent, aircraft carriers. The greatest difficulty in limiting naval auxiliaries involved submarines. At the Washington Conference, the French insisted on 90,000 tons of submarines. The British therefore believed that they could not limit cruisers and destroyers, their main defense against submarines. All the United States could do to resolve these disagreements was to guarantee security to the French, which it refused. Instead, Hughes proposed in December 1921 a general limit of auxiliary ships to 10,000 tons and of guns to eight inches, in accord with advice from the General Board.[15]

The treaties that came out of the Washington Conference are, of course, well known. The Five-Power Treaty established ratios in capital ships of 5-5-3-1.67-1.67 for the United States, Britain, Japan,

France, and Italy. In addition, all powers would observe a ten-year holiday from capital-ship building. The treaty limited carriers to 27,000 tons and eight-inch guns, save for two heavier battle cruisers that the United States could convert and two *Hood*-class battleships the British could refit. Finally, it incorporated Hughes's suggestion for auxiliary-vessel limits of 10,000 tons and eight-inch guns. A Four-Power Treaty signed by the United States, Britain, France, and Japan replaced the Anglo-Japanese alliance and stipulated that any signatory engaging in a dispute in the Pacific would, in the event of diplomatic failure, invite the other signatories to a conference. A Nine-Power Treaty pledged the five naval powers, together with other nations interested in the Pacific (Belgium, China, the Netherlands, and Portugal), to respect the territorial integrity of China and adhere to the Open Door policy of equal commercial access. Delegates initialed agreements that restricted further fortification of the signatories' Pacific possessions, in the hope of inducing the Japanese to accept the agreed-on lower capital ship ratio.

The Washington Conference hence promised some practical gains for participants. It ended the race in capital ships and, at least temporarily, Anglo-American competition. Japanese-American rivalry subsided, and the political situation in the Far East stabilized, at least until the Chinese revolution began spreading north. Because of the treaties, each naval power tacitly accepted the others' areas of naval dominance: the British in the North Atlantic, the Mediterranean, and the Suez route to India and the Far East; the Americans in the Western Hemisphere; the Japanese in the western and northern Pacific.

The treaties also contained weaknesses. In the eyes of American navy officers, the Five-Power Treaty did not really offer parity with Britain, as the Royal Navy would retain superiority in capital ships through the 1920s. Neither the British nor Americans scrapped all the capital ships specified but converted some to carriers, so the ten-year holiday in building was a sham. To employ a metaphor of the time, the race only slowed from "a fast gallop to a slow trot." Agreements about Pacific fortification rendered defense of the Philippines nearly impossible. The Nine-Power Treaty proved the "weakest link in the Washington treaty chain" because it placed much of the responsibility for protecting China on the U.S. without allowing it the means. But Hughes and Harding probably realized that Americans would never pay for the defense of China, or for that matter, of the Philippines anyway.[16]

Hughes made the best of the Washington Conference. His goal

had been to limit the capital-ship race; the alternative had been to gamble on congressional support for a building program. But he realized that the American public would not approve large arms expenditures. He thus remarked hopefully of the Five-Power Treaty that it "ends, absolutely ends, the race in competition of naval armaments."[17]

A majority of naval officers opposed the treaties. The General Board concluded that the treaties could prevent aggression against the continental U.S. and the Panama Canal, but not the Philippines. Captain Dudley W. Knox expressed the navy's opinion in a column in the Baltimore *Sun*, in articles in the Naval Institute *Proceedings*, and in a book, *The Eclipse of American Sea Power* (1922). The treaties, he correctly observed, had undermined the American strategic position in the western Pacific without a corresponding compromise by the Japanese: the U.S. could no longer defend the Philippines.[18] Although Knox's writings did not represent official opinion about the conference, they did represent the unofficial navy position, for articles submitted to *Proceedings* went through a screening board of six senior officers, and most authors understood that the Department of the Navy approved de facto all articles published.[19] Captain Schofield, one of the advisers to the conference and a member of the General Board, was another vociferous opponent of the treaties. Indeed, his memo had comprised much of the General Board recommendations to Hughes before the conference.[20] In a series of articles and speeches Schofield echoed Knox. Captain Pratt had played a more active role than any other officer at the conference and agreed with the strategic and technical objections of Knox and Schofield but believed that improved political relations in the Pacific mattered more than any technical difficulties.[21]

The Senate approved the treaties even though Senator Borah of Idaho contended that the treaties represented but a first step toward disarmament. Borah called for the abolition of submarines as well as for parity in capital ships between France and Japan. Still, such parity would have upset the British government and probably scuttled the accords. Most senators backed the administration, and the treaties received approval by a large majority, despite debate over the Four-Power Treaty, which the senators were reluctant to accept as a substitute for the Anglo-Japanese alliance.[22]

President Harding gained much from the Washington Conference. He held off Borah during the negotiation and, on approval of the treaties, united the Republican party behind his leadership. He could now turn his attention to such domestic issues as tax revision.[23]

Most Americans approved of the Washington treaties, which garnered praise in the press, especially in the *New York Times* and the conservative financial journals. Steel men such as Charles M. Schwab of Bethlehem Steel and Judge Elbert H. Gary approved of the government's course during the conference, and most businessmen came to support disarmament because they hoped that government economy would bring welcome tax relief at home.[24]

Organized peace groups, which had done much to promote the conference, including the World Peace Foundation, the American Association for International Conciliation, the Carnegie Endowment for International Peace, the Women's Peace Society, the Women's World Disarmament Committee, the Women's International League for Peace and Freedom, and the Federal Council of Churches of Christ in America, endorsed the treaties and applauded the American delegation. One group, the International Conference of Women, headed by Jane Addams, meeting at The Hague in December 1922, held that universal disarmament by land, sea, and air was necessary for lasting peace: "In view of modern scientific development there is no practicable half-way measure in respect to disarmament." But, as a wry British observer noted, it was natural that American private groups should admire naval restriction, which promised them financial relief or moral satisfaction or both.[25]

It is interesting, particularly in comparison to later naval disarmament conferences, that Secretary Hughes arranged to guide public opinion during the conference by having President Harding appoint an American Advisory Committee to represent various public viewpoints.[26] Elihu Root had suggested a group to monitor and influence public opinion; the committee therefore included prominent citizens, including politicians, defense officials, four women, and Secretary of Commerce Herbert Hoover, who was supposed to keep the politicians in line.[27] Pacifists and most other peace group members were not among those selected. Although the Foreign Policy Association and the National Council for the Limitation of Armaments later attacked the Committee for rejecting contrary views, the Committee served its purpose for Hughes: it deflected direct public criticism from him and it prevented independent peace-group interference.

If Harding gained from the conference, so did Prime Minister Lloyd George. Although not a firm adherent of disarmament, the nimble Welshman had been able to hold his coalition cabinet together by giving the chief British delegate in Washington, Arthur Balfour, leeway in forming a position. Lloyd George had bolstered his own position while reducing government expenditure (a necessary move if his long-cherished welfare reforms were to come), all the while repairing Anglo-American relations. The treaty had left Britain the strongest sea power, though weakened in the Far East.[28]

Lloyd George's achievement was all the more remarkable because Britons displayed no strong public desire for disarmament.[29] Peace groups, although not as strong as in the United States, focused on the League of Nations rather than on disarmament. The League of Nations Union (LNU), largest of Britain's peace groups in the early 1920s, stressed a moderate course and attracted a wide following, including such members of Parliament as Robert Cecil and adherents of the still-powerful Liberal party. The LNU promoted arbitration and multilateral disarmament, as well as the League. But because of links to establishment figures, poor relations with some Labourites, especially future prime minister J. Ramsay MacDonald, a refusal to cooperate with other peace organizations, and an ambiguous stance on the powers of the League, the group never became politically powerful.[30]

Hara, as mentioned, had hoped to strengthen his control over the military and to claim more power for Japan's political parties through his participation in the Washington Conference. Unfortunately, he was assassinated on November 4, 1921. Although close relations between the navy and Hara's successor, Takahashi Korekiyo, did not develop as Hara had hoped, it was more because of Takahashi's deficiencies as a leader than Hara's miscalculation about the naval conference.

The treaties received favorable comment in influential Tokyo dailies and support from the fledgling Japanese peace organizations. In educational programs aimed at students and members of the Diet, the largest peace group, the Japanese Peace Society, warmly applauded the treaties. The chairman of the society, Eiichi Shibusawa, emphasized cooperation with the West and used his influence to urge ratification of the treaties. The other large peace group, the League of Nations Association of Japan (LNAJ), had even greater contacts with government leaders, as it depended on business contributions and government subsidies. This was both a strength and a weakness, for, although LNAJ had access to important people, its independence was limited; the Foreign Ministry in 1924-25, for instance, contributed 100,000 yen to the organization. In 1922 the LNAJ urged action on the treaties.[31]

But the Washington treaties also angered a segment of Japanese society. The British ambassador to Tokyo reflected that the Japanese seemed to regard the Washington Conference as "a secret coalition between Great Britain and the United States."[32] Certainly the conference had an important effect in creating two competing factions within the navy (treaty and nontreaty) and in persuading Japan to turn away from British naval technology toward that of Germany. More and more Japanese naval personnel traveled to Germany during the 1920s rather than visiting Britain as in the days of the Anglo-Japanese Alliance.[33]

THE CRUISER ISSUE

After the Washington Conference, the so-called treaty cruiser became the leading issue in naval disarmament. In fact, the purpose of the Geneva Naval Conference held in 1927 and the London Naval Conference of 1930 was to limit treaty cruisers. Before the cruiser matter had run its course, it had created much trouble between the United States and Britain, harmed Anglo-French relations, and involved Japan in a compromise at London that resulted in another assassination, that of Premier Hamaguchi Osachi, which contributed to the fall of the last liberal cabinet in pre-1945 Japan.

In discussions during the 1920s, there was no question about the usefulness of the type of warship known as the cruiser. Since its appearance in the 1890s, when it was known as the protected or armored cruiser, it had become more lightly armored, and by the time of the First World War was primarily a scouting ship for battleship fleets. It displaced from 3,000 tons upward, and normally displaced between 6,000 and 7,500 tons. Yet its armor was strong enough to withstand hits from other cruisers, it could survive destroyer fire, and it could handle independent tasks. The cruiser hence could function as a commerce destroyer, a guardian for convoys, a minelayer, or even a minesweeper. Given the holiday on battleship construction dictated by the Five-Power Treaty, cruisers assumed even more importance, as they were not restricted and could perform various tasks according to each naval power's strategy.

Cruisers assumed greater importance too for the American navy because of changes in strategy and in fleet strength. Strategists had constructed their war plan for the Pacific, War Plan Orange, on the belief that in a war, the Japanese would capture Guam and the lightly defended Philippines and remain in the western Pacific.[34] Americans would respond by sweeping through the Mariana and Caroline islands to retake the Philippines before moving on to Japan, which they would blockade if necessary.[35] Though older members of the

General Board disagreed, young officers of the Plans Division of Operations, who served on the important Joint Board Planning Committee, emphasized that Britain would probably not participate in an American-Japanese war but that Japan probably would in an Anglo-American war.[36] Reflecting this new concern with security in the Pacific, the navy had transferred much of its fleet after the war to this area. Since war with Britain was indeed difficult to imagine, the Navy needed War Plan Orange and the interests of the Far East to justify not only a treaty navy, but especially the treaty cruiser.[37] Indeed, the negotiation of the Five-Power Treaty had been predicated on it.

After the Washington Conference, American navy men began to reconsider their cruiser needs. British and American cruisers had usually carried six-inch guns before the war. But after that conflict many American naval officers began to prefer larger cruisers, if only because of greater fuel capacity needed for the long cruises in the Pacific between the few American naval bases. The American navy had commissioned no cruisers between 1908 and 1923. Many officers believed that the *Omaha*-class cruisers, the first of which was due to be finished in 1923, would prove inadequate because they did not possess enough range for the long Pacific voyages.[38] They also preferred cruisers heavier than the *Omaha* to offset Japanese numerical superiority in light cruisers, which had been constructed during the war. Japanese naval doctrine favored aggressive action, causing American planners to worry about defense of the nation's Pacific possessions. Curiously, as William Braisted has noted, American planners never seem to have surmised that perhaps the Japanese were building because of concern for the great American building plan of 1916.[39]

American officers also preferred a fast cruiser. Many of the U.S. Navy's cruisers had been built between 1893 and 1908, and their slowness rendered them unsatisfactory for offensive operations. The General Board worried about the speed achieved by new Italian designs and feared that the Japanese might follow suit. A fast cruiser might well run circles around the older, slower American variety. As a consequence, the General Board insisted on a larger propulsive mechanism.[40]

American officers pointed to the lessons of the war in regard to firepower and argued that the weight of shells and the calibers of guns had provided the means for victory. Admiral Graf von Spee's squadron, they noted, had been destroyed off the Falkland Islands by the great rifles of the *Invincible* and the *Inflexible*. Commanders of the British and the German fleets at the Battle of Jutland had agreed that the heavier armament of the British ships had been helpful—even though superior German gunnery had turned that great encounter into a virtual German victory. Larger cruisers were therefore required because heavier guns required larger platforms.[41] After the war, most members of the U.S. General Board became alarmed about British construction of the *Hawkins*-class cruisers, which displaced 9,750 tons and carried 7.5-inch guns. The board recommended that new American cruisers possess greater firepower than British treaty cruisers so the U.S. ships could patrol freely—unless confronted by pre-treaty British battle cruisers, which carried bigger guns. Similarly, board members would allow a larger propulsive mechanism, thereby permitting more speed than any British or Japanese cruisers.

The General Board easily reached agreement on problems of optimum displacement. Board members concluded that a 10,000-ton cruiser—the heaviest cruiser permissible under the Washington Five-Power Treaty—should have a range of 10,000 miles and a speed of thirty-five knots. These specifications would allow for mounting larger (heavier) guns than the *Hawkins* class; the U.S. Navy wanted eight-inch guns. And larger displacement would allow larger fuel tanks, giving more radius. The *Omaha* class that so dissatisfied the board displaced only 7,050 tons.[42]

Interestingly, the navy had favored cruisers of 10,000 tons even before the Washington Conference. American officers in London during the war had been impressed with the *Hawkins*, designed for lengthy searches for German commerce raiders. The wartime chief of naval operations, Admiral William S. Benson, had asked for proposals for a postwar generation of cruisers. The navy department's planning section suggested a ship similar to the *Hawkins*, and Rear Admiral Thomas Badger presented a plan to the General Board in 1920 calling for ten so-called scout cruisers of 10,000 tons. The next year the board recommended a similar program to the then secretary of the navy, Edwin Denby.[43]

Given the board agreement on heavier guns, range, and speed, naval engineers had to wrestle next with the problem of adequate armor. They had provided several blueprints for the board's report in 1920, including some that called for a cruiser of 8,250 tons and some for one of 12,000. In 1921, the board asked for protection of the ship's bridge in a splinter-proof enclosure and suggested little armor elsewhere, only a waterline belt for the ship's machinery.[44]

According to the board in 1921, increased firepower would make up for lack of protection, and at this juncture the board favored the eight-inch gun. It commissioned studies that noted that both six-inch and eight-inch guns had advantages. The six-inch boasted greater—more rapid—fire. Yet it had less destructive power because of its lighter shell, could fire no better than that of probable enemy ships employed on similar duty, and fired less accurately over 8,000 yards. The eight-inch offered fire superior to enemy ships employed on similar duty because of its heavier shell and slightly greater accuracy over 8,000 yards. Fire control around the gunnery area was as good as that of the six-inch. The disadvantage of the eight-inch gun lay in less-rapid firing caused by the difference between hand- and power-loading of shells. A six-inch shell weighed 100 pounds and could be hand-loaded, whereas an eight-inch shell weighed 250 pounds and had to be machine-loaded. Power-loading eight-inch shells took much more time than hand-loading six-inch shells. In brief, the studies concluded what perhaps should have been self-evident, that the eight-inch gun could achieve fewer hits than the six-inch but threw more metal. Still, after weighing the pros and cons, the board came out for the heavier gun—one suspects because it was larger.[45]

In addition to stressing the tactical advantages of bigger guns, officers mentioned the moral effect of the heavier cruiser. Such a ship would encourage cruisers of enemy navies to think twice before engaging. Curiously, the American officers championing what became known as the heavy cruiser—that is, the cruiser bearing the eight-inch guns—overlooked a possibility that might have solved their other problems. The leaders of the U.S. Navy desired a large radius and speed, but, although they did not mention the fact publicly, they were concerned about the lightness of the armor on their proposed large cruisers. They really were trying to pile too much into a fairly small (even at 10,000 tons displacement) package. Here they might well have looked again at their desire for the eight-inch gun. The General Board, unable to imagine Congress building many small cruisers (an expensive proposition), spent little time exploring the possibilities of the six-inch gun. The board produced a memo stating that to put six-inch guns on a 10,000-ton cruiser violated the American principle held from earliest times, that ships should carry the heaviest armaments possible for their size. The six-inch gun ran counter to "the fact that in the World War, in every action, the side which had the largest number of heavier guns was successful." Or, as a captain supposedly once advised a midshipman: "Boy, if ever you are dining, and after dinner, over the wine, some subject like politics is discussed, where men's passions are aroused, if a man throws a glass of wine in your face, do not throw a glass of wine in his; throw the decanter."[46]

The British Admiralty based its strategy on policies adopted by the Cabinet in 1919. The Cabinet held it unlikely that a European war would occur in the next five to ten years, that service levels of 1914 should be maintained, and that guarding imperial trade routes would be the most important task in the decade to come. British naval men regarded Japan with more apprehension than they did the United States when identifying possible threats to trade routes. The British nevertheless anticipated attacking quickly in American and Japanese waters in case of world war, destroying the enemy fleets and securing victory through blockade. But for the short-term future, guarding trade routes was most important.[47]

The British, like the Americans, faced problems of cruiser design. The Admiralty's decision to build to the Washington Treaty limits created a host of planning problems for naval engineers. They also had to deal with gun caliber and armor. By late 1926 they had begun emphasizing armor over guns.[48] Admiral Lord Jellicoe, commander at Jutland, had written in *The Grand Fleet* that lack of protection had cost the Royal Navy its victories. The argument had been made, he continued, that the best defense was offense. "Although this argument is very true when applied to strategy, the war has shown its fallacy as applied to *matériel*. Ships with inadequate defensive qualities are no match for those which possess them to a considerably greater degree, even if the former are superior in gun power."[49]

British interest in protection also derived from problems in designing a satisfactory eight-inch gun. Engineers had failed to increase the rate of fire, speed of loading, and elevation (between ten and seventy degrees) of eight-inch guns. In February 1926 the controller of the Admiralty therefore suggested that a smaller caliber for cruisers might be considered, perhaps in the range of seven or seven and one-half inches, because, in his opinion, the new *Kent*- and *London*-class cruisers were overbalanced with guns and lacked protection, especially around magazines. He also naturally wanted to save money. A report on the eight-inch gun proposed by Lord Forbes, director of naval ordnance, in October 1926 for the "B" type cruiser (the last type adopted before the Geneva Conference) listed several problems encountered since 1922. Guns on the *Kents* and *Londons* had failed to achieve high shell velocity for more than a few rounds. A longer charge might require redesign of guns and mountings and decreased magazine- and handling-room space. Worse, a quick redesign to meet the timetable for the cruisers of the 1926 and 1927 programs was impossible. The director of gunnery development, S.

Brownrigg, recommended either a new design or more smaller-caliber guns, since lighter guns had advantage over eight-inch in deck penetration at closer ranges. He halfheartedly suggested abolishing the eight-inch gun.[50]

Japanese strategy after the Washington Conference called for building a fleet as strong as any other fleet in the western Pacific and, like the British, guarding important parts of the empire as well as commercial and communication routes. Because of its proximity and interests in the Pacific, the Japanese regarded the United States as their most likely enemy and designed their war plans accordingly. In the event of a war, the Japanese would wage surprise attacks on U.S. bases in the Pacific, such as Guam and the Philippines, to capture them before a declaration of war. The American navy would eventually be defeated, Japanese planners believed, because the long island hopping required to gain position to attack Japan itself would give the Japanese navy ample opportunity to bleed the American fleet dry. To succeed, the Japanese navy would have to clear American screens and engage in raids before taking on the remaining American fleet in a decisive battle.[51]

The Japanese needed cruisers to do this, but they needed ships capable of raids even more: larger, quicker submarines, destroyers armed with torpedoes to engage an enemy fleet at night, and carriers that could launch planes to attack fleet auxiliaries. The large Japanese building plan of 1920 that so worried foreign observers included twelve cruisers, five gunboats, thirty-two destroyers, twenty-eight submarines, and two aircraft carriers.[52] Yet in designing cruisers the Japanese encountered some of the same problems as the Americans and the British, especially in trying to place sufficient firepower and protection on a ship displacing only 10,000 tons. The Japanese did not have to worry as much as the Americans about range, of course, for Japan had many bases within the western Pacific and now controlled the mandated islands which could be used in any war against the United States.

A TREATY NAVY OR NOT?

Designing cruisers was one thing. Obtaining the money was another. Whereas the British Parliament and the Japanese Diet had approved spending for new cruisers between 1922 and 1926, the question arose whether the American Congress would support such construction—for cruisers would be very expensive. The American public believed that the Washington Conference had rendered further large naval appropriations unnecessary. If indeed the navy needed cruisers, Congress favored keeping the older cruisers in commission, as they were cheaper and many of them carried heavy guns.

Although congressional big-navy supporters managed to score some compromises in the appropriation bills of 1922 and 1923, so-called small-navy advocates, led by Representative Patrick H. Kelley of Michigan, chairman of the naval subcommittee of the House Appropriations Committee, generally prevailed in holding appropriations below the level recommended by the General Board and Secretary of the Navy Denby.[53] When the naval subcommittee sought to limit the appropriation bill for fiscal 1923, it cut the navy's budget by one hundred million dollars, trimming the building program and reducing personnel from 100,000 to 65,000, just over half that of the British navy and below that of the Japanese. Kelley argued that reducing the size of the navy would not impair its strength. Congress would still be able to furnish the men and equipment necessary for the battleships, the air service, sufficient destroyers and submarines, and other auxiliary craft required. He based his proposal on the assumption that the appropriation figure, double that of the pre-war navy, would serve the navy well enough. He counted on savings from ships scrapped according to the Five-Power Treaty of 1921, retirement of surplus destroyers and antiquated cruisers, and elimination of 254 smaller vessels. The savings, he concluded, would be more advantageous than a large peacetime navy.[54]

Navy supporters were soon relating that the condition of the navy was critical. The reduced appropriations permitted little expansion, modernization, or even maintenance—officers noted that four battleships broke down during fleet maneuvers in the spring of 1924. Congress seemed not to care about cruisers. Japan and Britain, meanwhile, were building large cruisers. Japan began building four cruisers of the 10,000-ton *Nichi* class in 1923, each with twelve eight-inch guns. That same year the British naval staff recommended seventeen cruisers of 10,000 tons. The General Board, therefore, asked for sixteen 10,000-ton cruisers, eight to be laid down in fiscal 1924. Ironically, the board benefited from the Immigration Act of 1924, which, by excluding Japanese and straining U.S.-Japanese relations, seemed to diminish anti-navy sentiment in Congress.

At first the House, gladdened by the work of the Dawes Commission on reparations, passed a resolution that the president should call a new naval disarmament conference. But naval supporters need not have worried, for, although Coolidge—Harding's successor after his death in 1923—did call for a conference in a broadcast address (April 1924), his proposal was vague and indicated that he would await the results of the Dawes Commission and a stable European political situation. The president may have sent up this trial balloon to please Congress, with which he had been at odds over tax reform, divesting government plants at Muscle Shoals, Alabama, and new farm legislation.[55]

Naval champions such as Congressman Burton L. French of Idaho, the new chairman of the naval subcommittee of the House Appropriations Committee, supported an appropriation for fiscal 1925 of $410 million for the navy. Congressman Thomas S. Butler of Pennsylvania, author of the Naval Act of 1916, also introduced a cruiser bill to be considered jointly with the appropriations bill.

In addition to these efforts, naval publicists presented Congress with warnings. William B. Shearer, a gregarious Beau Brummel and self-proclaimed naval expert with ties to many naval officers (resulting from his lobbying for higher navy pay in 1920), charged that oil reserves were dangerously low and that the U.S. Navy was being outbuilt by the two other naval powers. He complained that the range of U.S. guns was inferior, and that the British enjoyed a 4-1 advantage in cruisers. Shearer used the 5-5-3 battleship ratio of the Washington Conference to demonstrate that the navy had deteriorated. He released tables comparing the fleets of the naval powers (based on access to General Board records), testified before congressional committees, and wrote editorials for such newspapers as the *New York Times*. He recommended construction of cruisers and fleet submarines, more oil reserves, more bases, and an increase in navy personnel.[56] Other writers submitted articles to newspapers and journals and organized public events for the navy's benefit. William H. Gardiner, president of the Navy League, composed a comprehensive report, using General Board records, that detailed weaknesses in tonnage, firepower, and men. He established Navy Day on Theodore Roosevelt's birthday, which included the participation of ships and bands, together with speeches and fireworks. In the 1920s, Navy Day underlined the navy's need for cruisers.[57]

Navy men also attempted to demonstrate that because the Washington treaties prohibited further fortifications in the Pacific, the navy would be unable to prevent an attack on the Philippines, even with three-fifths of its capital ships now in the Pacific, based at San Diego and Pearl Harbor. Strategists argued that without ships of sufficient number and range the fleet would not reach the islands in time to support the army against any Japanese attack.[58]

The navy pressed its case with Congress in early May 1924. By this time Secretary Denby had resigned, disgraced by his transfer of oil reserves to President Harding's corrupt secretary of the interior, Albert B. Fall. His replacement was Curtis Wilbur, who, although a graduate of the Naval Academy, had studied law rather than accept a commission. He had been chief justice of the California supreme court and proved effective before Congress in requesting money for a study of oil reserves to support the conversion of remaining battleships from coal to oil, and for more cruisers and personnel.[59] Assistant Secretary Roosevelt also appeared before House and Senate subcommittees pleading the navy's case. Admiral Coontz made a report to Congress about the battleships which had broken down during the fleet's winter maneuvers.[60]

Opponents fought back. Congressman Thomas L. Blanton of Texas challenged Shearer's allegations, declaring that the U.S. had attained parity in battleships and probably in other categories by means of the Washington treaties and remained well ahead of Japan. Repeatedly he picked away at navy supporters by asking for definitions of terms, raising questions about points of order, and refuting the assertions of Congressman James F. Byrnes of South Carolina and others in favor of the navy program. Reflecting the mood of many members of the House, he hoped for the gradual elimination of all naval armament. Fearing an arms race, he argued that the U.S. should act as a leader of moral forces throughout the world and avoid naval increases.[61]

President Coolidge now entered the fray. The slight, sandy-haired Vermonter was known both for his economy of speech and for his laissez-faire philosophy. In many ways he was a throwback to the "shadow presidents" of the late nineteenth century who viewed themselves more as administrators than as leaders directing legislation through the Congress. A president, Coolidge believed, drew up legislation and submitted it to Congress, which then shaped it and filled in details. He had no particular program and, as a contemporary observer wrote, "followed no gleam, stormed no redoubt."[62] He valued law, order, and thrift and held to his credo when he considered such foreign affairs as international law, defense, and disarmament. Above all, he wished to avoid competition in arms for he believed, as did many of his generation, that the world war had come about because of the arms race prior to 1914. He also thought that public opinion, properly focused, could help diplomats seek solutions short of war. He therefore took a middle ground, approving the proposed appropriation but hesitating to increase naval tonnage because of concern with economy. He opposed demands that more cruisers be built immediately. For naval supporters he seemed a halfhearted ally.[63]

Congressional approval for construction finally came when the House passed a bill on March 24, 1924, allocating money both for battleship modification and for construction of six gunboats for river duty in China. House passage of the Butler cruiser bill followed in late May, providing for eight cruisers displacing 10,000 tons and carrying eight-inch guns. The Senate passed the regular navy bill and the Butler bill in December as well, but the latter only as an authorization, without appropriations. Although the Congress had been alarmed by reports of strained relations with Japan, members still hoped that a disarmament conference might relieve the need to build.[64]

In contrast to the Americans, the British Parliament did not try to limit cruiser construction in the first years after the Washington Conference. Their navy, unlike the American navy, had long stood as a symbol of the nation's imperial greatness. Its operations, in addition, were linked with those of other ministries, which had to agree before cuts could be forced on the Admiralty. Ministries and the Cabinet also were preoccupied with such domestic affairs as unemployment and labor strikes and, in foreign affairs, France's occupation of the Ruhr and economic distress in Germany and France. Moreover, many members of Parliament accepted the Admiralty's dictum that national security required cruisers to guard trade routes and shipping on the North Sea, the Mediterranean, and the Atlantic.[65]

Prime Minister Stanley Baldwin, whose Conservative government replaced Lloyd George's coalition in 1923, considered limiting the navy but settled for a letter to ministers for the armed services suggesting economic restraint. In a speech at Plymouth in October 1923, Baldwin announced the building of several cruisers to replace outdated *County*-class cruisers. He hoped, he said, that construction would ease the serious unemployment problem, and he identified certain hard-hit naval yards where the cruisers might be built. The fall of the Conservatives in late 1923 did not halt the construction of cruisers. MacDonald and his short-lived Labour government only cut the number of cruisers to be built from eight to five.[66]

The return of Baldwin to power in 1924 saw opposition to cruiser construction from Chancellor of the Exchequer Winston Churchill. Although a former First Lord of the Admiralty, Churchill sought limits on building because he understood and, more important, was willing to admit, that the government could not achieve welfare reform and also build more cruisers. Further, he saw no threat to British interests in the Far East that required additional cruisers.

Cabinet members waited for Baldwin to make a decision. A short, stocky, pug-nosed industrialist who often longed for the peaceful prewar days, the prime minister was never happier than when walking in the quiet hills above Aix-en-Provence in the south of France. He was usually efficient, but complacent, and had no clear national program. He permitted his cabinet ministers, especially Sir Austen Chamberlain at the Foreign Office, much freedom, with the result that ministers often were at loggerheads. It is also true that the Cabinet system of government, emphasizing harmony, together with the multitude of subcommittees working on defense issues often rendered decision-making responsibility obtuse.[67] A prime minister, ever mindful of parliamentary opinion, did not have the maneuvering ability of, for example, an American president. Nevertheless, when confronted with issues requiring decision, Baldwin used "his natural ability in sliding off a troublesome point" to avoid resolution, hoping that delay would dispel problems.[68]

Baldwin found himself between the Admiralty and its opponents. Concerned for his welfare reforms, he saw the point of Churchill's argument, but the First Lord of the Admiralty and the Parliamentary Secretary to the Admiralty were two of his close friends, and both condemned Churchill's proposals. Baldwin supported a strong national defense. He had chaired the Committee on Imperial Defense after Lord Curzon's death, instituted a Joint Planning Committee, and established the Imperial Defence College.[69] Above all, Baldwin wanted to preserve his Cabinet intact. He guessed that Churchill would not resign if overruled, but that First Lord of the Admiralty William C. Bridgeman and other Admiralty officials would.

Baldwin yielded to the Admiralty in July, accepting postponement in construction of submarines and destroyers and modified construction for cruisers authorized by former Prime Minister MacDonald, since the Australians, for whom the British provided defense, were building their own cruisers. But he had won grudging Admiralty acceptance of naval limitation in principle, and the British hence could begin considering another disarmament conference.[70]

The Japanese Diet also appropriated money for cruisers, despite cabinet shuffles, party instability, and cuts in military spending. Following the assassination of Hara, the former finance minister, Takahashi, had become premier. An uncharismatic man, he proved unable to unite the Seiyukai party and resigned in June 1922. Three premiers followed in rapid succession before Kato Komei of the opposition Kenseikai party won election in 1924. Kato sought financial retrenchment, particularly in military expenditures. The nation's economy was sluggish and the government heavily burdened by the rebuilding of Tokyo and Yokohama after the disastrous earthquake of 1923. The new finance minister, Hamaguchi Osachi, acknowledged that Japan had trimmed its military budget from 1921 to 1923 but held that additional savings were necessary and proposed a cut of fifty million yen from the navy's estimates for 1925, some of which could be accounted for in retirement of obsolete, reserve, and training vessels. Hamaguchi tenaciously battled with naval ministry officials and obtained his figure.[71] But Japanese trimming did not extend to the cruiser program.

In spite of cruiser construction, the Japanese moved closer to disarmament, in large part because of the efforts of Foreign Minister Shidehara Kijuro, who served from 1924 to 1927 and again from 1929 to 1931. Shidehara, the former ambassador to the United States during the Washington Conference who had helped craft the Four-Power Treaty, favored closer ties to the West in order to attract Western investment and relaxed trade barriers. In so doing, he represented a link to the former Meiji elite of the late nineteenth and early twentieth centuries who similarly had looked to the West because of the prosperity it had afforded Japan.[72] Aloof, impatient, and married to an heir of the Mitsubishi fortune, Shidehara also favored cooperation with Western countries because he wished, at least until 1925, to tie Japanese noninterventionist policy in China with that of Britain. When Britain moved to a unilateral policy in 1925, Shidehara began to lean diplomatically toward the United States.[73]

By the mid 1920s, then, Japanese leaders showed interest in a disarmament conference because political stability seemed restored and public interest in disarmament had increased. People worried about British plans for fortifying Singapore, for with construction of cruisers, Britain could threaten Japan.[74] Japanese opinion, therefore, began to favor a disarmament conference that might forestall this danger.

NEW DISARMAMENT PROSPECTS

Political leaders and peace groups in the United States, Britain, and Japan desiring discussion of armaments were not long disappointed, for in December 1925 the United States agreed to participate in meetings of the so-called Preparatory Commission for a general disarmament conference, called by the League of Nations. The Treaty of Versailles had stipulated that Germany's virtual disarmament—its forces limited to a small army and a navy of 100,000 tons with individual ships of no more than 10,000 tons displacement—was only a preliminary to a general disarmament of all the nations. After the Dawes Commission had arranged a schedule of reparations payments by Germany, pressure to do something about international armaments forced the convening of the Preparatory Commission. Coolidge decided to take part in its work because public opinion seemed disposed toward disarmament, political stability appeared to have been achieved in Europe and the Far East, and, of course, because he hoped to avoid the expenditures that cruiser construction seemed to require.

The Preparatory Commission came together in late 1925, composed of representatives of members of the League Council and of specially interested nations. The idea for the commission had come from two standing League bodies that studied arms control issues. The Permanent Advisory Committee, established in 1920, advised the League about armaments of nations applying to the League for membership. It did little to promote arms control other than to offer expert advice to the League and its commissions. The Temporary Mixed Commission, established in 1919, examined particular problems of arms control and studied the state of armament of member nations. Both had had a part in organizing the Rome Conference of 1924, which discussed further limitation of capital ships, including those of Soviet Russia.[75] The Preparatory Commission now sought to draft a disarmament convention so that when a general disarmament conference might be called, figures would only have to be inserted into a document which had already been agreed upon. At commission meetings, the British favored limiting arms useful for immediate war, especially naval arms, and the French wanted to limit the power to wage all war, that is, to limit arms of the land, air, and sea. They could not agree on what to discuss. At length League officials hoped questions submitted by the Americans might break the impasse.

The individual in Washington to whom fell the task of devising the American stance before the commission was the sixty-nine year old secretary of state, Frank B. Kellogg, who had replaced Hughes in 1925. A white-haired and somewhat deaf man wary of quick action, Kellogg was a Minnesota lawyer and had been chosen by Coolidge because of his contacts in the Senate (in which he had served a term, 1917-23), and because he had been ambassador to the Court of St. James's during the following two years. The president knew little of foreign affairs and granted his cantankerous secretary considerable freedom, but Kellogg did not take advantage of it: he depended on his advisers, especially those at the West European desk, to a remarkable degree.

Reluctantly, Kellogg agreed to draw up proposals for the Preparatory Commission, even though he favored separate land, air, and sea conferences. He of course emphasized limitation of naval armaments. Like many Americans he considered the postwar army of 130,000 men and officers so small that it virtually exempted the United States from taking interest in armaments on land. He therefore suggested a 5-5-3 ratio for auxiliary ships; the Americans sought to extend the Washington ratios to these vessels. The League adopted a version of the American plan on December 12, 1925. Soon afterward Coolidge agreed to send American representatives to future meetings of the Commission, surprising Sir Austen Chamberlain, who believed that the Americans would reject the invitation to attend the meetings of the Preparatory Commission because they remained suspicious of League-sponsored activities.[76]

By the middle of the 1920s, the signatories of the Washington treaties therefore moved closer to a new disarmament conference, as the success of those agreements seemed to indicate that further naval reduction might be possible. Continuing world peace, economic stability, and the possibility of a race in cruiser construction encouraged the naval powers to attend the meetings of the Preparatory Commission. Delegates would first have to sort out two issues, however—an American desire for a halt in cruiser construction, and a French request for a security pact from either Britain or the United States. No one thought the task easy.

2

THE PREPARATORY COMMISSION

In agreeing to send American representatives to Geneva, President Coolidge was only recognizing the existence of what many Americans in the 1920s described as a peace psychology, in the phrase of what then was a new science. There certainly was something of the sort evident among the American people. It was a remarkable thing, this so-called peace psychology, for Americans had not suffered nearly so much as had Europeans during the recent war. American losses in battle had been fifty thousand soldiers compared to nearly one million for Britain and nearly twice that many for France. Still, the psychology existed, there could be no doubt about it, and for unbelievers there was both the correspondence between congressmen and their constituents, who deluged Washington in praise of peace, and newspaper accounts of private peace groups seeking to assure world peace.

But remembrance of the war was not the only motivation for many peace groups. Many peace leaders considered themselves progressives and had been active in advocating various reforms before the war. Some came to see greater American participation in international affairs, especially involving the new League of Nations, as an extension of their earlier domestic work. They saw themselves as no longer contained by national boundaries; they might now lobby for progressive and antiwar measures on a global scale.[1]

One measure that peace groups generally supported was American participation in the League of Nations Preparatory Commission, which began planning a program in 1925 for a general disarmament conference. Preparedness groups opposed American attendance, but President Coolidge was attracted because of the economies that accompanied disarmament. He also could not help but notice editorials favorable to the idea and public calls for action. The president at length decided to participate in the Commission's work, together with the other major naval powers.

THE SPECTER OF MILITARISM: THE PRESSURE GROUPS

This peace psychology of the 1920s really amounted to public opinion favoring American efforts to achieve peace and prosperity in the world, and had a tangible effect on presidents and government officials in deciding to seek disarmament.[2] It also apparently influenced leaders of the other great naval powers to varying degrees. But to gain a greater understanding of how public opinion, and especially pressure groups, contributed to disarmament in each country, one should first take note of recent public opinion theory. A brief discussion of this theory can establish controls for comparison and delineate parameters within which pressure groups operated.

Most scholars who have examined public opinion and foreign policy during the last thirty-five years have adopted one of two approaches. The first of these, more prevalent in the literature, emphasizes a top-down model. According to scholars holding this view, power elites, a small segment of the population, control foreign policy through their manipulation of a poorly informed mass public.[3] The other approach highlights a bottom-up model. These scholars believe that the mass public has considerable impact on foreign policy and that leaders generally respond to the wishes of the public at large.[4]

But both of these approaches suffer from defects.[5] The top-down approach fails to note that elites often go to great lengths to persuade the public toward one policy or another because they believe themselves politically beholden to the public. Forming public consensus on an issue through elaborate propaganda campaigns is therefore of great interest to elites. The bottom-up approach fails to account for fissures both among elites and among various elements of the mass public. In short, elites may be receiving mixed signals from the mass public, making it difficult to claim that the public has formed a consensus on a particular issue.

One or sometimes both of these approaches also suffer from other problems. The bottom-up approach often does not differentiate between segments of the public. Just who constitutes the public? Obviously, one must identify those members of the public who are involved in foreign policy issues and those who are not. Surely one must identify the segments of public that matter in foreign affairs as well as opinion that a leader, his advisers, and legislature deem important. Further, one must note the influence of involved citizens, both that of individual actors and of nongovernmental groups, as they may have a decisive effect on foreign policy decision-making.[6] Neither of the above approaches attempts this or moves on to the next step: evaluating the effect of these actors and groups, possibly because it is easier to describe opinion than to gauge it.

If neither of these approaches is satisfactory, then what is left? Recently scholars in such disciplines as political science and sociology have investigated a third approach toward foreign policy and public opinion, one that permits a controlled comparison between cultures of particular foreign policy issues. Calling their method the *domestic structure approach*, these scholars particularly note the activities of nongovernmental groups and actors.

The domestic structure approach holds that the nature of different democratic political systems is the most important element in foreign policy decision-making and the level of influence that different social groups may have on this process. Seeking to explain the stability of social coalitions interacting with established political players, scholars have identified two aspects of democratic political systems: the degree of openness or closure and the relative weakness or strength in dealing with social groups.[7]

An open political system has certain characteristics, including an independent legislature that pays heed to public demands; a number of political parties presenting different political concerns, making it harder for established interest groups and government bureaucrats to prevail; and an electoral process that allows public input into the political process. A closed system, in contrast, typically has a less independent legislature, a smaller number of political parties, and an electoral process offering less opportunity for public participation. One may measure the strength or weakness of a particular democratic system by noting the facility with which the executive is able to institute policy and reject alternative viewpoints.[8]

Social coalitions not surprisingly show greater stability in an open system in which they have greater access to members of the political elite. They can then create political networks with the elite to promote causes and hopefully institute policies through interaction with the executive and the bureaucracy. In a closed system, however, social coalitions tend to be unstable: they enjoy less interaction with the elite and have little opportunity to influence the decision-making process. Because of this situation, groups suffer from a volatile membership and an ad hoc strategy. They matter less in helping shape the public debate.[9]

Domestic structure theory is useful because it stresses the limitations as well as the possibilities that political and social institutions of liberal democracies present to social groups seeking to enter the political ring. As one scholar notes: "Visible changes in policy, political rhetoric, and the policy-making process can create a political space for movements. Within that window of opportunity, movements can mobilize dissent, make political gains, and alter the structure of opportunity for subsequent challenges."[10] In short, domestic structure has a great deal to do with the probable success or failure of various social groups vying for influence.

Domestic structure theory therefore offers a way to compare the disarmament process in the three great naval powers.[11] To do so, however, one must establish controls in order to focus attention on domestic structure and social groups as variables that proved important. Then, one might compare the domestic structure of the three nations to understand the political conditions that pressure groups faced.

Four sociopolitical aspects of the three major naval powers were similar between 1922 and the early 1930s. First, the international situation was relatively stable until the early 1930s. All three governments were also democracies, with executives, legislatures, and voter input. The economies of all three powers, though suffering from time to time, essentially were robust. And finally, all these governments sought naval disarmament, though not always at the same time or with the same enthusiasm.

In the terms of domestic structure theory, the United States may best be described as an open, weak society, permitting social groups opportunities to interact with political players. This description was true of the 1920s, when the American legislature was independent of the executive, especially in foreign affairs because treaties required an approval margin of two-thirds in the Senate. Political parties were also relatively weak in that they could not dictate policies. Tensions between bureaucratic departments meant that differences of opinion on various policy issues abounded. In addition, in the American system the press could debate policy and influence foreign policy decision-making. This decentralized political system featuring a strong press and a government endowed with little power to terminate public debate offered social groups of the 1920s "windows of opportunity" to build coalitions to discuss such policies as disarmament.[12]

The British system at the time may be described as open and relatively strong. An independent Parliament represented the last word on legislation and could often stymie the best laid plans of a prime minister. Political parties could control elections and policies because prime ministers were party leaders above all and had always to heed party members' wishes. Prime ministers also had to contend with the entrenched bureaucracy, such as the Admiralty, which upended more than one prime minister's policy. An active press tended to take sides according to party affiliation and was active in pushing or panning particular policies. Social groups operating in the British system often found they could make their voices heard, but almost as often found their policies assimilated and watered down by the government.

Japanese domestic structure during the 1920s and early 1930s was closed and strong. The Diet was weak and provided little counterweight to the executive branch. Political parties, although stronger in the 1920s than they had ever been, still were limited in power by western standards. A strong bureaucracy, especially the military—which could appeal directly above the heads of civilian leaders to the emperor—paid increasingly less attention to party leaders. The press, never prone to reporting stories that might prove embarrassing to the nation in the eyes of foreigners, also suffered from external censorship by the late 1920s. Social groups in Japan, therefore, faced a moderately repressive government dominated by a small group of established interest groups, including the *zaibatsu* (business elite), the Privy Council, and military groups.

Operating within the above political boundaries, social groups in all these countries pushed their agenda in the public arena. But they had to decide whom they wanted to target for their campaigns and they had to develop strategies to achieve their aims. Indeed, the question arises: Just what were the segments of the public that social groups attempted to swing toward their position? After all, many citizens the world over, as mentioned, pay little attention to foreign affairs unless these directly affect their lives.

Certainly many Americans in the 1920s, as now, were blissfully unaware of international affairs, being more concerned with domestic affairs, especially in their own communities. Most were content to leave foreign affairs to the government unless they saw danger that could affect their lives. The attentive public was that 5 to 10 percent of the population that had knowledge of foreign affairs and followed international events; of this group, perhaps half make up the influential public, citizens belonging to foreign policy organizations or having access to government policymakers. Public opinion refers to the views of the attentive and influential public and to those of a "middle mass" of the public, comprising perhaps 75 percent of the population. This middle mass, although less well informed, moves in and out of politics, especially when administration elites disagree on issues, such as the League fight or the decision to go to war in 1941. During these periods many more people may join in foreign policy debates.[13]

Social groups and elites, therefore, must identify their publics and their political targets if they want to advance their policies. They also must decide how to gauge public opinion. Before the mid-1930s, when national opinion polls first appeared, the president and government officials were influenced by four major opinion sources.[14] Republican administrations of the 1920s looked first to the media to gauge public opinion, especially the New York dailies such as the New York Times and the Republican New York Herald Tribune.[15] They supplemented these papers with the New Republic, the Literary Digest, and the Review of Reviews. By the late 1920s both national political parties were beginning to use radio, but still concentrated on the more familiar print media. Presidents and their advisers also received opinions from friends, who were usually members of the influential public, well-informed on foreign affairs, as were the news correspondents whose letters arrived on the desks of the president and his top advisers. (Letters from the public at large were handled by White House secretaries, who seldom bothered the president and his advisers with their content.) Congress was a third source of information. Congressional hearings, debates, and resolutions received notice in the White House because they frequently offered insight into the views of the attentive public. Interest groups were a final source, composed of members of the attentive or influential public who sought to persuade Congress and the executive branch to follow certain policies. Pressure groups in the 1920s focused on such interests as education, farming, business and manufacturing, military spending, and peace. When it came to naval disarmament the interest groups most active were those advocating peace through arms control and those advocating preparedness, who opposed arms control.

As I have mentioned, Secretary Hughes managed to control public opinion and limit the influence of peace groups through the Advisory Committee at the Washington Conference during his term in office. But his successors in the 1920s were not as skilled vis-à-vis public opinion and often found it difficult to dispense with these groups. And the groups were certainly active, as presidents, premiers, diplomats, and admirals would complain.

American private groups for peace, far larger than their European or Asian counterparts, busied themselves in support of international harmony. Among themselves they appear to have agreed to some extent on the need for four measures. One was adherence to the protocol of the World Court. A second was some form of cooperation, mostly in support of committees for social and economic measures, with the League of Nations. A third category of concern was what for some years had been described both in America and in Europe as "militarism," though it is not very clear what that notion meant. Generally peace groups held it to mean either an arms build-up that they feared might lead to war or the attitude that sought to increase the presence of the military in different walks of life. The fourth area of agreement was a general belief that the world required a limitation, and ideally a reduction, of armaments. Arms reduction could serve as a curative to militarism, a way to reduce the influence of warmongers. This belief was based on the assumption, widely held in the 1920s, that if one reduced arms, international tension would subside.

Conservative peace groups in the United States focused on international law or collective security or both as a way to keep peace. These groups, composed of "political internationalists," attracted bankers, lawyers, politicians, and academics.[16] Almost all the members of these organizations came from the Northeast and many lived in or near New York City, the headquarters for most of the peace organizations. Included among these groups were many of the influential public, leaders in their professions, and many who were former public servants.

The largest organization in this category, the Carnegie Endowment for International Peace, was presided over by the president of Columbia University, Nicholas Murray Butler, assisted by one of his professors, James T. Shotwell, the director of the Endowment's Division of Economics and History. The Endowment was important because of its leaders' entrée to government, business, and academic circles in the United States and in Europe. Indeed, some eyebrows raised in 1925 when a former law partner of Secretary Kellogg moved from the Endowment into the State Department as assistant secretary of state.[17] The Endowment also financed other internationalist organizations such as the League of Nations Non-Partisan Association and the Foreign Policy Association. Butler, Shotwell, and other officials of the Endowment preferred indirect influence— informal visits to political leaders and other elites and providing experts and studies for the government—to the pressure techniques favored by more radical peace groups.[18]

The League of Nations Non-Partisan Association (which became the League of Nations Association in 1928) and the Council on Foreign Relations (CFR) were two other important internationalist groups. Elites made up these organizations as well, including the chairmen of important New York City banks, former Supreme Court justices, and members of past presidential administrations. In fact, the boards of these groups often had the same men serving as directors.[19] The League of Nations Non-Partisan Association, as its name implies, viewed the League of Nations with favor and desired to use it or its agencies as a means to expand American economic and ideological power. The CFR preferred a more subtle and indirect role as an internationalist group. Its membership comprised former members of the American Inquiry group active during the Versailles negotiations and many conservative Republicans who looked to Elihu Root as their leader—men, in short, used to wielding great power behind the scenes. The CFR therefore strove, especially through its journal, *Foreign Affairs*, to serve as a bipartisan repository of international experts. Some prominent Anglophile members of the CFR desired naval limitation but favored an old-style balance of power arrangement rather than international arms reductions. They favored an American and a British naval sphere of influence, as well as one for Japan in the Western Pacific, based on economic cooperation.[20]

Internationalist organizations at this time especially sought, albeit unsuccessfully, U.S. participation in the World Court. Particularly active were the Endowment and the League Association, together with the World Peace Foundation (subsidized by the Boston publisher, Edwin Ginn), the Foreign Policy Association, the Woodrow Wilson Foundation, and the American Foundation (sponsor of the Bok Peace Plan Award of 1922).

More liberal peace organizations, some dominated by religious groups and by women, distinguished themselves from the conservatives not so much by their objectives as by their crusading zeal. Most of these "community internationalists" (so called because they emphasized an international community of social interests rather than the expansion of American economic might and power), agreed with conservatives about the World Court and supported some sort of American relationship with the League of Nations but disagreed both with the conservatives and among themselves about militarism and disarmament.[21] Foremost among the groups advocating disarmament was the National Council for the Prevention of War, headed by Frederick J. Libby, a pacifist Congregationalist minister turned Quaker. A pacifist group led by Jane Addams (international president) and

Emily Greene Balch (American branch president), the Women's International League for Peace and Freedom, also supported disarmament, as did the National Committee on the Cause and Cure of War, founded by the former suffragist leader, Carrie Chapman Catt, and the American Committee for the Outlawry of War, organized by an energetic lawyer, Salmon O. Levinson of Chicago, and supported by the philosopher, John Dewey. These groups, joined by the Church Peace Union and the Commission on International Justice and Goodwill of the Federal Council of Churches of Christ, produced leaflets and sponsored lectures attacking militarism and advocating disarmament. They of course encouraged Congress to limit naval appropriations.[22]

Pro-navy organizations, notably the Navy League, sought to counter the disarmament proponents. Although most of the American newspaper press was anti-navy, the Hearst press, the *New York Herald Tribune*, and the *Chicago Tribune* sought to make up for such criticisms. These papers received backing from Irish Americans (always anti-British), steel and shipbuilding interests, chambers of commerce, the American Legion, and national organizations of manufacturers.

The Navy League, composed of retired officers and of civilians interested in the navy, fought for a strong navy. Besides sponsoring an annual Navy Day, which featured speeches and tours aboard navy ships, it produced reports comparing the strengths of the signatories of the Five-Power Treaty of 1922, showing that the U.S. lagged in construction. The Navy League especially argued that the U.S. Navy was essential in protecting foreign trade and the expansion of the American economy.[23]

Another group wholeheartedly supporting the navy was the National Security League (NSL), founded in 1915 by a New York corporate lawyer, S. Stanwood Menken.[24] The group had originally been involved in the preparedness movement during the period of American neutrality, then supported the decision of President Wilson to enter the war. In the early 1920s, the NSL lost prestige in some quarters by its participation in the Red Scare: the group had drawn up lists of possible communist sympathizers to be investigated by the government. Nevertheless, its members included many prominent politicians and educators. And many NSL members were likewise members of the Navy League. In April 1922, Menken scheduled mass rallys to apply pressure on congressmen who opposed building the fleet up to treaty limits. This was only a part of an NSL propaganda effort that included writing letters to editors and contacting influential congressmen. Menken and others also helped organize a national Defense Day in September 1924.

The American Legion also confronted those who opposed building the navy. It specifically targeted pacifist organizations because many pacifists called for a worldwide governmental organization, an idea in opposition to the nationalism that the Legion espoused. Many pacifists, particularly those on the far left, favored a socialist economic system, anathema to Legion members, and many, of course, also worked for disarmament, while Legion members worked for preparedness.[25] The president of the National Civic Federation, another pro-navy group, perhaps pointed to the Legion's greatest value to preparedness supporters when he noted in 1924 that the Legion was the major organization that all anti-radical groups could work with.[26] But the Legion did not focus as much attention overall on the disarmament question as did other pro-navy groups. It tended to work more on such issues as veterans' benefits, education programs, and anti-immigration legislation.

Yet the Navy League, National Security League, American Legion, and other navalist groups and pro-navy newspapers could boast of only limited success by 1927, principally in the construction bill of 1924. They were unable to push through a bill for twenty-two cruisers in 1924 or prevent the House Naval Affairs Committee in 1926 from shelving a measure for ten cruisers. Sentiment against navalism, in short, appeared stronger in the U.S. than pro-navalism.

Peace groups, in the meantime, had formed in other countries, such as Britain, where their members hoped that the League might support disarmament. In London, the League of Nations Union (LNU) called for a freeze in armaments and for an international percentage-of-budget reduction in naval expenditures or manpower. The LNU felt that if universal reduction were impossible, regional arrangements between neighboring nations would suffice. This position varied from the LNU report of 1921, which saw the League of Nations as an international policeman settling disputes. Many members of the LNU realized that such a program would be difficult to achieve and turned to limitation of naval arms, which seemed a more realistic goal. The LNU report of 1926 sought to restrict cruisers to 6,000 tons and battleships to 10,000 tons, figures much lower than the Washington limits. Smaller British peace groups, such as the Congregational Union, passed resolutions asking the government to take the lead in disarmament.[27]

Preparedness groups were also active in Britain, especially the Navy League which, like its American counterpart, had close ties to naval officers. The Navy League and other groups publicized appropriation debates in Parliament and supported Britain's cruiser program of the 1920s.

Japanese peace groups, more varied than the American or British, focused on world understanding or better Japanese-American relations. They were less effective in publicizing their message of peace and cooperation than British or American groups because Japanese society emphasized respect for authority, limited free discussion, and did not permit peace groups the latitude that groups in the Western democracies enjoyed. Nevertheless, the Institute of Pacific Relations, established in Honolulu in 1925 to encourage the study of countries in the Pacific area, opened a branch in Tokyo soon after. The branch received a government subsidy and enjoyed little independence. A League of Nations Association in Japan sponsored study groups and meetings in support of disarmament but had little effect on members of the Diet or on government officials. Perhaps the most active disarmament group in Japan was the Society of Friends, which enrolled many pacifists.[28]

Navy groups were also prominent in Japan, but were smaller in size and influence, probably because naval officers held more power in government than in the U.S. or in Britain, negating the need for special coalitions.

THE QUEST FOR NAVAL APPROPRIATIONS

Outside of the peace sentiment, one of the major reasons President Coolidge considered disarmament in 1925 was that a cruiser race among the naval powers had occurred since the Washington Conference; the trouble was that Britain and Japan had built cruisers while the U.S. had not. But by 1926 all three powers became more interested in disarmament. Indeed, naval proponents in the United States, Britain, and Japan had begun to find the task of obtaining appropriations for cruisers difficult. In America, congressional resistance remained almost as strong as it had been immediately after the Washington Conference—despite authorization for cruisers in 1924. In Britain and Japan economic and domestic unrest worked against increased naval appropriations. Aware of the large portion of national budgets going to naval appropriations, government leaders looked to a new disarmament conference that might make more ships unnecessary.

"A veritable cyclone of opposition" arose in Congress when big-navy supporters sought increased budgets in the United States, and

advocates had difficulty appropriating money for cruisers authorized in the act of 1924.[29] In the end, the House Appropriations Committee provided for only five of the eight cruisers authorized. Navy
supporters did defeat an amendment that would have delayed construction of three of the remaining five cruisers for a year. Congress
voted the money for all five cruisers in 1926.

Opposition to a big navy appeared from another direction—the
White House. Although President Coolidge had not contested the
appropriation for the five cruisers, he made clear his opposition at a
press conference when he said he would avoid an arms race. He, not
Congress, had prevented the navy from building auxiliary ships, and
he would support a new treaty reducing naval strength below present treaty limits. In his annual message to Congress, Coolidge repeated his hope for a new conference to reduce arms. In a budget
message the next day, he opposed an amendment to a recently introduced bill requesting appropriations for the remaining three cruisers authorized by the act of 1924.

For these sentiments Coolidge received a letter of protest from
Chairman Thomas Butler and nineteen of the twenty members of
the Naval Affairs Committee, and Butler introduced a bill in the
House that proposed ten more cruisers. He announced that he
would seek both authorization and appropriations during the current session of Congress. Coolidge at first opposed the Butler bill,
but after discussion with the Navy Department he changed his
mind, though he could not agree to the appropriations asked. He
apparently agreed to support Butler's bill in order to use the threat
of new cruisers to persuade other nations to attend a disarmament
conference.[30]

The Butler bill appeared too late to be included in the appropriations for fiscal year 1927, but big-navy proponents hoped that Congress might include the funds for the three remaining cruisers of the
act of 1924, despite the president's disapproval. But when the naval
appropriations bill was reported, it did not provide for the cruisers
because, according to Congressman Burton L. French, it would appear premature, considering the president's opposition and the work
of the League of Nations Preparatory Commission in Geneva.[31] In
the ensuing House debate many Republicans supported the naval-
ists, emphasizing British cruiser construction and expressing skep-
ticism about a new disarmament conference. The administration
had trouble attracting enough votes to defeat the cruiser amendment, though the measure did fail by two votes on January 7, 1927.
In the Senate, Frederick Hale (R-Maine), normally a spokesman for

the administration, offered his own amendment for the three cruisers, which was passed by a two-to-one margin on January 24. Coolidge reiterated his opposition but, faced with subsequent House approval of $450,000 to begin construction of the cruisers, reluctantly signed the bill into law on March 2.

In Britain, the House of Commons debate over the naval estimates of 1927 turned on the question of the navy's role and its strategic aims. Was the navy little more than a police force for the empire, as British delegates had argued before Sub-Commission A of the Preparatory Commission? Or did it have more substantial duties? Critics of the Royal Navy cited an article from the *Economist* charging that the Admiralty had maintained a two-power standard in cruisers that could induce the United States or Japan to build cruisers; in the event of a cruiser race, they warned, Britain would lose. Further, cruisers could not defend the trade routes, even with a two-power standard. Labour argued that the supposed savings that William Bridgeman, First Lord of the Admiralty, described were misleading, for the Admiralty had simply transferred money from one account to another to make savings appear. One Labourite said he lacked "great confidence in the First Lord's enthusiasm for disarmament."[32] Another called for publication of the Colwyn Committee Report (critical of high military estimates), though Prime Minister Baldwin had refused to show it outside of the Cabinet. Pacifists proposed amendments to the estimates that would force reductions or eventually eliminate warships over 5,000 tons. Other members of Parliament asked if the navy was building against Japan, because the United States posed little threat to British interests. They noted that the Japanese regarded enlargement of the naval base at Singapore, accommodating more British warships, as a threat.

Admiralty officials provided a spirited defense of battleships against a 5,000-ton limit and defended the need for cruisers. One remarked that "naval disarmament is not in itself an end, but that, if it is to be of value, it must tend to promote a feeling of security and the avoidance of a feeling of suspicion." Reduction of naval arms was useful only in a political sense, as it could lessen tensions.[33] Admiralty officials also observed that since the Washington Conference the French had rebuilt their fleet, gravely damaged in the war. Any calculation of British defense needs must also consider increasing numbers of French submarines.[34]

In the mid-1920s, Winston Churchill as chancellor of the Exchequer attempted to curb Admiralty expenditures, but failed abjectly. His critics, and he had many in British politics, claimed that he was in the pocket of the Admiralty—over which he once had presided. He doughtily pointed out that the Exchequer could manage no economies until the country either abandoned the one-power naval standard or reached an arms-limitation agreement. He hoped to maintain the former while pursuing the latter, provided Britain's needs as a worldwide empire were recognized. He acknowledged that the Admiralty had found funds to pay for the cruisers it wanted.[35]

In Japan, parliamentary consideration of cruiser construction took place amid turmoil. Following a period of mourning for the late emperor, politicians braced themselves as the Diet reopened early in 1927, in part because of instability of the Wakatsuki cabinet, in part because of fist fights on the Diet floor during the previous session. They turned to the budget, of which naval estimates formed a part, while Tokyo dailies reported bribery, especially regarding General Tanaka Giichi, leader of the opposition Seiyukai party. Despite all the uncertainty, the government gave attention to the navy's needs, especially the request for cruisers. The minister of the Marine had submitted a seven-year building program asking the equivalent of $147 million, only to see it rejected. The ministry then proposed a new program asking the equivalent of $130 million over five years. Premier Wakatsuki defended the part of the program providing appropriations for three cruisers, as he deemed the ships necessary for national defense. He vowed not to drop them from the budget.[36]

The Diet passed the budget in March 1927, shortly before it adjourned, because of another outbreak of violence on the chamber floor. Physical attacks linked to disagreements about government aid to failing banks and to charges of corruption had become so commonplace that older party members took seats surrounded by younger, more hardy men for protection. After more fisticuffs, the speaker of the house, Karuya Gizo, resigned, and the Diet closed the next day.[37]

Unable to convince either the Diet while in session or the Privy Council after parliament closed that the failing Bank of Taiwan needed a twenty million yen emergency loan from the Bank of Japan, Wakatsuki too resigned, in April 1927. His government had also been subjected to severe criticism over Foreign Minister Shidehara's noninterventionist policy in China after the Nanking Incident. Stepping into the political turmoil, General Tanaka of the opposition then formed a cabinet, taking over the foreign minister portfolio as well.

Tanaka was a prominent military officer who differed from

many in the army and navy in that he cooperated with the party politicians and was well regarded by many of them.[38] He had served in Premier Hara's cabinet as a minister of war and had headed the Seiyukai party since 1925. Tanaka was no political ideologue: he was by nature a man of action and he particularly abhorred Shidehara's policy of nonintervention in China (even though Shidehara had in recent months departed occasionally from this policy in order to protect Japanese nationals). Tanaka was determined to take a stronger hand in China if the need arose, and, as the civil war in China spread northward, few doubted that Chinese nationalists and Japanese interests would soon clash anew. Not long after he became premier, the general announced that he favored appropriations for cruisers.

BEGINNINGS OF THE PREPARATORY COMMISSION

In part because of antimilitarist feeling, in part because of foreign cruisers, in part because of the need for economy, many Americans looked to the League's Preparatory Commission to bring arms limitation. In his annual message to Congress in early 1926, Coolidge dealt mostly with a definition of the limitation of armaments and with technical questions, noting the general European assent to arms reduction following the signing of the Locarno Treaty. He emphasized that disarmament might remove part of the burden of taxes and reminded his audience that the work of the Preparatory Commission carried no obligation on the part of the U.S. to attend any disarmament conference or support any arrangements by League-sponsored bodies. He explained that representatives of interested governments and members of the League Council made up the Commission and that it would only suggest disarmament figures for delegates to consider. He asked Congress for $50,000 to send a delegation to Geneva, and Congress voted the money.[39] The first session of the Preparatory Commission had been set for February 15, 1926, but because of a French request the date was pushed back until late May.

Secretary Kellogg named the American delegates to the conference, who would operate under the leadership of the minister to Switzerland, Hugh S. Gibson, recently vice chairman of the delegation to the International Conference for the Control of Arms. The choice of Gibson was auspicious. Educated in California and Europe by a doting, ambitious mother, the forty-two-year-old Gibson possessed, according to one observer, an "almost inhumanly polished and suave exterior that concealed a singularly able and resourceful

mind."[40] His assistants included Allen W. Dulles and Dorsey Richardson of the State Department (counsel and general secretary, re-
spectively), several War Department representatives, and Rear Admirals Hilary P. Jones and Andrew T. Long, together with Captain
Adolphus Andrews and Lt. Comm. Harold C. Train. The officers
from the War Department did not figure prominently in the work of
the Commission, as the United States possessed a small army, but
the delegates from the Navy Department would labor for months to
arrive at some sort of naval agreement. They were led by Admiral
Jones, an attractive figure with ever-present cigar, straw hat, and
light gray suit—the white-haired Jones might have been taken for "a
Mid West banker on a holiday trip." Alas, his charming personality
did not diminish his stubbornness and Anglophobia.[41]

Kellogg informed the delegates that the U.S. would insist on
limiting immediately usable armaments, especially naval arms.
The administration would not agree to international inspection and
enforcement and would rigorously uphold the naval ratios established by the Washington Conference. He declared the reduction of
land armaments impracticable, as circumstances differed in Europe
and in the Western Hemisphere (Kellogg he favored separate land
and naval conferences). As for air arms, limiting aircraft might be
the most troublesome issue at the conference, he noted, though it
was of slight concern to Americans.[42]

The long-delayed first session of the Commission at last opened
in Geneva in May 1926. The British delegates, led by a sixty-two year
old patrician orator, Sir Robert Cecil, Viscount of Chelwood, recommended the establishment of two subcommissions—one military,
with an army, navy, and air expert from each country, the other economic, with economic and social experts. The Americans refused to
participate in League committees in the military subcommission,
Sub-Commission A, such as the Permanent Advisory Commission
or the Temporary Armament Committee, and the subcommission
had to be reconstituted, leaving membership essentially the same,
save for the addition of Americans. The Americans, not being League
members, had made their complaint with an eye on domestic politics. The military subcommission would study technical aspects of
limitation and demonstrate different ways of limitation.

During the first days of the meeting of the Preporatory Commission the British and the French presented their positions on a
questionnaire submitted to the delegations prior to the conference.
On behalf of the American delegation, Gibson refused to participate
in this exchange of information, saying that he desired opinions of
the other countries and instruction from his government. For the

most part Americans did not participate in debate during the first session and offered suggestions only when their interests arose or when acting as mediators between views.

Divergent opinion abounded, as one observer noted, especially among the British and French, whose positions represented differing ideas of war.[43] Possessing the world's largest navy, the British could control access to their shores, they could afford to send troops into territory where they controlled the adjacent seas, and they could pick the time and place for engagement. The French preferred to limit their ability to wage war and focused especially on reserve strength, because they possessed a large standing army. The French general staff adhered to the Clausewitzian theory that one had to confront enemy forces, especially countries with great reserves such as Germany. Worried about proximity to Germany, their nation's low birth rate, and weaker industrial position compared both to Britain and to Germany, the French were more concerned about land than naval arms.[44]

Focusing on their navy, British delegates called for national armies proportional to overseas commitments and air forces comparable to countries of similar military power. A subcommittee of the Committee of Imperial Defence, presided over by Cecil, had formulated the delegation's instructions, stressing that the British navy depended on cruisers for overseas commitments and that their limitation might prove difficult. In his opening remarks Cecil discussed British concern about cruisers and alluded to the American demand for parity:

In the case of the Navy there is no doubt a certain element of—I will not call it competition, but dependence on the size of other navies. That was very carefully considered from the point of view of certain kinds of ships at the Washington Conference, which ended in an agreement which was very warmly welcomed in my country. The Washington Conference, however, only dealt with certain kinds of ships. It is possible that further agreements may be made in respect of submarines and cruisers, but I ought to point out that the number of cruisers in the British Navy is also largely a question of overseas commitments and not of the size of foreign navies, or only very slightly a question of their size. While the number of cruisers may therefore not come within the scope of the question, their size undoubtedly does, and there is no reason why by general agreement the size of cruisers should not be diminished.[45]

The French then responded, reflecting not only strategic disagreement with the British but also a far different attitude toward disarmament in general. In short, Paris distrusted disarmament. Although willing to discuss the issue, the French insisted on coupling it with security and arbitration, as they had since at least the discussions of the Geneva Protocol in 1924. Although many League observers believed that Aristide Briand, at the Foreign Office since 1924, supported disarmament (as he often spoke approvingly of it), they did not always note that he carefully added caveats calling for security and guarantees first.[46] So too did other French delegates involved in the disarmament discussions, no matter how enthusiastic about the League. This attitude was partly philosophic, and partly an acknowledgment that a small number of men, fewer in number than in the U.S., Britain, or Japan, controlled the disarmament issue in France. These men controlled French disarmament policy through two organizations, the Conseil Supérieur de la Défense Nationale (CSDN), an interministerial consulting body that issued instructions to delegates at Geneva, and the Service Français de la Société des Nations, another interministerial body under the auspices of the foreign office. The French military, even more hostile to disarmament than the politicians, dominated both organizations during the 1920s, in part through long-serving military observers in Geneva with close connections to politicians, journalists, and the military high command.[47]

The French presented their proposals, led by Joseph Paul-Boncour, a curly-haired dynamo famous for his oratory in the Chamber of Deputies, and vice-president of the studies commission of the CSDN. Paul-Boncour called for linkage of land, sea, and air armaments, with naval limitation measured by total tonnage rather than class of ship. The distinction meant that the French could continue building submarines, their most effective vessel, while limiting classes in which they lagged. They also championed enforcement of limitations. Cecil rightly fumed that the French sought a guarantee of security from League members, as they had with the Geneva Protocol; to a French member of the League secretariat he confided that he would not be surprised if the American delegation left because of it. But the Americans gave no sign of leaving.[48]

Disagreement between the British and French led to temporary adjournment of meetings on May 26. Delegates arranged for subcommissions to prepare reports. The British foreign secretary, Austen Chamberlain, echoed the thoughts of many Europeans when he cautioned about the effect disarmament questions might have on the Treaty of Locarno.[49] He preferred that treaty to a stronger League, not only for reasons of defense, but perhaps also because it represented a personal political triumph. The aristocratic, aloof foreign secretary viewed disarmament with suspicion, afraid that Britain's navy might be irreparably harmed.

Talks continued, as did meetings of the subcommittees of Sub-Commission A. By early July, discussion had narrowed to naval affairs, but agreement between the French and British seemed no closer. The French and Italians wanted comparison of vessels by total tonnage and convinced a majority of the subcommittee to exclude comparison by class, as they had at Washington. The British delegate, Walter Roberts, reported that "discussions have been tortuous and at times heated."[50] In describing the minority report filed by Britain, the United States, Chile, and Argentina against the notion of total tonnage, the *Journal de Geneve* commented that a committee majority, made up of representatives of Czechoslovakia which had no navy, and Poland, which had next to none, was attempting to impose decisions on the British Empire and the United States. Admiral Jones wrote home that "the attitude of the French and Italians is so antagonistic to all that was done at the Washington Conference, that I am convinced there is little possibility of reconciling the points of view." Things looked bleak: "I confess it looks to me as if we are on a circle of talk of infinite radius. Such is the result of 'the Atmosphere of Geneva.'"[51]

After a recess, the technical committee meetings resumed on August 2. One of the issues in the Sub-Commission and its subcommittees was a French proposal for international supervision and enforcement. The Americans "threw up their hands in horror at the mere reference by name in a proposed report to the detested idea." Roberts confessed puzzlement that the French fought so hard for supervision, since both the United States and Britain opposed it.[52]

By early September the delegates had made little progress. Jones did not know when they would finish, and agreed with a Swedish delegate who said that "the great trouble with us is that we are a body of technical experts working under purely political instructions." Jones asked: "If political instructions can be largely eliminated so that we may deal with the questions from purely technical viewpoints, we may make more rapid progress." He meant French insistence on tying together land, sea, and air solutions because of the Franco-German political situation. In other ways Jones believed that affairs at Geneva were becoming ridiculous. On the eve of the second session of the Preparatory Commission, set for late September, he wrote: "Just now Geneva is full of self-appointed American Ambassadors to the League of Nations (elderly ladies of both sexes) who apparently delight in expressing to anyone who will listen, for-

eigners particularly, shame of their country for not being in the
League. I am glad none had so expressed him or herself to me be-
cause I am afraid my language would not be fit for publication in
The Ladies' Home Journal."[53]

The second session of the Preparatory Commission opened September 22. Perhaps the most important discussion of this session
took place informally two days later between Gibson and Cecil,
who agreed that before a disarmament conference convened, experts from their countries should discuss an agenda, especially regarding cruisers. Cecil said that the Admiralty would reduce the
size of cruisers but must have a certain number to guard imperial
communications. The American government understood, Gibson
replied, but could not easily agree to build fewer cruisers than the
British. The Americans desired a "navy second to none" to guarantee that a blockade hampering neutral shipping such as the British
had imposed on Germany during the war could not happen again.
Although they had far more need of cruisers because of their empire, the British appeared to accept parity. In Cecil's words, "I said I
did not understand that our naval authorities objected in any way to
that. It was not so much the relative number of cruisers, it was the
absolute number that was essential to us."[54]

As a result of this conversation, Jones went to London to meet
with the First Sea Lord, Admiral Sir David Beatty, who agreed on
parity in all classes. Beatty conceded that the British could accept
parity with the U.S. Navy even in cruisers. They could not accept a
5-3 cruiser ratio with the Japanese, but that problem might await
the conference. To make sure he understood Beatty's position, Jones
said, "Now, let us understand each other perfectly so that there can
be no doubt as far as the United States is concerned: Great Britain
accepts equality in all categories. In any conference we would establish a level of armaments in all categories in which each nation
would have an equality." Beatty agreed "unequivocally."[55] Nevertheless, it is not clear how seriously Beatty meant what he said.
Many of his colleagues did not accept this position, and he himself
had not in the recent past. Perhaps he wished to sound out Jones on
other matters and deferred to him on the one issue he knew the
American held dear.

Delegates reassembled in Geneva in March 1927 for the third
session of the Preparatory Commission. Secretary Kellogg had written to the impatient chairman of the House Committee on Foreign
Affairs, Stephen G. Porter, reiterating that the Commission would
only survey problems and, he hoped, draw up an agenda for a confer-

ence.[56] The British and the French exchanged their proposed plans, the British giving theirs to the French a few days before the meeting because portions had already appeared in the French press. The British then formally presented their draft, which encompassed proposals they had already championed. They urged limitation by class instead of tonnage and opposed international supervision. Not wanting to hinder technological changes, they argued against budget restrictions, and they asked no limit on naval reserves in order to maintain flexibility in assigning personnel in time of crisis. The French countered with a draft promoting limitation by total tonnage and enforcement by international supervision. They supported limits on reserves because they had neither a large navy nor air force. And in proposing budget restrictions, they hoped to limit new weapons, particularly on land. But the French proposal ran so counter to American wishes and placed so much stress on League involvement that an exasperated Gibson described his French opposite (Paul-Boncour) as an "impenitent idealist." Gibson announced that the United States would take little part in debate until he knew his government's views.[57]

By this time the American position was fairly clear. Gibson had proposed that the United States, being outside the League, oppose international inspection and submit no draft agenda. Americans would regard a universal standard of disarmament—fixed total tonnages as offered by the French—as unwise and would favor a final draft with two parts, the one for arms limitation, which would include the United States, the other for matters concerning only League members. Secretary Kellogg cabled that he thought Gibson was inviting other nations to arrange terms of supervision. The United States disapproved of international control not because the nation remained outside the League, the secretary wrote, but because Americans objected to supervision.[58] Supervision impugned national honor and dignity. Although he still thought League members might agree to enforcement, Gibson suggested a single draft plan without enforcement, fearing that the United States might become the scapegoat for the failure of Commission efforts on enforcement.[59]

The French rejected limitation by class. Britain's First Lord of the Admiralty, William Bridgeman, a delegate to the Commission, feared the discussions at Geneva would produce little of value and failure of the Commission might affect the disarmament conference scheduled by President Coolidge for Geneva in June. Described by Chamberlain as "a really good fellow with a slightly surly manner but as straight as they are made," Bridgeman remained optimistic, on the condition that conference participants not arrive committed to programs.[60] At the Commission's meeting on April 11, Gibson suspected that Cecil believed that "the three powers . . . were more concerned with what might happen at the said Conference than with the present labors of this Commission." Americans did not "denigrate" the work of the Commission in favor of the later conference, Gibson said. Jones wondered if the British might have set up the Americans. But Cecil supported the Commission as much if not more than the forthcoming conference. He was surprised that Gibson chided him for emphasizing the naval conference above the Commission and took pains to point out the good work of the Commission. In fact, Cecil concluded, Gibson's attitude seemed "far more pro-League than that of our own Admiralty."[61]

The British and Americans had reason for pessimism about the Commission, even if they applauded its work, for Paul-Boncour gave a speech that implied that he wanted to break up the meetings. It was a "direct slap at those countries that said they could not agree to supervision and control." He suggested that the Commission answer four questions: Did all participants accept an exchange of information? Would an international organization collect and collate information? Would delegates agree that this organization was more than an information gatherer? If any country came before the League Council could the Council decide its case?[62]

In the end, conferees achieved a modest compromise. They agreed to limited sharing of information, without participation of the League. The delegates made little headway, however, toward resolving differences over disarmament. Gibson thought that more might have been accomplished if the French had not held out for international control. Final meetings proved frenzied, and nerves frayed. The mercurial Cecil complained to Chamberlain about his naval advisers:

I feel bound to add that throughout this rather difficult task in which I have been engaged, I have received no assistance, direct or indirect, from the Admiralty, except such as has been extorted from them by yourself and my other colleagues who have been good enough to come to my assistance. The First Lord of the Admiralty [Bridgeman] throughout has adopted an attitude of what may be called 'Malevolent neutrality' towards the whole of our proceedings here. . . . In private he continues to express the opinion that he would be glad to see these negotiations come to an end, or words to that effect. . . . This attitude will perhaps not surprise you, in view of the continual pretension of the Admiralty to run their own policy irrespective of that which has been adopted by the Cabinet. . . . I felt it was proper for me to give you some account of how it has been that, with respect to naval officers at any rate, our efforts here must be regarded as so far having failed.[63]

A NEW NAVAL CONFERENCE

Disappointed in the Preparatory Commission, distressed by the British Admiralty's decision to build sixteen heavy cruisers, and dismayed by Japanese-American tensions, Coolidge issued invitations on February 10, 1927, for a naval conference. The president, having considered the idea for some months, permitted Gibson to draft the text of the messages, proposing that the powers use their Preparatory Commission delegations in Geneva for the task. Gibson prepared the ground for the invitations for two months, meeting with personnel from the State and Navy Departments. He reported to his mother after a meeting with Coolidge that the president genuinely desired arms reduction, that he had "followed what we have been doing and has a clear idea of our problems."[64] The invitations went to powers that had attended the Washington Conference.[65] Coolidge wondered if the Japanese would extend the 5-5-3 ratio to auxiliary vessels and if European powers, having signed the Locarno pact, might consider a conference. At a press conference the previous October, Coolidge had hinted that he would like to call a conference on both land and naval disarmament, and European responses had been unenthusiastic.

Kellogg, too, had considered a new conference. While ambassador in London in the early 1920s he and MacDonald had discussed the possibility but judged the timing inauspicious. When he and Chamberlain met after the Conservative victory in 1924, Chamberlain favored a conference but Kellogg still hesitated. After becoming secretary of state, he had called for regional meetings on land armaments and for great-power naval meetings. Even so, according to William R. Castle, Jr., assistant secretary of state, Kellogg remained skeptical of the idea of a conference and had agreed only when the cabinet, at a meeting on February 1, 1927, proposed unanimously that the president issue invitations. From then on, Castle noted sardonically, the conference became Kellogg's idea.[66]

The initial reaction to the invitations was disappointing. France declined the invitation because the agenda proposed to deal only with naval affairs and ignored the French position on global tonnage. The French chose to follow events at Commission meetings where, they said, the true work of disarmament was continuing. The Japanese accepted, suggesting that the conference not meet before June. Premier Wakatsuki explained indelicately that the U.S. was Japan's best customer and "one does not fight one's best customer." He hinted that Japan would not accept the 5-5-3 ratio for auxiliaries, as the international situation had changed since the Washington Conference. The Italians refused to attend, citing poor relations with the French—although the American ambassador thought that the general staff and Fascist leaders had overpowered Mussolini, who wished to attend. London belatedly accepted, after communicating with the Dominions; the latter were irritated that no diplomatic talks had gone on before the invitations were issued.[67]

Coolidge had serious reservations about the value of a three-power conference. Castle reported to Gibson that the president wanted to "get Italy in" to the conference and was so preoccupied with the matter that he seemed to have forgotten that he had given the State Department leave to propose three-way discussions to London and Tokyo. Happily, Castle wrote, answers from the British and Japanese reassured the president. But Coolidge reacted strongly to a rumor emanating from London that, as discussions would be among the three powers only, negotiations would be restricted to the Pacific. He labeled the rumor nonsense and reiterated that delegates would focus on naval disarmament everywhere, subject to review with changing conditions.[68]

Little more then occurred before the opening of the three-power conference in June. Kellogg left Washington in late February for a two-week vacation and made no provision for communicating with the powers in his absence. He may have regretted this action, for on his return he found himself overburdened with preparations for the impending conference.[69] Nevertheless, he believed that differences between Britain and the United States were slight, based on the conversations between naval staffs and between representatives at the Preparatory Commission.[70] Kellogg wrote Ambassador Houghton in London: "I do not think there will be any great differences between Great Britain and ourselves. Of course, Great Britain would be willing to cut the size of cruisers but she will not insist on that and I do not think she will insist on anything that will make an agreement impossible." He was relieved about arrangements for the conference because the League of Nations had offered its personnel and buildings.[71]

Between March and June 1927, the only subsequent correspondence between the participating nations related to the appointment of delegations. The Japanese appointed a prestigious delegation: Saburi Sadao, Ishii Kikujiro (ambassador to France), and Admiral Viscount Saito Makato (governor-general of Korea); for the British,

Bridgeman, Cecil, Admiral Sir Frederick Field, and Lord Jellicoe. Coolidge attempted to send a ranking delegation, asking former secretary of state Charles Evans Hughes, who refused, ostensibly because he was involved with a Chicago drainage case but also because he saw little chance for success since French feelings had not changed about limiting auxiliary vessels. The president then suggested that Kellogg attend, with Secretary of the Treasury Andrew Mellon and Senator Claude Swanson, ranking minority member of the Naval Affairs Committee, but Kellogg declined, objecting that "it would look like overloading the delegation and make it appear to the other countries that we were overanxious to have an agreement." In the end, the president appointed Gibson and Admiral Jones, the American delegates to the Preparatory Commission, as they were well acquainted with the subject, together with Hugh Wilson, the new minister to Switzerland (Gibson had been transferred to Brussels).[72] For his part, Gibson wished that a more prominent figure such as Senator David Reed of Pennsylvania had been selected and complained privately that he would not have time to read the technical material before the conference.[73]

There remained the cruiser problem. In Britain, most naval experts opposed parity, especially in cruisers, despite Beatty's assurances to Jones. As Sir Esme Howard wrote years later, "It is not publishing a secret to say that many of our leading Naval experts . . . could not understand why the U.S. government should need so large a navy as Great Britain."[74] Americans continued to demand parity, and Jones detected a whiff of future discord when he met Admiral Field, who implied that the British might desire many cruisers. Jones pronounced the notion unacceptable and hoped that Anglo-American agreement might lead to limits on Japanese cruisers.[75]

Kellogg now suspected possible trouble. Responding to a request from Secretary of the Navy Curtis Wilbur for suggestions for the General Board, he had proposed a reduction in capital ships and gun calibers and division of cruisers into classes of 10,000 and 5,000 tons. Kellogg recommended a clause allowing Britain more cruisers and destroyers with any increase in French and Italian submarines. The General Board ignored these ideas.[76]

Coolidge expressed his views at a meeting in early June attended by Gibson, Jones, and Admiral Long. The United States, he said, must have parity in cruisers, but conceded that he might consider a form of limitation that combined the French and British proposals—restriction by total tonnage and numbers of ships— "which would permit Britain to build vessels of less burden."[77]

As the weeks slipped away, the prospects of limiting the weapons of Mars in the realm of Neptune appeared bleak. Although the *Economist* described the task before the powers as "child's play" compared with the work of the Preparatory Commission, the Tokyo *Nichi Nichi* predicted that the conference would fail because of "special interests" mentioned in the British reply.[78] Indeed, France and Italy had refused to participate, and the draft convention, the dubious result of the first three sessions of the Preparatory Commission, left many questions unresolved. Success appeared to lie in compromise, perhaps achievable yet exceedingly difficult.

3

OPENING GAMBITS

After a long train trip from Paris, Rear Admiral Frank Schofield trudged up the stairs of his hotel in Geneva, La Residence, in the early evening of June 18, 1927. Small of stature, gray-haired, sixty-two years old, looking like "an emeritus professor of economics," the humorless Schofield would call the hotel his home for the next six weeks.[1] President Coolidge's invitation had suggested that the conference would convene three weeks earlier, on June 1, but it had been postponed to June 20 because the Japanese delegates pleaded for time and officials of the League of Nations asked for a delay so the League Council could discuss naval issues. Confident that it would achieve some limitation, Schofield had no indication that the conference would take longer than the summer, as initial meetings between American delegates and technical representatives of the other powers had not seemed troublesome to him.[2]

Having recovered from his fatigue after the third session of the Preparatory Commission, Lord Cecil similarly settled into his spacious quarters at the Hotel Beau Rivage, situated near Lake Geneva with Mont Saleve in the distance. On a clear day he could even see snow-clad Mont Blanc. A tall, ascetic man with bowed shoulders, he shared Schofield's presumption that the conferees would quickly fashion a treaty. To Austen Chamberlain, temporarily in Geneva for a meeting of the League Council, he optimistically predicted success in three weeks, "since even Admirals ought not to be able to spin out a negotiation on the principles of which we are all agreed for more than that time."[3]

NAVAL POSITIONS

Unhappily for the two men, the disagreement over cruisers hinted at in the meetings of the Preparatory Commission and the informal naval talks of the spring soon appeared in the Geneva Conference. The General Board of the U.S. Navy emphasized parity with Britain because it had lagged in cruiser construction and was determined to build a "navy second to none." Remembering the *Dreadnought*, the all-heavy-gunned battleship that outclassed all other battleships when launched in 1906, the board favored treaty cruisers. It viewed with concern both the British preference for light cruisers and German experiments in designing a "pocket battleship" which combined speed and heavy guns within a displacement of 10,000 tons. Yet the U.S. Navy had launched no treaty cruisers. It had laid down the 10,000-ton *Pensacola* only in October 1926, the *Salt Lake City* six months later. The navy would not receive the first of these ships until at least 1929.

The board proposed extending the Washington ratio, 5-5-3, to cruisers. It suggested a single cruiser class, not two classes as the British had mentioned at the Preparatory Commission. It opposed lowering displacement or allowing other nations to build more small cruisers because it believed the small cruiser could not guard commerce. The board also suggested caliber of guns no larger than eight inches, with no maximum for guns per ship, in part because it realized that the eight-inch shell would pierce the thin armor of Japanese and British battle cruisers. The board further recommended that delegates ask a total cruiser tonnage of 300,000 tons, and accept no more than 400,000 tons. Finally, it proposed changing cruiser age limits to twenty years. This would reduce the number of British cruisers, the oldest being only sixteen years, and force Congress to replace American cruisers, some of which were thirty-four years old.[4]

In London, Admiralty officials sought to avoid mention of the Royal Navy's lead in cruisers. British cruisers included those of the *Kent* class (10,000 tons, eight eight-inch guns, four four-inch antiaircraft guns), and the *London* class, including both a "B" type, which displaced 8,400 tons and featured six eight-inch rifles in twin turrets and four four-inch antiaircraft guns, and an "A" type, which displaced 10,000 tons.[5] The Admiralty advised Cecil to turn any talk of limitation toward discussion of the possibility of war in the Far East. They anticipated completion of nine cruisers, the first since the Washington Conference, by 1927-29, compared to two for the United States and four for Japan.

The Admiralty favored a large number of light cruisers, both because Britain already had great numbers compared to the U.S. and Japan, and because the large merchant marine included several dozen ships that could mount six-inch guns in war. Admiral Beatty outlined this position at a cabinet meeting on May 20, advocating extension of the Washington 5-5-3 ratio to other classes. He said that, although the treaty cruiser had been forced on Britain at Washington, the Admiralty preferred not to limit such ships. If forced to restrict them, he preferred limiting the heavy eight-inch type but not the light six-inch. If driven to limit ships carrying the smaller gun, he favored an absolute number of cruisers, namely seventy, instead of a number based on the cruisers of other powers. Churchill impatiently asked Beatty whether, if the U.S. and Japan insisted on parity with Britain's seventy cruisers, the Admiralty would give in. Beatty replied that it would not, since he based the figure of seventy on the estimated strength of the other powers. Protection of trade routes required seventy cruisers and he did not suppose any argument would arise at Geneva against the proposal. Bridgeman said he believed the U.S. would not agree that trade routes justified more cruisers. Churchill responded that not all routes needed patrolling, which might mean fewer cruisers. Beatty admitted that Britain might benefit by limiting small cruisers if the small naval powers, France and Italy, agreed to reduce submarines and destroyers, for fewer cruisers would then be needed to patrol the Mediterranean routes.[6]

The Admiralty viewed the Far East with the least concern of any strategic area. Officers believed that the widening civil war in China rendered Britain's interests there vulnerable, and they warned of a possible Sino-Japanese war. That problem would perhaps solve itself, even though it might make a debating point at Geneva. It showed the need for the base at Singapore.

The Japanese came to Geneva determined to improve their nation's security and at the same time achieve economy. They feared for security in the western Pacific because they considered neither the League of Nations, the Washington Treaties, nor occasional discussions about limiting or outlawing war as compensation for a large British base at Singapore and loss of the Anglo-Japanese alliance. Addressing the Japanese Council of the Institute of Pacific Relations, Vice Admiral Nomura Kichisaburo, assistant chief of the naval staff, doubted that Japan could halt British construction at Singapore or American construction at Pearl Harbor. He expected little financial benefit for Japan in disarmament, reflecting the sentiment of many in the navy.[7] Admiral Kobayashi Seizo believed that Japan needed to guard against China and the Soviet Union, both of which could create "situations that no one can predict." He also had doubts about the conference: he did not think that the British had changed their minds about cruiser limitation since the Washington Conference, when they rejected the idea because of the high number of French submarines. Kobayashi noted that the French had even more submarines in 1927.[8] In his first message on disarmament since assuming office, Premier Tanaka on June 13 repeated the pledges of his naval spokesmen that Japan's naval needs were defensive; the nation needed only to guard its trade routes.

In reality, the Japanese wished to safeguard their position by achieving either equality or at least a better ratio with the other powers if ratios were applied to auxiliary ships. Editorials in a majority of Japanese papers opposed the 10-6 ratio because of economic uncertainty and political dislocation in China, and some, such as the Tokyo *Asahi* and *Hochi*, reminded their readers that the political and naval arrangements of the Washington Conference would be affected by the outcome of the Geneva Conference.[9] In Paris en route to Geneva, the personable Saito, who was closely associated with the chairman of the Mitsubishi Shipbuilding Company, suggested Japanese dislike of the Washington ratio.[10] But at the same time, Tokyo desired lower naval costs in the future, especially in auxiliary ships, following the disastrous bank emergency that spring. Given this situation, the instructions for the delegates at Geneva approved by Wakatsuki's government were reaffirmed by the Tanaka government at a ministerial conference May 3.[11]

OPENING DISCUSSIONS

In addition to Schofield and the voting delegates, Rear Admiral Jones and Ambassador Gibson, the American delegation at Geneva included Rear Admiral Andrew T. Long, a member of the General Board and a veteran of other conferences, notably the Paris Peace Conference; Captain J.M. Reeves (promoted to rear admiral during the conference), commander of Aircraft Squadrons, Battle Fleet; Captain Arthur J. Hepburn, the quiet, studious director of Naval Intelligence; Captain Adolphus Andrews, who had been present at the Preparatory Commission meetings; Captain W.W. Smyth, a gunnery specialist; Lieutenant Commander Harold C. Train (promoted to commander during the conference), who had been at the Preparatory Commission meetings; and Lieutenant Commander H.H. Frost. Also included were Allen W. Dulles, the former State Department official and disarmament specialist, then in private legal practice and Hugh R. Wilson, the newly appointed, young (Schofield thought too young) minister to Switzerland, who would serve as secretary-general of the conference.

Some American officials worried that naval representatives, lacking finesse and imagination, and little fearing the junior diplomats of the delegation, might interfere in the diplomatic activity at the conference. Yet Gibson wrote that Jones "is a lovable old boy but it takes him forever to make up his mind and somewhat longer to explain his ideas. As a result he did not produce one idea during our recent meeting and I was to all intents and purposes our naval expert. We got away with it but it is too big a chance to take next time."[12] But William Castle wished that Kellogg would go to the conference because the secretary might monitor the navy men and, if needed, "sit on them with great vigor." Castle was probably overly optimistic about this, as Kellogg did not do it in Washington. Castle also worried about the effect the undistinguished delegation from the U.S. might have on the outcome of the conference.[13] Castle concluded that "all in all, I feel that we may be riding for a great fall unless we are extremely careful."[14]

The British delegation included—in addition to the leading delegates, Cecil and Bridgeman, and Admirals Field and Jellicoe—Rear Admiral A.D.P.R. Pound, assistant chief of the naval staff (who would take Field's place when he became ill); Captain W.A. Egerton; Lieutenant Colonel W.W. Godfrey; and Vice Admiral Aubrey Smith, liaison officer, together with representatives of the Dominions.

Accompanying the Japanese delegates, Saito and Ishii, were Saburi Sadao, the director of the Bureau of Treaties and Conventions in the Department of Foreign Affairs; Vice Admiral Kobayashi; Rear Admiral Hara Kanjiro; Captain Hori Teikichi; Captain Toyoda Teijiro, naval attaché at London until March 1927 and close to Saito; Captain Koga Mineichi, and various junior officers.

As Castle had feared, the Japanese delegation expressed concern to Bridgeman in early June that Gibson was to preside over the conference, for he was inferior in rank both to Japanese and to British delegates.[15] Ambassador Matsudaira pointed out to the Americans that Gibson, although respected, did not rank with Saito, the most prominent statesman in Japan, or with Ishii, the most senior foreign office official. The Japanese, however, later sought to reassure the Americans when the new navy minister, Admiral Okada, stated that he wished to "shatter the illusion" that the Japanese objected to American personnel.[16]

Delegates of all three nations considered informal discussion at the outset, but time was short between the end of the third session of the Preparatory Commission and the opening of the conference. Also, the delegates had only recently been selected, and many remembered the tactic of Charles Evans Hughes, who had made the well-remembered American proposals at the first session of the Washington Conference. In opposing preliminary talks, Beatty remarked: "There is no doubt that the United States scored tremendously at Washington by withholding her proposals for a Naval Holiday till the first public Session. The idea caught the imagination of the world, and made it difficult for any Power to oppose it. There is not so much credit to be expected this time, but what there may be we should endeavour to obtain. Therefore if the Conference is to hold Public Sessions, I consider we should not communicate our proposals to the other Powers. . . . I would give nothing without a quid pro quo."[17] The other delegates agreed. The Americans assumed preliminary talks were unnecessary because of Jones's conversations with the British. The Japanese refrained because they wished to determine the positions of the other powers and only then promote their own demands. The press reports from Geneva, especially in the French newspapers, and the reports of Wythe Williams, correspondent for the *New York Times*, gave the participants hints and started many rumors about the probable substance of each power's proposals. Williams wrote that Britain should dismantle naval bases that might threaten American coastal and trade routes since this would be an equivalent sacrifice to the one the American navy made at Washington in scrapping capital ships and not fortifying Guam. On June 1, Williams described the British preference for six-inch-gunned cruisers as a trick to prevent attacks on armed merchantmen, which could not mount eight-inch guns.[18]

The first plenary session of the conference opened on the afternoon of June 20, 1927, in the League of Nations' Glass Room, which held about three hundred people. After photographs, the Americans sat at the head of a large U-shaped table, with the Japanese on their left and the British on their right. Minor officials and observers took chairs around the sides of the room.

Gibson welcomed delegates in a voice barely audible and oversaw the establishment of procedural matters. He outlined the American proposals, concentrating on reduction of tonnages and continuation of the Washington treaty limits; Kellogg had forbidden the delegates to introduce the nonfortification issue. Gibson proposed that the ratios and principles of the Washington treaties apply to auxiliary vessels. Auxiliary ships, he suggested, should be divided into classes— cruisers, destroyers, submarines, and other vessels. He recommended total tonnages for cruisers of 250,000 to 300,000 tons for the U.S. and Britain and 150,000 to 180,000 for Japan. For destroyers he suggested 200,000 to 250,000 total tons for the U.S. and Britain and 120,000 to 150,000 for Japan. He concluded that submarines might displace 60,000 to 90,000 tons for the U.S. and Britain and 36,000 to 54,000 for Japan. The American proposal sought low tonnages in all classes because the Congress probably would refuse higher limits.[19]

Bridgeman offered the British proposals in a loud, clear voice, declaring he would "not be revealing any secrets hitherto unknown." Indeed, he continued, "I am more likely to be accused of repeating well-worn platitudes." He suggested extending the lives of ships, from twenty to twenty-six years for capital ships, twenty-four for eight-inch-gun cruisers, twenty for destroyers, and fifteen for submarines. He advocated reduction in displacement and gun size for battleships and aircraft carriers. Turning to cruisers, he recommended that the 5-5-3 ratio apply to eight-inch-gun cruisers and, after the numbers of eight-inch-gun cruisers had been set, a limit of future cruisers to 7,500 tons and six-inch guns. For destroyers, he suggested guns of five inches and displacement of 1,400 to 1,750 tons. He noted British willingness to eliminate submarines, but, as powers not at the conference might object, he stood ready only to apply limits. He avoided the issue of total tonnage and noted that any agreement at the conference would have to please France and Italy, who were not participating officially. Whereas the Americans proposed limiting cruisers at 5-5-3, according to total tonnage, then, the British wanted the 5-5-3 ratio for heavy cruisers, based on tonnage, armaments, and age, but not on cruisers less than 7,500 tons and carrying six-inch guns.

Finally, Viscount Saito submitted the Japanese proposals, observing that capital ships and aircraft carriers (for which the Japanese wanted a higher ratio) were not in his outline. He suggested that the powers not increase tonnages of authorized ships. He excluded ships under 700 tons, carrying guns under three inches (or no more than four guns, between three and six inches), and aircraft carriers under 10,000 tons. Destroyers, together with submarines, would have a life of twelve years, and larger ships a life of sixteen years. Excess tonnage should be destroyed and "appropriate regulations" cover replacement construction, to avoid sudden tonnage differences between the conferring powers. In line with the Japanese strategy of "wait and see," his suggestions appeared vague.[20]

It is interesting that each power's proposals followed the recommendations of its admirals. Flag officers in the 1920s received respect, since they had not gotten into trouble in the world war—aside from the Battle of Jutland. Admirals at Geneva encountered little resistance on technical issues from civilians. In the case of the Americans, as noted, navy men were more senior than their State Department counterparts. Diplomats rarely felt able to counter the technical experts' advice because the president appeared to back the navy men. Admiral Beatty dominated discussions in London, while the prime minister appeared ambivalent about the conference. In addition, the British may not have seen the conference as more than a technical meeting: Ian Nish has claimed that the British did not consider limits on auxiliaries as an extension of the "Washington System."[21] Navy men in Japan were more prominent in the government and many held political or diplomatic posts, making the distinction between political and technical responsibilities hazy.

At any rate, after the opening plenary and executive sessions, the admirals dominated proceedings for the next two weeks, both informally and in technical sessions. They dealt first with battleships, a subject unexpectedly brought up by the British. The Americans, diplomats and admirals, were upset by London's proposal to discuss modification of battleships before 1931, the date set by the Five-Power Treaty. Gibson and Dulles visited Saito and the cautious Ishii to find out the Japanese position, and Ishii, who spoke better English, replied that the Japanese government might like the economies provided by further reduction in capital ships, but he would have to await instructions from Tokyo. The American delegates did not come away reassured, for they wanted to prevent the Japanese from increasing their battleship ratio, in light of the Washington limit on fortification of the Pacific islands.[22]

Despite American concerns, humor managed to leaven the discussion. Admiral Jones and Captain Hepburn met Admiral Kobayashi and Saburi in Jones's office at the Hotel Les Bergues on June 25 to consider an approach to the battleship and cruiser problems. During the conversation the Japanese inadvertently demonstrated their concern about ratios, which they preferred to describe by other names, possibly thinking the term "ratio" insulting. As Hepburn noted later; "At one point Admiral Kobayashi used the word 'ratios,' which caused both Mr. Saburi and Admiral Jones to laugh; the latter saying that he was glad to see that the Japanese delegation had apparently got over their objection to the use of that term. Admiral Kobayashi said something about its only being a term, and Mr. Saburi still laughing said they were going to propose a five-franc fine for every mention of it." The Americans remained uncertain how the

Japanese would stand on capital ships, and with reason, as the Japanese announced on June 27 that they might accept the British proposal to reconsider age limitation and tonnages of that category.[23]

But the cruiser issue overshadowed this problem and, indeed, all others, so the technical committees turned to the subject of light and heavy cruisers. Describing heavy cruisers, the British opined that "this type will . . . eventually disappear," although it currently operated with the battle fleet, and that the Washington-dictated displacement of 10,000 tons was unduly large. In conversation with Gibson on June 23, Bridgeman and Cecil suggested informally that the United States might not want to build to the level that the British deemed necessary for their security and that of the Dominions. Gibson responded that they could settle the matter when Washington decided on its program, but the right of parity remained fundamental. Bridgeman said again that the British favored dividing cruisers into two classes. He reported to London that in informal discussion the Americans held that small cruisers were of little use but conceded that if tonnage of light cruisers went as high as 7,500, they did not foresee difficulties in dividing cruisers into classes. The Japanese favored limiting large cruisers, probably at the Washington ratio of 5-5-3, but preferred a total tonnage for small cruisers and would probably build more.[24]

Although the Americans would accept the division of cruisers into classes, British demands for cruiser tonnage at 607,950, compared to the proposed U.S. total of 511,945, or a 6-5 ratio, shocked them, as Schofield confided in his diary. The United States wanted to cut total tonnage drastically, not expand it, and refused to consider any increased British tonnage. To keep track of the informal talks, Gibson ordered a record book for the American Chancery at Les Bergues; members of the delegation were to read and initial the minutes. (Foreign offices in the 1920s still maintained the pretense that they did not record informal talks.) Gibson's arrangement appears to reflect his concern over the proposed high British tonnage, and perhaps also his desire to document intransigence in case the conference failed.[25]

In Washington, Secretary Kellogg took offense at the British demand for a large number of cruisers. He declared to Gibson that the only nations with navies large enough to threaten the British were the U.S. and Japan, and their representatives were at Geneva for the purpose of limiting navies. Although Kellogg still hoped for agreement, he began to distrust the intentions of the British.[26]

The Japanese expressed surprise at the high British figure, but held to their plan, which vaguely advocated a status-quo arrangement with a holiday in auxiliary ships. They wished to preserve their lead in cruisers over the Americans and, as Saito told Gibson, would not accept a 5-5-3 ratio. Asked about rumors that Japan would demand equality, Saito remained noncommittal, answering only that his government would ask for tonnages on the basis of its requirements. The opposition in Tokyo, the newly formed Minseito party (made up of smaller opposition groups), joined with Premier Tanaka's majority Seiyukai party in approving Saito's position.[27]

Seeking to head off speculation about his government's plans, the vice minister of the Marine in Tokyo explained to a British naval attaché that the Japanese press remained poorly informed about the negotiations. When told that it was too early for the ministry to make a statement about the talks, Japanese journals fell back on conjecture, he said, which might explain the articles attacking the British and American positions at the conference. He assured the attaché that the government was considering proposals and would make its position known.[28]

In a thoughtful article, the American journalist Frank H. Simonds speculated that the Japanese might propose a limit on cruisers based on existing strength, a reasonable idea, since the Americans had used that basis at the Washington Conference in the cases of France and Italy. But he cautioned that Americans would not accept permanent inferiority with Tokyo. He offered little hope for success in Geneva, as Americans expected both Japan and Britain to give up any thought of cruiser supremacy, as the U.S. had done with battleships at Washington. Those countries, he reminded his readers, had different strategic needs than those of the U.S.[29]

As the month of June came to a close, delegates and observers began to realize that a treaty might not be possible. While the Japanese made little comment, Bridgeman warned Baldwin that negotiation on cruisers would be difficult; he complained that the other two delegations had proved slow in furnishing material for the British and that the Americans answered questions reluctantly and seemed to be playing for time. Cecil sounded a more pessimistic note in his report to London, in which he recognized American financial ability but overestimated the desire of the American government and public to increase their navy:

The conference here is not going extraordinarily well so far. I am afraid the Admiralty made a mistake in insisting upon such profound secrecy about our proposals before we came. No doubt it was tempting to play the part of the leading advocate for disarmament, but the fundamental fact of the situation is that we have got to do what the Americans wish, since they alone are able and willing to build to any extent if we do not reach an agreement. Unfortunately, as they had no guidance as to what we were going to propose, they arrive here in a rather suspicious frame of mind.[30]

Kellogg predicted to Gibson that even if the British put forward its cruiser claims seriously, analysis of them would justify failure to conclude a treaty in the eyes of the public: "It might even have the effect of stimulating [the] zeal of Congress for competition building." From his vacation in South Dakota, President Coolidge sent his encouragement to Kellogg.[31]

A CRUISER IMBROGLIO

Shortly thereafter, the Americans thought they detected a ray of hope. Gibson reported that Bridgeman had consented to parity in cruisers with the United States. In informal discussion, Schofield suggested to the British a cruiser limit to last until 1936, based on a formula for avoiding construction.[32]

But the British had not backed down. Churchill argued against a treaty that granted parity with the United States, complaining that the Americans had put forward the demand for reasons of prestige, not need. He sagely suggested that as long as Britain led in cruiser construction, and set a slow pace, the U.S. would probably follow, as Coolidge seemed disinclined to increase the navy. With ill temper he concluded that "it always seems to be assumed that it is our duty to humour the United States and minister to their vanity. They do nothing for us in return, but exact their pound of flesh."[33] After consultation with London, Bridgeman explained that Britain would discuss a cruiser scrapping plan if America agreed to four principles: a higher age for ships, the six-inch gun for light cruisers, a 7,500-ton displacement for new light cruisers, and a limit on cruisers with eight-inch guns. The United States responded by sending the cruiser question back to the technical committee, and the Japanese told Gibson the British tonnage figure saddened them.[34]

The cruiser imbroglio came to a head. An irritated State Department cabled its delegates on July 2 to insist on a maximum total cruiser tonnage of 400,000 tons. Over the Fourth of July weekend, while most delegates were out of the city, Schofield drew up a proposal for the next technical meeting: he was through trying to compromise with the British. Gibson added a final line to the document, per his instructions from Washington, which disclosed that the Americans would not consider proposals for limitation higher than 400,000 tons.[35]

When Jones revealed the terms on July 5, the technical committee members seemed stunned. Back at his office Jones apparently had second thoughts and worried that the proposal might sound to the British like an ultimatum; his fear was well-founded. Bridgeman cabled London that "we have reached something like a climax over cruisers." He could hardly believe that after the conference had accomplished so much in respect to other classes of vessels the Americans would break it up over the cruiser issue.[36]

The Cabinet in London split on the proper course of action. Foreign Minister Austen Chamberlain had arrived back in London from the League Council meeting and a vacation in the South of France in late June, ill-prepared to face the crisis. He had had no messages forwarded and knew little more about the conference than what he could read in the *Times*. He was confused by the sketchy details discussed in Cabinet, for the Committee of Imperial Defence (CID) and the Cabinet Committee for Disarmament headed by Lord Salisbury, Cecil's brother, had handled most of the work of the Geneva Conference. Nevertheless, Chamberlain apparently felt confident enough to attack Churchill's contention that a breakdown of the conference would not prove disastrous.[37] Churchill had argued that without an agreement, the Americans would probably build ten cruisers, which would not hurt Britain. Indeed, he had concluded, the collapse of negotiations might provoke a reaction in the U.S. that would assist limitation. Chamberlain replied that the British would be forced either to build eight-inch cruisers or to drop the one-power standard. He was anxious for success at Geneva because if naval reduction did not occur, there seemed little prospect of a general disarmament conference in the spirit of Locarno, a meeting which was dear to his heart. But Churchill and Beatty carried the Cabinet. Chamberlain therefore instructed the delegation at Geneva to reiterate the British position on total tonnages, grant no parity in light cruisers (a reversal of Bridgeman's assurances), and use the delegation's press connections to publicize the government's objectives.[38]

For their part, the Japanese repeated to Gibson that they considered the British tonnage totals too high. They proposed restricting cruisers to 450,000 tons for the U.S. and Britain and 300,000 for themselves, adding that they would welcome lower figures. Gibson considered withdrawing the U.S. proposal of 400,000 but his technical advisers, especially Schofield, talked him out of it.[39]

The day after the technical meeting, American and British delegates met in a stormy session. Cecil asked heatedly if the Americans meant the 400,000-ton proposal as an ultimatum, and Gibson assured him they did not. Perhaps he was too convincing, for the British left the meeting believing that he was more conciliatory than his naval advisers when, in fact, he had been responsible for the harsh presentation of his country's proposal. Whatever the impression Gibson created, the Americans were determined to hold their position, and Kellogg told Ambassador Esme Howard that the U.S. insisted on limits for all classes of vessels, including cruisers. As concessions, Washington would accept an agreement with an escape clause in the event nonsignatories increased naval armament and would discuss anew the capital-ship question.[40]

Kellogg approved the American delegates' position, even if the conference should fail because of it. A private meeting of American and British delegates and advisers might be beneficial, but he suggested adjournment for a week or so if breakdown appeared imminent. He agreed that in case of failure Gibson should make a statement that the Americans accepted the limit on cruisers and destroyers that Hughes had proposed at Washington—that is, 450,000 tons. President Coolidge telegraphed his support: "Tell Gibson what is needed is not excuse or soft words but clear strong statement of American position. Let blame fall where may. Your plan approved."[41]

Room remained for bargaining over cruisers, especially considering the Japanese proposal for total tonnage, but thus far neither Washington nor London seemed inclined to compromise.

It was a strange impasse, in which theory dominated fact. As mentioned, the British government really disliked the idea of building larger, so-called heavy cruisers, simply because the American navy desired to build them. The Americans themselves had created this issue but then chose not to build as rapidly as the British and Japanese. The nation most threatened by the existence of large cruisers was clearly Japan, and yet at Geneva the Japanese refused to offer any constructive proposals, preferring to choose their best course from among their opponents' proposals. The negotiation was largely a series of poses, not in accord with reality because, after all, none of the large cruisers had gone down the ways.

In such a situation one might expect the civilians, members of the governments in Washington, London, and Tokyo, to take charge—to decide what their national interests dictated. The success at Washington, they surely knew, had derived from the willingness of civilians to make choices in naval armament, not allowing the experts alone to decide what was best. Something, one must conclude, had happened to the heads of governments in the capitals of the major naval powers, for this time around they were not willing to suppress the building zeal of naval officers.

The root cause of the impasse at Geneva is difficult to know. It may have been the receding memory of the world war, which made issues of armament less pressing than they were in 1921-22. It may have been the appearance of prosperity throughout the world following the violence of 1914-18—fears of an economic collapse had somehow subsided, and national economies had gone from strength to strength. It may have been a lack of imagination among the leaders who, for some reason or reasons, were simply not up to the requirements of the moment, the need to move decisively for limitation at least, and if possible, reduction.

In any event, it was still not beyond the realm of possibility that the conferees could find a solution to the cruiser impasse, and early in July 1927 they turned to this possibility.

4

A DIPLOMATIC IMPASSE

All conferences come to an end, and so did the Geneva Naval Conference; the concern of the historian is how it happened. The enormously important problem of the limitation of arms, and, in 1927,
the limitation specifically of naval arms, seemed to have a real
chance of resolution in the 1920s; the first instance of this fortune
had occurred in 1921-22 at Washington. The second, presumably,
would take place at Geneva. The League of Nations was working
feverishly on a somewhat larger program—the limitation of all
arms, both on land and on sea. The League was pursuing this possibility in part, of course, because the Treaty of Versailles had limited
German armaments and related that Germany's limitation was
only the first step in general limitation. The purposes of the Washington and Geneva conferences were, one might say, more modest.
But in retrospect, considering that they involved the Japanese government, they were of almost equal importance. Japan would attack
the United States Navy at Pearl Harbor only fourteen years after the
Geneva Conference of 1927. The failure at Geneva hence held great
importance for the future, for the way in which failure came about
is an indication of why the powers could not maintain peace in the
interwar years.

THE SHEARER QUESTION

Part of the difficulties during the naval discussions of 1927 lay in
the animosity, the irritability, that surrounded Anglo-American affairs, and at the center of this problem was the American naval
publicist-cum-journalist William Shearer. Present during the talks
in Geneva, he circulated daily anti-British communiqués on naval

matters. The British Foreign Office on July 2 received an inquiry about him from its delegation at Geneva. The delegates believed that Shearer, while posing as a journalist, was really working for American steel interests and hoped to wreck the conference. They reported that the American delegation appeared equally anxious to stop him but had insufficient evidence for the purpose. Suspecting that Scotland Yard possessed a dossier on him, the delegates asked that it be sent to Geneva.[1]

Although the delegates might have overstressed American anxiety (after all, Shearer supported the American position), they accurately reflected the annoyance of Britons in Geneva, London, and Washington over the ability of the American press to discredit British proposals or, as Sir Esme Howard put it, to "queer the pitch every time."[2] Although leaks from the conference appeared most frequently in the French press (presumably through French observers at the conference), the British were more exasperated with American journalists who wrote scathing attacks on the British negotiating position or perennially favored other nations. In the latter instance they could cite the francophile Edwin James of the *New York Times* who had covered the meetings of the Preparatory Commission. At length Scotland Yard complied with the request and furnished the desired document on Shearer.

Shearer was indeed an interesting lobbyist. He was good-looking, a careful dresser, and a bright and easy conversationalist. A foe of the League of Nations, Britain, Judaism, Asiatic peoples, internationalism, pacifism, and communism (or, as he said, of pink, yellow, and red), he had published a novel in 1926, *Pacifico*, about an American naval officer who discovered a Japanese plot to crush the United States. A writer for *Collier's Weekly* surmised that "in the old days he would have sold patent medicine or lightning rods. Today he sells patriotism, a product with a much higher social status and more profitable to sell."[3] Shearer maintained good relations with Wythe Williams of the *New York Times* and Henry Wales of the *Chicago Tribune*, who arranged for him to secure press credentials from the *New York Daily News*. Reporters themselves believed that Shearer worked for arms manufacturers.

They were, of course, right. Shearer had lobbied for shipbuilders in 1926, and afterward officials of the National Council of American Shipbuilders engaged him. Any restrictions on construction of cruisers might cost the shipbuilders as much as $54 million,[4] they calculated, for the year 1926 had witnessed a sharp decline in orders. Shearer was hired on March 17, 1927, in a meeting with Samuel W.

Wakeman, a vice president of Bethlehem Shipbuilding Corporation, and Frederick P. Palen and Clinton L. Bardo of New York Shipbuilding, a subsidiary of American Brown-Boveri Electrical Corporation. He communicated with the shipbuilders through Henry C. Hunter, counsel for the National Council of American Shipbuilding, of which Bethlehem, New York, and Newport News Shipbuilding were the only members.[5]

In Geneva, the wily Shearer propounded the navy's case, vexed the British, but made little real difference in the course of the negotiations. For information he used a booklet prepared by the General Board of the Navy, and let other journalists see it, providing them with tables about gun caliber, elevation, tonnage, and other technical points. He occasionally dined with junior members of the American technical staff. But Rear Admiral Schofield remarked in his diary that in dealing with the press he and the other advisers talked only about reasons for American proposals and said nothing about decisions reached or progress made. After dining with Shearer one evening, Schofield wrote that, as usual, Shearer had done all the talking. Shearer did not learn much of importance during his time in Geneva. He even missed the biggest leak of the conference, for it was French journalists, probably with the assistance of French *informateurs*, who first revealed the large British figure for cruiser tonnage.[6]

Shearer tried to make up for lapses in his ability as a lobbyist by claiming that the British were already over the tonnage limit in capital ships established by the Washington treaty. Williams repeated the charges in the *New York Times*. Annoyed, the British filed a protest with the State Department.[7] In a cable to Gibson, Kellogg asked if reports about lobbyists for steel interests were true. Gibson said he had no idea of anyone in Geneva associated with steel interests and thought the British had brought this up to explain the critical attitude of the American press. It is interesting that by this time the British had shown Gibson their dossier on Shearer.[8] Gibson perhaps was embarrassed by his own ignorance.

At Geneva the essential problem was not press distortion, however, it was governments that could not agree on cruisers. Poor communication between delegates in Geneva and their governments, which, the delegates regularly complained, gave them no information, exacerbated this problem. Yet the French had leaked many secrets during meetings of the third Preparatory Commission and delegates had not complained as strongly. The admirals wanted cruisers.[9] The humorist Will Rogers wryly observed that "two more disarmament conferences and there won't be enough ocean to hold all the cruisers they want to build."[10]

THE PHANTOM OF PARITY

Delegates struggled to find areas of agreement, and the first progress came in the Technical Committee's meeting of July 8, when its members agreed on limitation of destroyers, fixing the maximum displacement for destroyer flotilla leaders, which carried additional equipment, at 1,850 tons, and that for ordinary destroyers at 1,500 tons. Flotilla leaders, they concurred, might make up 16 percent of each nation's destroyer tonnage. They designated a five-inch gun as maximum armament and sixteen years as an age limit. The British wanted 221,600 tons of destroyers, with 29,600 as leaders, while the Americans and Japanese withheld their figures until establishment of cruiser tonnage.

The committee also set tentative limits for other ship categories, limiting displacement for submarines to 1,800 tons, with maximum gun caliber of five inches and an age limit at thirteen years. The British had proposed dividing submarines into classes, one of 1,000-to-1,600 tons, the other under 600, but the Japanese and Americans had disagreed, and the British yielded. Technical experts also agreed not to limit any type of ship under 600 tons, provided it carried no guns over six inches, no torpedo tubes, and did not have a speed over eighteen knots.

But the experts on each side did less well with cruisers, as they largely maintained their previous positions. The British still asked fifteen heavy and fifty-five light, while the Japanese hinted that they might agree to a smaller cruiser class of 8,000 tons, albeit with eight-inch guns. The Americans asked for a total cruiser tonnage of 300,000 to 400,000.[11]

The conference's executive committee held its second formal session the same day and accepted the Technical Committee's report. Attempting to find a solution to the problem of total tonnage for cruisers, the Japanese suggested that the conferees group figures for cruisers and destroyers together, with totals of 450,000 for Britain and the U.S. and 300,000 for Japan. Gibson spoke against tonnage limits, and the committee decided to consider the question between that meeting and the next. The British insisted on a plenary session on July 11 to present their case, as they believed their position had been misrepresented in the press. Gibson and Ishii

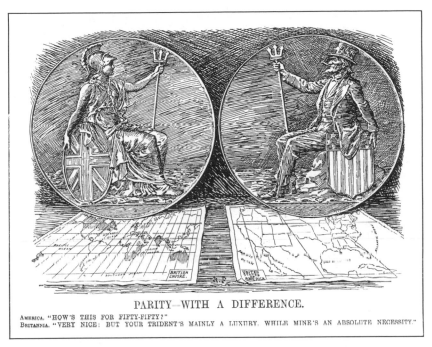

PARITY—WITH A DIFFERENCE.

AMERICA. "HOW'S THIS FOR FIFTY-FIFTY?"
BRITANNIA. "VERY NICE: BUT YOUR TRIDENT'S MAINLY A LUXURY, WHILE MINE'S AN ABSOLUTE NECESSITY."

Punch, August 3, 1927.

strongly opposed such an early date, fearing that views of delegations would harden when subjected to public scrutiny. In the end, the British did postpone the meeting for a few days, ostensibly to discuss the proposal of a temporary cruiser restriction and to honor a recently assassinated delegate from the Irish Free State, Kevin O'Higgins.[12]

Before the next executive committee session Britons and Americans sought a breakthrough on cruisers. Both delegations consulted with their governments, and naval advisers met in small groups. Gibson and Dulles considered a compromise in cruiser numbers, but their naval advisers persuaded them against it. Gibson had drafted a cable to Washington suggesting fifteen cruisers instead of twenty-five, but Jones and Schofield prevailed on him not to send it. Schofield told Hugh Wilson: "As between breaking up the conference and sacrificing national interests, I thought that we could quite well afford to break up the conference."[13]

On the British side, Admiral Jellicoe counselled Bridgeman and Cecil to hold for a total of seventy cruisers, although he thought that a new tack—limiting cruisers for a shorter period of time rath-

er than attempting an arrangement that would last until 1936—
deserved study. Jellicoe had returned from consultation in London
prepared to do battle for the cruisers. He had written in a private
letter that the American program had only one object, "equality
with Great Britain on the sea. We cannot help it if they build up to
our required standard, but we can avoid lowering our standard to
suit them, and we shall of course take this line."[14] At a private
meeting of leading delegates (except Jones), Cecil suggested study-
ing building programs for 1927-31 and concentrating on cruisers for
those years only. He proposed restricting all programs to 400,000
tons through 1931. Bridgeman and Cecil assured the others that the
British could assent to this, but not to setting cruiser tonnage lower
than 465,000 until 1936. Gibson said he would study the proposal.[15]

Bridgeman meanwhile pressed for seventy cruisers and equivocated on parity. At a press conference, he emphasized the requirements of empire, underscoring Britain's need for seventy cruisers
and questioning America's need for heavy cruisers. Although he
hoped for a settlement just before the plenary session of July 14, he
refuted Kellogg's charge that delegates at the Washington Conference had agreed to 450,000 tons as a maximum limit for destroyers
and cruisers. The journalists were openly skeptical of Bridgeman's
claims and interpreted them as a retreat from parity.[16]

Chamberlain also hedged on the issue of parity, appearing to offer
it in one breath and attack American need of it in the next. In London, Ambassador Alanson Houghton asked Chamberlain for the
minimum number of cruisers Whitehall would accept and wondered
if the British objected to the American figure of twenty-five. Chamberlain evasively replied that Britain desired the "same parity for
which you ask." He would scrap some of the fifteen heavy cruisers
then being built, and he offered to go to Geneva and meet Kellogg if
the Americans thought it would help. But at the same time, Chamberlain assailed the American position, claiming that he could not
understand U.S. opposition to light cruisers armed with six-inch
guns since American experts at the conference had never maintained
that the cruising radius of the smaller ship was too short. British
naval experts, he continued, could not believe that the Americans
would take such a position, as the argument had no technical foundation. The Admiralty had assured him that a 7,500-ton cruiser, armed
with six-inch guns, had a range of 3,000 to 4,000 miles at full speed
and 7,000 to 8,000 at cruising speed. Coming slowly to his point,
Chamberlain concluded that the Japanese posed a problem in the
negotiation, too, for if the U.S. embarked on a large cruiser program

(achieving parity with Britain), the Japanese would build more ships and the British would have to follow with even more. Britain in any event, he said, needed seventy cruisers, and he suggested that a maximum number be established that each power would agree not to exceed before 1936.[17] He apparently did not realize the incongruity of arguing for an absolute number based on the relative strength of other powers. In a speech to Parliament the same day, he added an obscure caveat: "We do not attempt to suggest that in any class of vessel they [the Americans] are not entitled to parity, without criticism or objection from us, that their needs require."[18] The key word, of course, was "needs," which the Americans in British eyes did not have.

In Washington, Ambassador Howard found Secretary Kellogg fuming about headlines in the *Washington Post* stating that he had rejected the British heavy-cruiser proposal. Kellogg protested that he did not even know what the proposal was. The secretary's irritation was partly the fault of Howard, who had spent part of the summer in cool Massachusetts out of direct contact with the State Department, while Kellogg dealt with a chargé d'affaires in sweltering Washington. But the ambassador had returned to Washington on July 7 when it appeared that problems at Geneva might require his presence in Washington. Kellogg was also himself at fault: he had neglected to delegate responsibility for communications received from Geneva, so few in the State Department could inform him of developments.

The conference plodded along. At the plenary session on July 14, each delegation stated its latest position, which had been presented to the other delegations in private the day before. Arguing for total cruiser and destroyer limits of 450,000 to 550,000 tons, Gibson charged that British figures were based on the strengths of the other powers and not on absolute need. He objected to light cruisers, which he privately called "woolly lambs" or the "kitten fleet," but conceded that the number of heavy cruisers could be negotiable after delegates set tonnage limits. Exasperated, he finally announced that if the Japanese and British reached agreement on main issues, Americans might make the decision unanimous. He made no comment on the British proposal for considering building programs only binding to 1931.

At this juncture Admiral Jellicoe extended the debate. He stressed the need for lines of communication and hence seventy cruisers: "It is a generally accepted view that in a fleet five cruisers are required for every three capital ships. With a British fleet of 15 capital ships the number of cruisers needed for fleet work, therefore, is 25, and

45 out of 70 are therefore left for direct trade protection. Of this number we must expect 12 to be refitting or fueling at any given moment. With lines of communication 80,000 miles in length, this gives one cruiser for every 2,500 miles of communication."[19] Jellicoe admitted that by any conceivable means the navy could not stop commerce raiders from entering non-Mediterranean ports. He thus succeeded only in demonstrating the opposite of what he intended—that seventy or any other number of cruisers would be inadequate to protect trade. Churchill had received similarly contradictory responses to earlier questions as to why the Admiralty desired seventy cruisers. Perhaps the Admiralty refused to adjust its figures because it surmised that seventy cruisers was the most it could expect from Parliament.

Lord Lee of Fareham, former First Lord of the Admiralty and a participant at the Washington Conference, now took a more realistic view of parity. As First Lord of the Admiralty, he had advocated building the fleet, as the Americans before the Washington Conference were augmenting their fleet. But in a letter to the *Times* he now averred that the British would gain more from granting parity, without proof of need, because they enjoyed a comfortable lead and, as Churchill said, the Americans probably would not build to limits.[20] At the same time, some Cabinet members worried that the call for 600,000 ships and 70 cruisers would lock the Cabinet into a cruiser-building program not yet committed to and wondered if these figures were new or related to those approved in the building program of 1925. Cabinet referred these questions for reexamination to the CID.[21]

The British were particularly annoyed with Admiral Jones, who had infuriated them by equating the lines of imperial communication and commerce with America's commercial routes, especially in the Pacific. Discounting the British need to maintain trade routes except in the North Sea and Mediterranean, he displayed no understanding of empire—that to a Briton defending Australia was as important as defending the Isle of Wight. He exaggerated American commerce in the Pacific, conveniently forgetting that U.S. trade with the Far East made up only 10 percent of the total and most of that was with Japan.[22] His lack of tact did not help—Hugh Wilson thought Jones's debating style, such as it was, lacked variety, and Admiral Kobayashi offered a backhanded compliment in an interview, saying: "there are some people who say that Admiral Jones . . . is a pigheaded old man, but my impression is that he is an earnest man not like a Yankee."[23]

THE ANGLO-JAPANESE COMPROMISE

Responding to Gibson's call for Anglo-Japanese conversation, the British and the Japanese held informal discussions for two days, as Bridgeman noted, in an improved atmosphere. The press hinted about a new Anglo-Japanese alliance, and the Japanese anxiously kept Americans informed about the negotiations. Captain Egerton told Schofield that the British hoped to compromise and that the Cabinet was considering some of the questions. Baldwin had considered calling the delegation home but permitted Bridgeman and Cecil to continue the talks at their request.[24]

Gibson received the compromise at a private meeting on July 17. Tokyo and London suggested up to 500,000 tons of surface auxiliary vessels for Britain and the U.S., 325,000 for Japan, and a heavy cruiser limit of twelve for the U.S. and Britain and eight for Japan. Light cruisers could carry only six-inch guns, and Britain could retain its four Hawkins-class cruisers, the United States its ten Omaha-class, and Japan its four Furutaka-class. All powers could maintain 25 percent of overage ships.[25]

The Americans asked for instructions from Washington and, in a cable to Kellogg, recommended rejection of the compromise. They objected to retention of overage ships, since those of the British and Japanese were newer than the American (Congress had not authorized any auxiliary ships between 1904 and 1916). They also found fault with the proposed increased ratio for Japan and the use of small guns on cruisers. Schofield had recast the cable because the original contained arguments why allowances could be made to the other delegations. His draft mentioned none of them and pointed out why the Americans could not offer concessions.[26] By allowing the Schofield draft, Gibson did not offer Kellogg much choice, unfortunately; the Americans soon rejected the compromise.

Curiously, the British delegates had almost given in to the American position. Cecil later wrote Baldwin that after the Anglo-Japanese compromise the British seemed "on the road to an agreement." Of course, he had largely been responsible for the compromise. But the Americans, he said, saw little difficulty with the proposals, save for the cruiser question. Compromise on this point had seemed possible. Bridgeman recorded that discussions were at "a critical stage" when the Cabinet recalled the delegates to London. He could not believe that members of Cabinet had been following the proceedings. He admitted he would have compromised on guns—perhaps because Cecil accused him of not wanting agreement. He recognized that the Japanese would prefer the eight-inch gun, "mainly because they were unaware that they could have mechanical loading for 6-inch guns as well as 8-inch (their men [were] too small to load the 6-inch by hand)." One wonders what might have been the reaction of the Cabinet if a tentative agreement had been reached at this juncture. Breakthrough, even if minor, might have given pause to critics.[27]

At any rate the Cabinet ordered its delegates home for consultation. Beatty, having doubts about an Anglo-Japanese compromise, had ordered Admiral Field home, and Churchill convinced Baldwin and other Cabinet members to recall the others, as Baldwin was about to visit Canada with the Prince of Wales. Admiralty officers and Cabinet members then argued against concessions. Beatty hesitated to scrap cruisers and was considering technical proposals for arming cruisers against eight-inch shells.[28] These circumstances, together with worries about Cecil's health and the fear that the British delegates might give too much away had encouraged the Cabinet to call a recess.[29]

The Cabinet did consider compromise on the eight-inch gun. Beatty reported that if the U.S. and Japan did not agree on the six-inch gun, the Admiralty might consider using eight-inch guns on smaller cruisers. He wanted to ensure that American and Japanese cruisers would not outclass British light cruisers before 1931. He tempered his proposal, saying it represented increased expenditure over the existing program, which anticipated construction of light cruisers. After a stormy session during which Cecil threatened to resign, the Cabinet supported Beatty and Churchill and found for the six-inch gun. In a speech before Parliament (part of a Cabinet plan to publicize its proposals), Chamberlain summarized the British position, paradoxically denying that the government had forbade parity for all cruisers with the U.S. while ruling it out for small cruisers. He held hope for a temporary cruiser agreement, much as the British and American delegations had discussed.[30]

When American representatives received news of the British delegation's departure, an exasperated Gibson wrote his mother that "if the show keeps on much longer the burden will pass to the naval experts to figure out the details and I hope to have an easier time."[31] In Washington, Kellogg conferred with Secretary of the Navy Wilbur and the chief of naval operations, Admiral Eberle. With American delegates idle, the secretary reported developments to the president in South Dakota and wondered privately just how closely Coolidge was following the conference. Kellogg wrote Coolidge condemning the suggested tonnage limit as high; he was more open to compromise on cruisers than the General Board because he thought the United States could use light cruisers based at continental ports and at Hawaii. But he concluded that he did not understand all the technicalities and had to take the opinion of the Navy officials.[32] Coolidge responded with a commitment to heavy cruisers. The president had to "confess that it is very disappointing to have the British position revealed to us, as it apparently shows a state of mind on their part which I did not suppose existed." He ruled out compromise: "We have made a perfectly straightforward and candid presentation of a plan for limitation. I do not think we should deviate from it. If others are unwilling to accept it, we can very well be content with having made a fair proposal and leave others with the responsibility for its rejection."[33]

If the British-Japanese proposal did not attract the Americans, neither did it appeal to many British or Japanese leaders. In London it had little support outside of Cecil and Bridgeman.[34] Japan's delegates had agreed with the British on some points, conceding on light cruisers because they wanted support for an increased ratio, even though they did not appreciate the British demand for seventy cruisers. Admiral Kobayashi received a cable on July 20 that directed him to advocate a ratio of 5-5-3.5, rather than the 3.25 he had recommended.[35] Bridgeman was aware of Japan's intent—"very anxious to stand with both us and the USA, while getting the most she could for herself out of our [Anglo-American] differences. . . . The main desire was to get some improvement on the 5-3 ratio against the USA." Ishii later speculated that if conversations had continued, the delegation might have found it difficult to avoid resentment over the Anglo-American-Japanese ratio. Although Foreign Minister Shidehara did not wish to upset America, one of Japan's best customers, opinion in Japan, he and the delegates knew, demanded a better ratio.[36]

DISACCORD

On their return to Geneva after the recess, the British found that the American attitude had stiffened on the gun and tonnage issues. Bridgeman attributed the change to fancied British concessions and wrote with typical vagueness: "It was not for me to justify such claim, or to sign an agreement to say it has right, but I was not going to oppose it."[37]

The final British proposal offered little compromise, as it demanded twelve or more heavy cruisers for the U.S. and Britain, prohibition of eight-inch guns on light cruisers, and an increase in total tonnage for submarines from 60,000 for all three naval powers to 90,000 for the U.S. and Britain and 60,000 for the Japanese.[38] The proposal dismayed the Japanese delegates. The delegations scheduled a final plenary session for August 1, but Gibson asked to have the date pushed back to August 4, so as to receive instructions from Washington.

The powers cast desperately about for a face-saving temporary solution, to no avail. Secretary of Commerce Hoover discussed the possibility of joint American and British peace propaganda with British Ambassador Howard during the last days of the conference, but the British ultimately balked.[39] Secretary Kellogg meanwhile suggested a clause allowing a naval power to call a cruiser convention with six-months' notice; if negotiation then failed, any limitation might be terminated in a year. Schofield opposed the secretary's proposal and pressed for adjournment, noting that "the longer we stay here, the greater the tendency is to look around for some compromise that is unsatisfactory from my viewpoint, and from that of most naval members of the delegation."[40] But he need not have worried, for conference delegates met at Hugh Wilson's house (surrounded by reporters) late the night before the final plenary session in a final futile attempt at agreement.[41] The other delegations rejected Kellogg's suggestion of another conference. The Japanese then proposed a holiday, based on building plans to 1931 and Anglo-American maintenance of parity until that date. The proposal represented a compromise between the Japanese government and the Naval General Staff, the latter having held for parity in cruisers with the other powers. After the new First Sea Lord, Admiral Sir Charles Madden (Beatty had retired July 30), rejected the Japanese compromise in a report to the Council of Imperial Defence on August 4, the British rejected the holiday scheme, as did the Americans.[42] After this plenary session the conference adjourned, a failure.

Repercussions came in the weeks that followed. Rumor circulated of an Anglo-Japanese secret pact (officially denied), a large new American building program, and gun elevation on American ships. Cecil resigned from the Cabinet on August 7, disgusted with Churchill, Baldwin, and Chamberlain, who did not share his conviction that the British should have used the conference to "erect an effective barrier against war."[43] Coolidge announced that he would not seek another term, though this decision was only remotely related to Geneva.[44] At the dedication of a "peace bridge" at Niagara Falls on August 8, Vice President Dawes, probably jockeying for presidential position, criticized the State Department's handling of conference preparations in the presence of Baldwin, Kellogg, and the Prince of Wales. In London, MacDonald leveled similar charges about British preparation.[45]

What had gone wrong? For one thing, it is clear that much had changed since 1921-22. At the Washington Conference, it seems, a miracle had occurred against the heaviest of odds. At Washington several factors had contributed to success: an esprit de corps among recent war allies, American willingness to cut its lead in battleships, and political calm in China. At Geneva other factors worked against success: European dissatisfaction with Washington's intransigence on war debts, British unwillingness to cut its lead in cruisers because of imperial obligations, American insistence on large cruisers and guns, and a Japanese conviction that civil war in China required naval strength.

Could the outcomes of the two conferences have depended on the varying quality of the American delegations? At Washington Secretary Hughes had dominated his delegation with skill. He also had been in close communication with President Harding. As head of the Department of State and by force of personality he had kept his naval representatives in check. Oswald Garrison Villard, the caustic editor of The Nation, concluded that "few men [such as Hughes] are capable of a stroke like that—witness the disaster of a second-rate man and a half-hearted admiral at the abortive Coolidge Conference at Geneva."[46]

But the American delegation at Geneva was not so noticeably inferior as to explain its failure. Although delegates did not perform brilliantly, Gibson and Jones did not function as poorly as Cecil, Bridgeman, or even Villard claimed. If neither as strong a personality as Hughes nor as able to guide technical advisers, Gibson nevertheless did a fair job in negotiating, given the narrow range of options he received from Washington. Jones often proved disruptive, only underscoring that he was a naval officer, not a diplomat. Still, Allen Dulles negotiated behind the scenes and received high marks from foreign representatives. Moreover, the delegation received sound technical advice from Admiral Schofield.

The difference between the Washington and Geneva Conferences lies in executive determination to achieve success. At Washington, economic, technical, and strategic differences among the powers, to be sure, played their part, but the strength of the United

States' large number of battleships had given it a strong bartering position. Perhaps more important, President Harding's desire for agreement overrode any negative considerations in the end. Harding wanted an agreement to demonstrate his leadership ability to his party and to the nation.[47] A stunning success in disarmament would help strengthen his relationship with Congress and thus his ability to direct domestic legislation. In contrast to Washington, the United States had nothing to offer at Geneva, as Kellogg noted.[48] And Coolidge, though he admittedly wanted an agreement for domestic reasons, did not want it enough to compromise. He commanded the loyalty of Republican party regulars and voters, having proved his popularity in the 1924 campaign. The American economy continued to boom, at least in most sectors, and the president benefited from this prosperity. He desired disarmament, but only if he could obtain it easily.

Indeed, Coolidge was weary of all foreign policy. He had spent trying months dealing with foreign affairs in the spring of 1927, as he came under attack for the U.S. occupation of Nicaragua and for U.S.-Mexican disagreement over Mexican oil leases. He had extricated himself from Nicaragua through the skill of his agent, Henry L. Stimson, but he still faced continuing strife with the Mexicans. As the president spent his summer in the Black Hills working on the budget, seeking the advice of western farm leaders, and mulling over whether to run for reelection the last thing he must have desired was a foreign complication. Even more irritating, Coolidge probably thought that he had already obtained agreement on cruiser parity, based on Admiral Jones's discussions with British officers the previous spring. When differences appeared, he showed little imagination in appraising the alternatives raised at the conference he had called. By refusing any significant concession, he signaled that agreement was not all that important.

Confusion within the British government also contributed to failure at Geneva. In assessing the effect of the conference, Chamberlain confessed to Howard that he worried more about the Geneva Conference than about anything else since he had taken office; Cecil's resignation had exposed him to criticism.[49] A League man, Cecil believed that "we ought to have regarded the American Navy and ours as two divisions of a great Peace Fleet, and if the Americans liked to provide the larger part of it, so much the better."[50] Cecil naively dismissed the opinions of military men out of hand. Bridgeman, for his part, vacillated over parity until his return to London shortly before the end of the conference. The Cabinet agonized but finally, with Chamberlain's reluctant support, opposed Cecil. Afterward it took a weak position, delaying heavy-cruiser construction and hoping that inaction would encourage similar behavior by the Americans.[51]

Like the Americans, however, the British found their biggest problem was executive leadership. Like Coolidge, Prime Minister Baldwin did not take much interest in the negotiations at Geneva. But neither did he allow the delegation there the freedom to shape proposals. The Committee of Imperial Defence and Salisbury's Disarmament Committee usually managed to keep tight rein on the moves of Cecil and Bridgeman. Baldwin reasoned that a failure of the conference would not harm his government. He was more concerned in the summer of 1927 with reform of the House of Lords, continuing unemployment, and maintenance of trade with the Soviet Union following a rupture in diplomatic relations in May. He did not, of course, count on Cecil's resignation, which embarrassed the government but did not wound it.

The French, who had sent unofficial observers to the conference, gleefully noted the disaccord. Philippe Berthelot, Briand's powerful assistant at the Quai d'Orsay during the 1920s, disdainfully noted that the conference had ended "a mess."[52] But Briand noted that the conference presented the French an opportunity to push their disarmament proposals at the Preparatory Commission meetings. He declared that France would respect the Washington Conference in the future but would reemphasize French security needs. He also hoped to put the French case before the Americans again and overcome their objections.[53]

Indeed, whatever its other effects, the Geneva Conference did manage to clear the air. Bridgeman noted that "in time the fact will emerge that there was a great deal of common ground disclosed." Kellogg concurred; in late October he wrote Coolidge (as part of his suggestions on foreign affairs for the president's annual message to Congress) outlining the conference's preliminary agreements on submarines, auxiliary vessels under 600 tons, and destroyers.[54] Negotiation had also displayed points of disagreement for future reference, especially about cruisers. Naval advisers were discredited for their narrow views—helping ensure that in future meetings the technicians would supply only testimony, not diplomacy.

Ironically, the lack of agreement offered hope for future disarmament. Geneva demonstrated that the Conservative government and the Coolidge administration were not deeply committed to disarmament. Their failure to resolve the cruiser impasse at once encouraged big-navy supporters in both countries and worried pacifists. Geneva therefore provided pressure groups a window of opportunity to pursue their goals with elites and with the mass public. Within months, pressure groups began to support new disarmament discussions or new naval building.

5

RECRIMINATIONS AND RAPPROCHEMENT

The Geneva Conference of 1927 was disappointing generally to Americans, and especially so to many in Congress, who had been urging disarmament resolutions on presidents for years. It was dismaying also to many peace groups in the United States, Britain, and Japan, who, with varying success, began agitating for new disarmament measures. Between 1927 and 1930 these groups, especially in the United States, would go far in publicizing antiwar efforts, including disarmament.

Discouraged by the failure of the Geneva Conference, Frederick J. Libby, head of the National Council for the Prevention of War (NCPW), decided that the duty of the American peace movement was "to educate America 'clear to the grassroots' that she may use her unique power wisely and effectively." Libby believed that Yankee ingenuity could point the way to sensible antiwar solutions for Europe and Asia that had not yet been considered. For Libby and many other peace activists, education meant working for the Kellogg-Briand Pact and a resumption of disarmament discussions, and against a large new naval bill proposed by the Coolidge administration. They also attempted to neutralize the effect an Anglo-French naval compromise would have on American leaders and encouraged British and Japanese associates to work for disarmament.[1] They took heart when the Quaker, Herbert Hoover, was elected president in 1928, for disarmament had been a strong campaign theme for the former secretary of commerce. Many of the radical groups distrusted his business philosophy and connections, however, and decided to approach the president gingerly as he opened new disarmament talks in the summer of 1929 with a new Labour government in London.

PEACE GROUPS, DISARMAMENT, AND OUTLAWRY OF WAR

Taking advantage of the openness of the U.S. political system that provided them easy access to elites, peace groups looked first to a treaty renouncing war. This idea had grown out of informal conversations between American peace leaders and the wily French foreign minister, Aristide Briand, in the spring of 1927. James T. Shotwell of the Carnegie Endowment for International Peace had visited Briand and suggested formal renunciation of war by the United States and France and possibly other nations.[2] Briand had sought to appease American public opinion since facing American anger over France's failure to pass the Mellon-Berenger accord of 1926. Later, when France refused attendance at the Geneva Naval Conference, American congressmen had accused France of being "armed to the teeth."[3] Briand therefore sent a draft treaty incorporating Shotwell's suggestions to Washington on June 20, 1927, the same day the Geneva Conference opened. The date was no accident, as Briand desired to demonstrate his country's unhappiness with the proceedings at Geneva while presenting an alternative to naval disarmament that would appeal to peace groups, especially in the United States.

Unimpressed with Briand's proposal, Secretary Kellogg ignored it as long as possible, and peace groups, puzzled by his hesitation, sought to change his mind. They were inspired by the League of Nations' approval of a Polish resolution that outlawed aggressive war and called for settlement of international disagreements.

American peace workers accordingly sent representatives to discuss strategy in Washington and New York, a significant action, for peace organizations had not collaborated much during 1926 and 1927. Occupied with other issues, conservative groups with closer links to elites, like the Carnegie Endowment, the League of Nations Non-Partisan Association, and the National Committee on the Cause and Cure of War (NCCCW), worked for entry into the World Court.[4] Indeed, the League's educational programs and pamphlets in 1927 focused on international economics, international law, and on the World Court, rather than on the subject of disarmament.[5] Meanwhile, such liberal groups as the NCPW, the Women's International League for Peace and Freedom (WILPF), and Fellowship of Reconciliation (FOR) labored for arbitration of the United States' dispute with Mexico over the nationalization of American oil holdings, with considerable success.[6] Several issues also divided these liberal groups, however, including the August 1927 execution of two Italian anarchists, Nicola Sacco and Bartolomeo Vanzetti, convicted of

Above left, Admiral Hilary P. Jones, a dubious disarmament supporter during and after his tenure at the Preparatory Commission, briefly served as a technical adviser at the London Naval Conference of 1930. Courtesy of the U.S. Naval Historical Center. *Above right*, Ishii Kikujiro, Japanese delegate and the empire's most prominent diplomat at the time of the Geneva Conference. He skillfully helped Japan sidestep the cruiser controversy between the U.S. and Britain in 1927. Courtesy of the Library of Congress. *Below left*, Robert Cecil, Viscount of Chelwood, was Britain's disarmament delegate during most of the 1920s, including stints at the Preparatory Commission and at the Geneva Naval Conference of 1927. Perhaps more than any other British politician, he supported the League of Nations and warmly embraced naval arms control. *Right*, Sir William C. Bridgeman, First Lord of the Admiralty and a personal friend of Prime Minister Stanley Baldwin. He and Cecil, his co-delegate to the Geneva Conference, often disagreed over the value of disarmament, leading to confusion about the British position on parity. The Cabinet came to monitor their activities at the conference closely. Both courtesy of the Library of Congress.

Above left, Hugh S. Gibson, the urbane and witty U.S. ambassador to Belgium, served as the leading American disarmament specialist during the Coolidge and Hoover administrations. *Above right*, Frank B. Kellogg, secretary of state from 1925 to 1929. Lacking much guidance from President Coolidge during the Geneva Naval Conference of 1927, the cautious Kellogg usually deferred to his navy advisers. Both courtesy of the Library of Congress. *Below*, Calvin Coolidge and Herbert Hoover during the presidential campaign of 1928, posing at the summer White House in Brule, Wisconsin. Of the two presidents, Hoover believed more strongly in disarmament and sometimes overruled his naval advisers. Courtesy of the Herbert Hoover Presidential Library.

Above, Admiral Frank H. Schofield (left), the influential technical adviser at the Geneva Naval Conference of 1927, who favored eight-inch guns on cruisers, and Admiral William V. Pratt, who held the same post at the London Naval Conference of 1930 but favored six-inch guns. They are shown aboard a warship in 1930. Courtesy of the U.S. Naval Historical Center.

Admiral David Beatty (right) Britain's First Sea Lord for much of the 1920s and a staunch opponent of disarmament, chats with King George V aboard a battleship during the king's visit to the Grand Fleet in July 1918. Courtesy of the U.S. Naval Historical Center.

Herbert Hoover and British Prime Minister Ramsay MacDonald on the steps of the White House in October 1929, shortly after their first meeting. MacDonald and American envoys had shaped the outlines of an Anglo-American cruiser agreement the previous summer. Courtesy of the Herbert Hoover Presidential Library.

Left to right, British Foreign Secretary Austen Chamberlain, Prime Minister Stanley Baldwin, and Winston Churchill, then chancellor of the exchequer, outside No. 10 Downing Street in January 1925. During the mid-1920s, Baldwin mediated between Chamberlain, who increasingly favored disarmament, and Churchill, who opposed it. Courtesy of the Library of Congress.

Above, Cabinet members of the government of Kato Komei in May 1925, some of whom dealt extensively with naval limitation. Left to right, back row, Hamaguchi Osachi, later premier during the London Naval Conference; Ugaki Issei; and Shidehara Kijuro, foreign minister during the Geneva and London conferences. Front row, Ogawa Heikichi and Okada Ryohei. Courtesy of the Library of Congress. *Below*, Wakatsuki Reijiro, Japan's lead delegate to the London Naval Conference of 1930 and a disarmament supporter, addressing the League of Women, a group of educators and social workers, in Tokyo, April 1926, when he was prime minister. Courtesy of the Library of Congress.

France's delegates to the London Naval Conference of 1930. *Left,* Foreign Minister Aristide Briand, longtime proponent of security and disarmament and co-sponsor of the Kellogg-Briand Pact. *Right,* Premier André Tardieu, a French representative at Versailles in 1919 and head of the London delegation. He had to contend with a shaky coalition government. Both courtesy of the Library of Congress.

Frederick J. Libby, executive secretary of the National Council for the Prevention of War, an American private group dedicated to disarmament and greater international cooperation. Libby unsuccessfully sought defeat of the Naval Building Bill of 1929. Courtesy of the Library of Congress.

Above left, Dorothy Detzer, executive secretary of the American branch of the Women's International League for Peace and Freedom, a pacifist group that strongly favored naval reduction, in 1929. Detzer was one of the more effective disarmament organizers. *Above right*, Laura Puffer Morgan, American disarmament lobbyist for the National Council for the Prevention of War during the Geneva and London naval conferences. Both courtesy of the Library of Congress. *Below*, Carrie Chapman Catt (second from left), American leader of the National Committee on the Cause and Cure of War, with NCCCW officers (left to right), Henrietta Roelefs, Ruth Morgan, and Josephine Schain, at the opening session of the annual National Conference on the Cause and Cure of War, Washington, D.C., 1931. Until 1928 the NCCCW focused more on international cooperation than on disarmament. Courtesy of the Library of Congress.

Above, Herbert Hoover signing the London Naval Treaty in the East Room of the White House, July 22, 1930. Surrounding him are (left to right) Senator Joseph T. Robinson of Alabama, a delegate at the London Conference; Secretary of State Henry L. Stimson, lead American delegate at London; Vice President Charles Curtis; Senator William E. Borah of Idaho; Senator Claude Swanson of Virginia; Navy Secretary Charles F. Adams; Senator James C. Watson of Indiana; and Senator David A. Reed of Pennsylvania, another delegate at London. Courtesy of the Herbert Hoover Presidential Library. *Below*, the *Salt Lake City* (foreground), one of the first of the American treaty cruisers, carries President Hoover and his party as it passes the aircraft carrier *Lexington* during the naval review of 1930. After all the controversy over cruisers during the 1920s and 1930s, these ships would prove less important than carriers in the next world war. Courtesy of the U.S. Naval Historical Center.

the murder of a paymaster in Braintree, Massachusetts; a campaign by the Federal Council of Churches of Christ against compulsory military training in colleges and secondary schools (which attracted the wrath of the American Legion, Daughters of the American Revolution, and the National Civic Federation); and a struggle to guarantee the civil rights of pacifist aliens.[7]

Despite differences, many peace leaders cooperated in 1927. Libby of the NCPW, Shotwell of the Carnegie Endowment, and officials of the Federal Council of Churches of Christ (FCCC) met at the Carnegie Endowment offices to organize an executive committee to advance Briand's proposal in Washington. Soon most of the peace groups were at work: Jane Addams and members of the WILPF called on President Coolidge and urged him to press for the outlawry of war. The president also received a petition against war with thirty thousand names. The third convention of the NCCCW, headed by Carrie Chapman Catt, met in Washington in January 1928, and Catt declared war on the war system. Delegates heard Secretary of War Dwight H. Davis, Rear Admiral Schofield, and Assistant Secretary of State Castle defend national security and describe ways that the U.S. sought to maintain peace in the world.[8]

For six months peace groups continued their crusade. The NCPW served as a clearinghouse for thirty-two smaller peace agencies through its journal, Peace Action, and its newsletter, and by publishing books, and sponsoring radio programs. It called for state conferences and appealed to other groups, offering to present peace "clinics," speeches, and programs. It sought to enlist farm and labor organizations, church denominations, Sunday schools and missionary societies, fraternal orders, the American Federation of Teachers, the Socialist party, and the U.S. Chamber of Commerce.[9]

Peace workers gave special attention to the newspaper press. The executive secretary of the WILPF, Dorothy Detzer, scheduled visits to congressmen or administration officials to coincide with votes or important speeches and engaged a clipping agency. Laura Puffer Morgan of the NCPW supervised her organization's publicity, making speeches and sending out press releases. Salmon O. Levinson, of the American Committee for the Outlawry of War, focused on getting his committee mentioned in midwestern newspapers, including the Chicago Daily News.

Many peace leaders rallied to congressional resolutions that called for antiwar measures. Mrs. Catt and executives of the FCCC and the World Alliance for International Friendship through the Churches supported the short-lived Capper Resolution in the Senate and the Burton Resolution in the House. Arthur Capper of Kansas and Theodore Burton of Ohio (who was also president of the American Peace Society) had sponsored resolutions urging treaties with France and other interested nations, acceptance of the Locarno definition of an aggressor nation, and refusal to help any aggressor nation or any nationals aiding an aggressor.[10] The eastern press took the Capper Resolution to indicate that the western United States was awakening to the peace campaign. Senator William E. Borah, chairman of the Senate Foreign Relations Committee, perennially concerned about neutrality and skeptical of American involvement in international activities, sponsored a resolution calling on the president to assemble a conference to draw up a code of maritime law that would include neutral rights. He hoped to replace the Capper Resolution and directed the Foreign Relations Committee to hold the measure. The House refashioned the Burton Resolution into a simple proposal for American neutrality.[11]

Meanwhile, Secretary Kellogg had reopened negotiations with Briand. Although doubtful about the value of a bilateral treaty outlawing war, Kellogg came to believe that a multilateral treaty might be useful.[12] He probably saw the latter as a capstone to his diplomatic career, for he planned to retire in March, 1929.[13]

Just who inspired the secretary and the president to expand Briand's suggestion into a multilateral treaty is unknown. Kellogg had been toying with the idea, as had Senator Borah. Although most officers in the State Department distrusted public opinion and opposed what they saw as idealism in Briand's idea, Kellogg often ignored State Department advice and took notice of public opinion—especially since his senatorial reelection defeat in 1922.[14] The secretary was quite aware of the high-powered campaign on behalf of Briand's bilateral proposal. He perhaps received encouragement from the president, who had met with the British journalist, Henry Wickham Steed, at the White House a few months after Geneva. Steed emphasized the relation between neutral rights at sea, naval armaments, and European security. He suggested that Coolidge reiterate the American position on neutral rights, as it seemed to him the main stumbling block to Anglo-American naval agreement. Coolidge hinted vaguely that Congress might pass a resolution forswearing American aid to aggressors and pledging readiness to consult with other nations.[15] But the president, still angry about Geneva, had no wish to take the initiative himself. He suggested that Steed continue the conversation with Senator Borah.[16] Although Coolidge perhaps favored linking American neutrality policy closer to the needs of

League members, he wanted above all to justify America's need for naval parity with Britain, on which he had insisted throughout the Geneva Conference. The State Department conveyed the president's feelings to the Foreign Office when Theodore Marriner of the West European desk told British officials in Washington that freedom of the seas had not been the issue at the unsuccessful conference in Geneva; parity had.[17]

As the president considered the problem of security in Europe, Kellogg pursued negotiation with Briand, keeping in touch with Borah, Shotwell, and Levinson. Kellogg attempted to persuade a reluctant Briand, who preferred a bilateral treaty, of the merits of a more general treaty. The Frenchman only relented when Germany announced its agreement with Kellogg's draft in July 1928.[18] Britain then joined.

The resultant multilateral treaty contained three articles that renounced war, prescribed pacific means in settling disputes, and established procedure for ratification. But the signatory nations attached reservations that considerably altered the original treaty, exempting wars of self-defense and those arising from the League Covenant or Locarno treaties—that is, war between signatories and nonsignatories and war with violators of the pact. In consenting to the treaty, the Senate attached amendments exempting use of force to maintain the Monroe Doctrine and matters of vital interest or national honor.

At first, the American peace groups were hesitant about the treaty. Although most of them had favored the original Briand proposal, many opposed Kellogg's version. The Carnegie Endowment and the American Peace Society, both with close links to the State Department, ultimately supported the treaty, as did Libby and most members of the NCPW, but arbitration advocates accepted it reluctantly, and World Court advocates, such as James Brown Scott of the Carnegie Endowment and Clark Eichelberger of the League of Nations Non-Partisan Association, disliked it because it ignored the World Court. Shotwell, who had played such a large part in the original idea of the pact, still preferred a bilateral treaty with the French, as he explained in correspondence with Admiral William V. Pratt.[19] Writing to a British friend, Dorothy Detzer of the WILPF admitted that she preferred bilateral arbitration treaties and had difficulty reconciling Kellogg's treaty with the U.S. action in sending marines to Nicaragua and imposing leaders on the Nicaraguans: "Many people feel that they are unwilling to support the Secretary of State's proposals for outlawing big wars while he continues to wage little wars." Still, she feared that the Senate might withhold consent and that friends of peace would undergo the same disappointment they had experienced with the World Court. The approaching presidential campaign of 1928 might also confuse matters: the Republican platform had endorsed the Kellogg-Briand Pact together with Coolidge's Nicaraguan policy and a new naval bill, and Detzer feared that the Democrats might make the Kellogg proposal a party issue, as the Republicans had when they opposed the League of Nations.[20] Although ill throughout much of 1928, Mrs. Catt urged on the NCCCW in its efforts to encourage ratification of the treaty. She planned to use the pact as pressure on Washington to join the World Court and engage in disarmament. Like Shotwell and Detzer she saw the pact by itself as weak without greater international involvement by the United States: "A pact to renounce war is a poor dike with which to hold back the flood."[21]

Perhaps the basic trouble was the naval bill. Detzer complained that Libby, rather than concentrating on the Kellogg-Briand treaty, was "so full of destroying the Navy program that he does not seem to want to take up this double issue." Libby was not alone, for congressmen had wondered about outlawing war while increasing the navy. Senator Pat Harrison of Mississippi asked: "Why do we in one hand hold a peace pact for the preservation of peace throughout the world and in the other a bundle of explosives to burst upon the world?"[22] Secretary Kellogg noted the high volume of mail to Congress favoring the treaty but opposing the naval bill and feared that linking the two issues would mean defeat for the treaty. He believed that people did not understand the need for ships, as the naval bill simply meant replacing obsolete or outdated cruisers up to 300,000 tons, just what the Americans had proposed at the Geneva Conference.[23]

In Britain, activity after the Geneva Conference was more restrained. Peace workers found that many of their proposals were coopted by the government or by the political parties. Once this occurred, the proposals were inevitably watered down and only partially adopted. The League of Nations Union, for its part, usually continued to cooperate with the government. It supported the Kellogg-Briand Pact, believing it would inspire a new campaign for disarmament, but did not see in the pact a substitute for the League, as did many American supporters. Cecil, MacDonald, and Lloyd George, along with many LNU members, primarily regarded the pact as a way to improve Anglo-American relations.[24]

Peace groups were less active in Japan. Little access to elites and a dependence on the government for financial support meant that peace groups controlled few resources for collective action. Few of their views were ever aired in the Diet, in contrast to the views of American and British groups in their national legislatures. Many of the most prominent, pro-Western advocates in Japan, in addition, were still angry about the American Immigration Act of 1924 and noticed that Californians supported further limits on Japanese land-holding. The Tanaka government meanwhile began repressing dissident groups. It did not encourage further disarmament and imprisoned thousands of Marxists and fellow travelers under a so-called Peace Preservation Law. Under such circumstances, advocacy of disarmament diminished in Japan.

THE ANGLO-FRENCH COMPROMISE

If observers hoped that the Kellogg-Briand Pact would soon lead to international disarmament, they were mistaken, for the British and French began bilateral discussion of naval limitation, resulting in an agreement that infuriated Americans. The Europeans initiated informal talks during meetings of the Preparatory Commission for a General Disarmament Conference because they doubted the success of the Commission.[25] The British saw advantage in conversation, for they were still smarting from their experience at Geneva and the Americans at the Preparatory Commission seemed little inclined to discuss naval subjects anew. In a memorandum to Foreign Secretary Chamberlain, Lord Salisbury listed reasons why the British government might negotiate with France. He and Lord Cushenden, the delegate to the Preparatory Commission meetings in Geneva, had agreed that Britain should avoid diplomatic isolation, and they therefore proposed approaching either the French or the Americans about a naval accord. They perceived two obstacles to this plan: Briand's influence with the French admiralty, and the possibility of a Franco-American agreement.[26]

The Cabinet in London had already accepted a memorandum describing the future of Anglo-American relations. The conference, it stated, "strengthened enormously those elements in the United States whose object it is to 'show the world' conclusively that, while the nineteenth century may have belonged to Britain, the twentieth century undoubtedly belongs to the United States." The report predicted an "almost certain" increase in the U.S. Navy but doubted if it would affect relations, unless "more fuel were added on, in the shape of further naval disagreements." The Disarmament

Committee headed by Lord Salisbury—including Bridgeman—had also presented its post-Geneva Conference report and concluded that the government should postpone immediate disarmament discussions at the Preparatory Commission, but if that were not possible, then it should mention anew its proposed battleship cuts and emphasize recent cuts in British cruiser construction.[27]

Chamberlain, a true francophile, hardly needed encouragement to pursue the French connection and proceeded forthwith. Following conversations between the two naval staffs, he visited Briand, who informed him of France's need for a navy larger than that of Italy. The two men met again in Paris, as did their naval staffs. At Preparatory Commission meetings in Geneva, Admiral Violette of the French Navy suggested to Vice Admiral David Kelly of the British Navy an absence of limits on six-inch-gunned cruisers, since armed merchantmen could be included in this class. Instead, Violette proposed limits on heavy cruisers. The Admiralty approved the idea, and the British presented a draft incorporating the French suggestions.[28] The British had accepted the French demands on July 4, after Chamberlain stressed the awkwardness with Germany that would result if the British and French failed to agree. Ironically, the Germans were upset by the agreement itself, as they thought it signaled a new entente containing secret agreements aimed at Germany.[29] Lord Crewe, the departing ambassador at Paris, reported that French officers agreed in substance to British proposals, including a system of classification for cruisers and submarines. The French accepted the British draft, and the Cabinet Committee on Policy in London recommended acceptance.[30] The British acted quickly out of fear of a Franco-American agreement and out of ministerial weariness caused by continued discussion of detailed technical matters.

A few British officials, nevertheless, opposed the compromise before its final acceptance. Cushenden, with an eye toward the U.S., with whom he had to contend at Geneva, declared that Washington would never accept the compromise. Sir Victor Wellesley of the Foreign Office argued much the same, noting that such an agreement with Paris would likely doom further naval parleys with the U.S. Salisbury continued to worry about the effect the compromise would have on the U.S. and Germany, yet he also dreaded Britain standing alone diplomatically.[31]

The Anglo-French proposal suggested two classes of cruisers, one subject to limitation, for ships with guns of seven inches or more, and one not limited, for ships with guns under seven inches.

All great powers would receive parity in heavy cruisers and in submarines over 600 tons. After news of the proposal leaked out of Paris, London sent the basis of the Anglo-French agreement to Washington, Tokyo, and Rome.[32]

As Cushenden and Wellesley had predicted, the Americans were hardly pleased. Secretary Kellogg received a telegram from the president, then summering near Superior, Wisconsin. "Please," Coolidge directed, "make no commitment concerning limitation of armaments." He expanded in a letter of the next day: "I have your wire relative to the British naval proposals. What I desire to have done in relation to these at present is nothing at all. I shall be back in Washington within a few weeks and we can take the matter up at that time. I would not have you even ask the British Government for any explanation of the proposals which they have made. Let the entire matter stand in abeyance." Perhaps Coolidge thought that the issue might disturb the ceremonial signing of the Kellogg-Briand Pact in Paris, which Kellogg would soon attend. At any rate the president instructed Kellogg to discuss neither disarmament nor war debts while in Europe, and asked the secretary to cancel a planned personal visit to London after the signing.[33]

Washington regarded the compromise as the British way of getting the League of Nations to approve what Americans had opposed at the Geneva Conference. "If the limitation is to have a beneficial effect in securing peace and saving expenditures," warned Admiral Jones, "it must be a real limitation and must not be restricted to a small number of classes that are especially adapted to the use of one country and excite competitive building in unrestricted classes by others. In other words, we must not close the spigot and leave the bunghole open."[34] As the British had sent only the general terms of the compromise, Washington asked for more information. Kellogg had Jones look over the draft American response to the compromise, and Jones made suggestions that the secretary used in the final version. The Americans unofficially rejected the proposal on September 22, 1928.[35]

For a while the cruiser issue rested. In London, Lord Cushenden, acting foreign secretary, wanted to send a soothing message to Washington, but Churchill, who regarded President Coolidge as a "New England backwoodsman," favored a sharp response. While defending the Foreign Office's handling of the affair, Cushenden explained to the Cabinet that Washington would not likely change its mind. The British government nevertheless retained the proposal but ordered details of the agreement withheld until receipt of an official American note. Cabinet members wanted to demonstrate the British view of disarmament and, just as important, put forward the Unionist view and take the wind out of Labourite sails. To avoid antagonizing the Americans further, the Foreign Office did nothing, for it recognized that the impending American presidential election would bring in a new administration. Also, because Congress would soon meet and the Senate had scheduled debate on the naval bill, any British move might appear as an attempt to influence that discussion.[36]

Briand had written a letter meant for Kellogg's eyes to the French chargé in Washington on July 23, 1928, stating French goals for the compromise. Briand affirmed in a subsequent letter to the chargé that he believed the compromise tilted largely toward American views on disarmament, but he recognized, he said, that many American officials opposed the compromise. He also believed that an American press campaign against the proposal hurt chances of its acceptance by Washington.[37]

Coolidge's call for an expanded navy on Armistice Day 1928 did not bode well for the Anglo-French proposal. The president apparently agreed with Secretary Kellogg, who had concluded a few days after receiving news of the compromise that the "best answer" was to "pass the Naval Bill as soon as possible." Coolidge and Kellogg also disliked reports that delegates at the League of Nations had attacked the United States for its silence on the proposition, and they suspected that League members might blame them in advance for future difficulties in disarmament.[38] The president ignored foreign affairs as much as he could. To Hugh Gibson's complaints that he had not received new instructions about naval disarmament at the Preparatory Commission, Assistant Secretary Castle replied: "Although the President wants results, he is so thoroughly disgusted with the result of the Geneva Conference, so bitterly anti-British, that it is unlikely that instructions could be drawn up which would really be helpful."[39]

Thus the Anglo-French proposal quietly died. Although Prime Minister Baldwin gave a speech explaining the compromise, attempting to show that it would be satisfactory to the United States, few in Washington believed him. Castle met with the prime minister shortly afterward and, seeking to smooth relations, told him that Herbert Hoover, the president elect, was not anti-British. In conversation with Briand, Chamberlain explained that without American concurrence the compromise was dead and that the British would hold to their current modest naval program.[40]

THE AMERICAN NAVAL BILL

Like politicians, peace workers turned their attention to a new naval building bill after the signing of the Kellogg-Briand Pact. In working toward defeat of the impending bill, peace workers were challenged by navy supporters who used the Anglo-French compromise in a drive for increased naval spending. Peace workers recognized the damage done their campaign by the agreement: "The case of the [American] navy," Laura Puffer Morgan confided to a British peace worker, "has, of course, been made infinitely stronger by the activities of your own Foreign Minister and the Anglo-French Naval agreement. We are following with great interest the attacks of the *Manchester Guardian* upon the Government for this piece of secret diplomacy."[41] Mildred Wertheimer of the Foreign Policy Association called Secretary Kellogg's protest against the Anglo-French Compromise a "model state paper," and she added that Kellogg had "dealt a well-deserved blow to the antiquated methods of secret diplomacy."[42] Oswald Garrison Villard, the assertive, pacifist editor of *The Nation*, wrote Ramsay MacDonald: "Everyone in Washington says that the Fifteen Cruiser Bill will go through with a rush 'just to give the Britishers what's coming to them.' . . . There can be no doubt whatever that Baldwin's blunder in the matter of Franco-British Alliance has done infinite harm. . . . People here have the feeling that Baldwin, Bridgeman, and Churchill were caught . . . cheating at cards as it were, and the fact that they have now dropped their cards on the floor in no wise satisfies people here."[43] Yet Morgan and most of her colleagues commented little publicly on the compromise because they hoped it was less important than the Kellogg-Briand Pact. With governments committed to outlawing war, a limitation of weapons seemed the next logical step. But first the NCPW and its allies had to upend the navy's request for increases.

Emboldened by the failure of the disarmament conference at Geneva, the Navy General Board had fashioned a large bill for Secretary of the Navy Wilbur that had Coolidge's backing. In final form it asked for five aircraft carriers, twenty-five heavy cruisers, nine destroyers and flotilla leaders, and thirty-two submarines at a total cost of $725 million—in short, the largest building program since the Naval Act of 1916.[44]

Peace promoters moved quickly. A variety of witnesses, including representatives of the World Alliance for International Friendship through the Churches, appeared before the House Naval Affairs Committee during hearings on the bill. The American Friends Service Committee inundated congressmen and the White House with letters and telegrams. The FCCC asked each city federation to send a hundred telegrams from leading citizens. The NCPW engaged two able lobbyists who had worked for the National Women's Trade Union League and the Anti-Saloon League and produced a handbook for peace workers.

After an eight-week battle, Congressman Fred Britten, chairman of the House Naval Affairs Committee, announced withdrawal of the bill, and a few weeks later the navy produced a more modest proposal—instead of seventy-one new ships it proposed fifteen heavy cruisers and one carrier, at a cost of $224 million. When Congressman Loren M. Black of New York asked if the peace groups had had an effect on reducing the original appropriations request, Britten did not reply directly, but said that the Naval Affairs Committee had listened to all kinds of groups and that the new bill was fashioned after considerable opposition from a "number of so-called peace societies, pacifists, and communistic societies."[45] Neither did Britten remind his audience that England, responding to the size of the new American bill, had declared that it was canceling construction of one of its cruisers scheduled for 1928.

Pro-navy forces, to be sure, opposed the peace activists. After Professor William I. Hull of Swarthmore College testified before the Naval Affairs Committee in opposition to the bill, Chairman Britten asked a friendly witness, an official of the Daughters of the American Revolution, to recommend a DAR resolution asking Swarthmore to dismiss Hull. She agreed and added that "if there was any other country that would like to have Dr. Hull [we] would gladly give him to them." The national president of the American Legion criticized Libby and his fellow pacifists as "white-livered yellow people" and questioned their right to live in a democracy. The *Chicago Tribune* and the St. Louis *Post-Dispatch* also attacked the peace activists.[46]

On the floor of the House during the debate on the naval bill, Congressman Britten called Libby "communistic," and claimed that he was responsible for Britten having received "hundreds of letters from people" who, according to Britten, were "misguided." Britten also quoted from a letter during the debate from Laura Puffer Morgan who criticized his handling of the Naval Affairs Committee hearings. Britten's reply, also read into the *Congressional Record*, simply noted that he had had a hard time maintaining order because of the "many women [peace activists] clamoring for attention." Finally, Britten took aim at Dorothy Detzer and the WILPF, declaring to the House that the WILPF was a "dangerous . . . socialistic, communistic organization which has sent out much trash against preparedness." In short, Britten concluded, the WILPF was a "real menace" to the government.[47]

In the end, more members of the House could accept the pared-down version of the bill, for the failure at Geneva weighed heavily on their minds. Voicing the opinion of many, Congressman Charles L. Abernathy of North Carolina said on the floor that until the failure of the conference, he would have voted against new ships. But Alan Treadway of Massachusetts perhaps put it best: "The fact that the conference failed puts an entirely different aspect on the whole proposition [of naval building]. We must all recognize that we have gotten into a position of internationalism and are, to a certain degree, a creature of the nations of the world. If our views are not accepted by the other nations, whether we wish it or not, we arc practically forced to keep up with whatever programs they may set up."[48] The House passed the bill and, as it had for every such bill since 1922, inserted a clause inviting the president to initiate a new disarmament conference.

When the Senate withheld consideration of the bill until a later session, the Navy League launched a new campaign, led by its president, William Howard Gardiner, who created most of the group's publicity and monitored both peace groups and the international situation. Indeed, he "practically wore a groove between Capitol Hill and Navy League headquarters," providing committees, witnesses, and the press with volumes of reports and statistics supplied to him by Navy officers. The Navy League emphasized the similar patterns of British and American trade, pointing out that, like Britain, the U.S. was a net importer of food. It attacked Britain but not Japan because the latter possessed a smaller navy and because Americans on the West Coast, the site of most anti-Japanese sentiment, already largely supported the navy.[49]

Navy officials also found receptive audiences among many business groups, which had become more critical of disarmament by 1927. Small manufacturers and medium-sized businesses paid as little attention to news from Geneva as they usually did to news of foreign affairs. Export manufacturers also paid little heed to the failure of the conference because they considered the chances of war with either Britain or Japan remote. Financial and banking organizations, better versed on foreign affairs, were most critical of the administration's handling of the conference. Sectional differences also mattered: midwest businessmen reported more displeasure with the outcome at Geneva than did those in the east and the south.

Still, most business groups opposed disarmament because they had already received one of the benefits that they had sought when supporting disarmament at Washington in 1922: tax relief, which had come about independently of disarmament in 1926 through the efforts of Treasury Secretary Andrew Mellon. Many businessmen, in addition, saw the navy by 1927 as important in protecting overseas commerce lines.[50] Indeed, Thomas W. Lamont, the House of Morgan partner and White House confidante who participated in most European financial conferences during the 1920s, had made no mention of disarmament when he addressed the annual convention of the Chamber of Commerce of the United States just a month before the Geneva Conference.[51] Navy proponents, therefore, found interested audiences among many of these groups when they talked of preparedness and naval construction.

Many senators began to favor the new naval bill for much the same reasons that a majority of House members had: they ruefully recalled Geneva, resented the recent Anglo-French action, and, though noting the high-powered disarmament campaign, realized that they could not allow the navy to decline. The Senate at last passed the House bill in February 1929, authorizing fifteen cruisers (five in fiscal 1929, five in 1930, and five in 1931) together with the carrier (fiscal 1931). Isolationist senators such as David Reed of Missouri, Thomas Walsh of Montana, George Norris of Nebraska, and Borah added an amendment reaffirming the traditional American position of protecting ships of neutrals from search and seizure. Although their actions attracted the attention of the British Foreign Office and opposition leader Ramsay MacDonald, neither President Coolidge nor his successor, Hoover, valued neutral rights above achieving a disarmament agreement. They believed the one would lead to the other.

Through their publicity blitz and their dogged emphasis on the goals of Kellogg-Briand, peace groups had probably helped force the navy to reconsider its original request, and they kept up a vigorous campaign against the naval bill even when it appeared that the Senate would pass it. The NCPW sponsored a conference in Washington that included prominent peace workers such as Reinhold Niebuhr, Oswald Garrison Villard, and Morgan. Libby engaged Jeannette Rankin, the pacifist and former congresswoman from Montana, and at the last moment Nicholas Murray Butler campaigned. Detzer encouraged the British section of the WILPF to take a stand against cruiser construction.

Given their hard work and the attention they received, why

couldn't peace groups bring on the bill's defeat? In a report to the International WILPF Detzer blamed internal divisions within the peace groups. She believed that they had built effective coalitions against the bill until they began to disagree over tactics. The League of Nations Non-Partisan Association, for example, had lost its president and appeared to have little direction.[52] After supporting the Kellogg-Briand Pact, in addition, church groups did not have enough time to organize against the cruiser bill. At the same time, international politics and economics favored passage of the naval bill. The Franco-British agreement did not affect the person in the street but did provide propaganda for big-navy interests to use in lobbying congressmen, the White House, and businessmen. Detzer also blamed shipbuilding firms in need of contracts. Yet she underestimated the effect of the failed Geneva Conference and of the Franco-British pact on Coolidge, Kellogg, and congressional leaders. Disgusted with what they regarded as European maneuvering, they were determined to augment the navy.[53]

It is interesting to observe how the progress of the American naval appropriations bill in Congress coincided with British actions.[54] Seeking to save money, deflect international criticism of the British position at Geneva, and possibly help restrain the size of the proposed American naval bill, Bridgeman announced in the House of Commons the postponement of the cruiser program of 1927—the government would not lay down the two remaining keels. On January 21, 1928, he canceled the heavy cruiser in the 1928 program.

In Britain, peace groups enjoyed less independence from the government than their American associates, and their workers did little to protest the American naval bill, as Kathleen Courtney, head of the British branch of the WILPF, wrote Detzer. The British WILPF never concerned itself with the number or tonnage of cruisers or the caliber of guns, but simply demanded the greatest possible reduction without going into technical details. Courtney commented on the great success of petition campaigns of the WILPF in the United States and added ruefully: "We had a disarmament petition here a couple of years ago. It was not very well organised, the number of signatures was not large, and at the same time it has somewhat 'queered the pitch,' as we say in this country. The petition method is now rather out of favour and for all these reasons we are on the whole not inclined to attempt anything in this direction."[55] The LNU stepped up its disarmament campaign in late 1928 following the collapse of the Anglo-French naval compromise, and established a disarmament study group. The British government did not always

view these efforts favorably: Chamberlain complained to Gilbert
Murray of the LNU even before the push for disarmament that the
LNU was preoccupied with antigovernment speech.[56] Nevertheless,
no British group won a similar influence or engaged in as many
activities as their American counterparts.[57]

In Japan, peace advocates failed for other reasons. After the Tanaka government sent troops to Shantung four times between May
1927 and May 1928, the interest of Japanese groups shifted from
disarmament to Manchuria and China by 1929. Civil war in China
threatened Japanese economic interests, particularly in Manchuria,
and caused the Chinese and Japanese armies to clash. In particular,
the angry Chinese maintained a boycott of Japanese goods, and the
Chinese Nationalist government proposed a tariff protection for its
textile industry that endangered Japanese cloth exports to China,
their biggest foreign customer. This action augured ill for the Japanese economy, just emerging from a bank panic. Aside from economic concerns, Japanese agents assassinated Chang Tso-lin, the
Chinese military governor of Manchuria. Scandals related to these
events caused the fall of the Tanaka government. Meeting in Kyoto
in late 1929, the Institute of Pacific Relations looked to the Manchurian problem and paid small heed to naval disarmament, as it
had enjoyed scant success in promoting it. Other peace groups in
Japan, similarly distracted by the turmoil in China, did the same.[58]

NEW LEADERS, NEW OPTIONS

Despite the recent discouragements, new interest gradually evolved
for disarmament. It began slowly, for the League of Nations Preparatory Commission for a General Disarmament Conference, meeting
in 1927 and 1928, accomplished little. At the latter sessions the
Soviet delegation under Maxim Litvinoff submitted a proposal for
universal and immediate disarmament. Along with most other delegations, the Americans rejected the proposition because it sought
to limit well-armed powers in favor of the poorly armed Soviet
Union.[59]

Meanwhile, the Conservative government in Britain and the
Coolidge administration inched ever so slowly toward new naval
conversations. Despite his anger over the outcome of the Geneva
Conference, Coolidge had not jettisoned the idea of future naval parleys with Whitehall. He had offered some encouragement in conversation with Ambassador Howard only a few days before the hardline

Armistice Day speech in 1928.[60] After the naval bill passed a few months later, he appeared ready to discuss disarmament with Gibson anew, but Kellogg vetoed the idea because the work would likely be redone by the incoming Hoover administration in March. But Coolidge had little new to offer anyway, as he still insisted on parity.[61]

More noticeable change took place in London. Foreign Minister Chamberlain confessed to Ambassador Howard in February 1929: "What worries me in the conduct of foreign affairs, as in other things, is when I myself do not know what I want—in short when I have not got a policy. This has been my position ever since the breakdown of the Geneva Conference and it has caused me more anxiety than anything else in our foreign relations."[62] Following this remarkable admission, Chamberlain began mending fences with Washington. He participated in arbitration discussions and intimated to Washington that Whitehall would be interested in bilateral naval discussions preceding any that might occur during meetings of the Preparatory Commission.[63]

The pace of naval negotiation increased considerably as new leaders took to the fore in Washington and London during the spring of 1929. Herbert Hoover, more sympathetic toward disarmament and somewhat more so toward peace groups, took the oath of president in the United States. The former secretary of commerce, best known for his relief work during and after World War I and after the disastrous floods of the Mississippi River in 1927, was a shy, self-righteous man distrusted by Republican party regulars. But he was a talented, hard-working, and intelligent administrator and, at fifty-four, had traveled abroad more than any president in a decade, having spent much of his engineering career in China and London. A Quaker, Hoover believed even more than his predecessor in the power of moral suasion in diplomacy and in the probability of continued peace in the world.[64] He disliked military men and solutions and looked kindly on limiting arms.

Hoover's secretary of state, Henry L. Stimson, had served as secretary of war for President William Howard Taft and was Hoover's fourth choice for the State Department post. The two men had never met prior to Stimson's appointment and never established a warm rapport, as Stimson preferred to run his own department and Hoover rarely granted him the freedom Coolidge had given Kellogg. Tall and stern with little sense of humor, Stimson was often callous toward State Department underlings, and he depended on them far less than had his predecessor. But he was intelligent and a quick

study, and, although he admired military men and methods, he believed in disarmament and in a diplomacy that strongly stressed
international law, being himself a lawyer. Stimson also supported
American participation in the World Court, had corresponded with
Salmon Levinson, and worked with Senators Swanson and Walsh on
the matter of disarmament in early 1929, having no confidence in
Borah.[65] Despite his general support of disarmament, however,
Stimson had served most recently as governor of the Philippines,
and he remained more interested in Far Eastern affairs than in arms
control. Nevertheless, he had discussed disarmament with Prime
Minister Tanaka and Minister of the Marine Okada in Tokyo on his
way from the Philippines to Washington to assume the position of
secretary of state. Okada had done most of the talking and explained
to Stimson that he favored a naval conference in 1930 rather than
1931 so Japan could design new ships permitted by the Washington
treaties more quickly, once they knew what changes in ship design
a new conference might require.[66]

Hoover quickly began considering new approaches to disarmament, in spite of discouraging advice from Coolidge. Coolidge had
brought Hoover up to date on disarmament efforts and possibilities a
few weeks after Hoover's inauguration. Although he had considered
discussing disarmament anew with Gibson in December 1928—
probably because he denied opposing further arms-control talks after
the *New York Times* accused the administration of such after Geneva—Coolidge revealed to Hoover that his attitude had changed
little. In fact, Coolidge held little hope for success:

The Peace Treaty requires the allies to disarm, which they have not done. The
French Army remains and the British Navy has been increased. . . . We have
disbanded our army, reduced our navy and are building scarcely enough replacements. The allies would be glad to be able to say that they cannot disarm
on account of our attitude. I am not very familiar with the French proposal
but so far as I recall it seemed to offer possibilities. I doubt much headway can
be made with any discussion of parity. Certainly our country would not accept inferiority. It may be possible to agree on a navy of reasonable size for
each country.[67]

Hoover entertained Gibson, an old friend and colleague, in the
White House, where the two men discussed disarmament after
morning sessions of medicine ball—an activity that left Gibson
bruised and sore.[68] Together they fashioned new disarmament proposals based on a meeting between State Department officials and
navy men in February 1929.[69] Returning to Geneva for the sixth

meeting of the Preparatory Commission in April 1929, Gibson startled some delegates of the Preparatory Commission, though not the British, by agreeing with a French proposal assigning each nation a total tonnage divided between ships in specific displacements. In other words, he moved closer to the French position advanced in earlier Preparatory Commission meetings calling for disarmament according to class of ship. More important, he suggested a "yardstick" to achieve "equal tonnages" of classes by displacement, gun caliber, and perhaps speed and other factors.[70] Gibson's colleague, Admiral Jones, not surprisingly, distrusted the idea, calling it privately "a mess . . . merely a method of approach" without quantitative proposals.[71] This was a somewhat surprising revelation, for Jones had attended the February meeting at which the idea of a yardstick had been discussed, and he had made no objection to the idea at that time. But Lord Cushenden, the British delegate, having received advance warning of the speech through secret meetings between Gibson, Hugh Wilson, and Sir Robert Craigie, endorsed Gibson's proposal because it promised to appraise ships in terms of fighting effectiveness instead of tonnage and gun size, thereby providing new diplomatic openings.[72] As other delegates fell in behind Cushenden, President Hoover emphasized the importance of disarmament and of the new yardstick proposals at Memorial Day exercises at Arlington Cemetery.

A change of leaders occurred in London at the same time. Ramsay MacDonald, a sixty-three year old Scotsman who had briefly served as the Labour prime minister in 1924, succeeded Baldwin as prime minister in the spring of 1929. The son of a farm laborer, MacDonald had made his way in the world through hard work, good looks, and charm, and by marrying money. He eschewed revolutionary action, preferring gradual change. Hardly the intellectual equal of Hoover, he was nevertheless a resourceful politician. Like the president, he supported disarmament. He had already proclaimed that the causes of war, including armaments, were no more irremediable than the causes of smallpox. Although he worked harder for a new disarmament conference than had Baldwin, MacDonald could not fully meld his desire for disarmament with his nationalism. When the American naval bill passed in early 1929, MacDonald claimed in a letter to the American socialist leader, Norman Thomas, that he would "let America build ships so that she packed the Atlantic from New York to Southampton and would not lift . . . a little finger to prevent it or to restore parity." Yet in the same letter, he blamed the Americans for the failure of the Geneva Conference and implied that the American case for parity was weak: "The cause of the failure was just as much America's as ours, and at any rate we were facing geographical and industrial reality, whilst the United States were not."[73] In great measure, MacDonald was also facing political realities in his call for more cruisers: his was a minority government that could not directly antagonize the Admiralty, which had agreed to drop its demand for light cruisers from seventy to sixty shortly after the Labour victory.[74]

The tensions of the past at last seemed open to remedy. With new leaders in both countries a diplomatic solution to the cruiser issue now seemed possible.[75] Although before his defeat Baldwin had concluded that private negotiations were necessary before another conference, he had nevertheless accepted Chamberlain's questionable conclusion that neutral rights on the sea were the main source of discontent, rather than cruisers needed for the Pacific against Japan, America's most likely enemy according to naval estimates.[76] MacDonald instructed Ambassador Howard to begin discussions with Stimson, and the result in Washington was agreement that civil leaders, not naval officers, should handle future disarmament negotiations, for only they would show the needed imagination.[77]

When the new American ambassador to Britain, former vice president Dawes, arrived in London, he established a warm relationship with the new prime minister. Both declared another naval conference desirable. Dawes afterward described for Secretary Stimson MacDonald's desire to avoid upsetting the Washington treaties, his support of parity in cruisers, destroyers, and submarines between the U.S. and Britain, and the need of a yardstick to establish cruiser equivalents. He related MacDonald's postponement of the construction of two cruisers of the 1928 program.[78] He also requested Gibson's presence in London.[79] Gibson handled most of the day-to-day negotiating for the United States and thought little of Dawes's participation or judgment.[80]

Stimson directed Dawes and Gibson to commit the British to parity and make certain that any new treaty did not contradict the Kellogg-Briand Pact. The U.S. would scrap enough destroyers and submarines to come down to British levels. If necessary, it might also scrap all submarines. It would postpone capital-ship replacements and establish age limits for all ships—twenty years for cruisers, sixteen for destroyers, thirteen for submarines. Many of these ideas had arisen during discussions at the Geneva Conference.

MacDonald generally agreed with the American proposals, but disclosed that the Royal Navy needed forty-five light cruisers to defend trade routes, in addition to fifteen heavy cruisers. For the U.S. Navy he proposed eighteen heavy cruisers, to avoid upsetting the cruiser ratio with the Japanese. After agreement with Japan, France, and Italy, he might propose a decrease in heavy cruisers.[81]

Stimson disliked MacDonald's suggestions because he suspected that the Admiralty had won over the prime minister.[82] MacDonald was also disappointed with the American position. To him, a yardstick did not make much difference: "We seem to be like the fox and the stork who invited each other to dinner which each served up in turn in utensils from which only one could eat." He discounted the importance of small cruisers, believing that one large cruiser equaled two and a half to four and a half small ones. Indeed, in a letter to Dawes MacDonald said that large cruisers were "worth almost an infinity of smaller craft."[83]

During these exchanges MacDonald also engaged in conversation with the Japanese. The government of General Tanaka fell in July 1929, as mentioned, because the assassination by Japanese agents of the Manchurian warlord, Chang Tsu-lin, left Tanaka's policy of bilateralism with China in shambles. But Tanaka's cabinet first approved a course toward naval disarmament should a conference be called: Japan would require a 10-7 ratio rather than the 10-6 that the Americans favored for Japan. The incoming government of Hamaguchi Osachi accepted the decision, probably because the Japanese Navy staff had reacted to the failure of the Geneva Naval Conference by appointing a committee to study post-1927 building policy. The committee's report, approved by Chief of Staff Kato Kanji and Minister of the Marine Okada Keisuke in March 1929, had identified the United States and Britain as Japan's main enemies and suggested that Washington treaty limits be forsaken.[84] Shidehara once again resumed his position at the foreign ministry and moved anew toward greater internationalism, largely because the Japanese planned to lift their gold embargo and link their economy more closely with the West. But to achieve greater internationalism Tokyo needed Western credits to assure steady transition to the gold standard; the easiest way to obtain the loans lay in diplomatic cooperation with the West.[85] One sure way to proceed, Shidehara knew from past experience, was to pursue disarmament. He accordingly directed Ambassador Matsudaira Tsuneo in London to inquire about a new naval conference. Matsudaira told MacDonald that Japan welcomed a conference but suggested two preliminary steps: a tentative adjustment of the levels of Anglo-American parity and Japanese-American examination of Japan's strategic needs. Matsudaira also

PREPARING FOR THE NEXT BIG REDUCTION SALE
—*The Daily Express* (London).

Literary Digest, February 1, 1930.

warned Ambassador Dawes that Japan would press for a higher ratio than the 5-5-3 accorded at Washington.[86]

But, as MacDonald announced in Commons some weeks later, any Japanese desire for a higher ratio in cruisers would probably anger the Americans. Ambassador Matsudaira informed MacDonald that Japan would agree to eighteen heavy cruisers for the United States and fifteen for Britain, so long as Japan received twelve. MacDonald continually advised the U.S. to consider Japan in any cruiser formula, leading Stimson to suspect that the British were using the Japanese requests to bring down U.S. demands.[87]

Stimson and Hoover began to hope a simple agreement on parity might encourage reduction, and they backed away from their earlier proposal of a yardstick. They feared that a yardstick, which would necessarily involve technical discussion, would persuade other countries to turn to bilateral parleys and encourage public opinion to focus on kaleidoscopic issues. The General Board also opposed a yardstick on the grounds that it was impossible to compare one ship class to others, and that a yardstick could put the U.S. in an inferior position.[88]

Hoover and the General Board meanwhile came to an agreement. The board reiterated its opinion that the navy needed heavy cruisers, that the cruiser category not be divided, and that limits extend only to total cruiser tonnage. It asked for twenty-one cruisers instead of eighteen. Hoover eventually agreed to twenty-one, as well as ten more *Omahas* and four cruisers of 7,000 tons.[89]

During his negotiation with the board, Hoover used a controversy involving shipbuilders and the journalist, William Shearer, to garner public support for a disarmament conference. As was noted earlier, Shearer had been accused of influencing statesmen to oppose disarmament at the Geneva Conference. Later, he claimed that shipbuilders had paid him to work for them at Geneva and had promised to take care of him afterward. Although he received over $6,000 in late 1928 as "hush money," he was not satisfied and sued the shipbuilders for back pay. Hoover encouraged Congress to investigate Shearer and the builders for, as he wrote Stimson, the Shearer case might be a "useful public example and one that we will need before we are finished."[90] The Senate Naval Affairs Committee named a subcommittee to investigate Shearer in September 1929 after several senators, including Senator Borah, mentioned the discussion of the case in the *Washington Post*.[91] The affair inspired calls for an examination of lobbying and went far in turning editorial and congressional opinion against the arms builders and big-navy supporters.[92] A State Department investigation indicated, however, that Shearer had had scant influence on American delegates and technical advisers at the conference.[93] Investigation of the shipbuilders' records indicated that Shearer had been paid as a lobbyist in 1926-28, but had provided little return for his wages.[94]

Herbert Bayard Swopes, the editor of the *New York World*, also interviewed National Security League officials at the direction of the White House to determine what links might exist between Shearer and Stanwood Menken, the NSL founder. Shearer was a member of the Speakers' Bureau of the NSL and had made NSL radio broadcasts arguing against a new naval agreement with Britain. Ultimately, neither Swopes nor the FBI discovered any strong ties between the two.[95] NSL membership, which had jumped as Hoover called for disarmament, nevertheless declined after the investigation.[96]

Satisfied that the British and American cruiser positions had moved close enough for a negotiated agreement, Hoover now invited MacDonald to visit the United States, an invitation for which MacDonald had been pushing all summer. The president did so because the positions of both countries had recently narrowed in that he would limit heavy cruisers and build light ones, whereas the British had reduced their total demand from seventy to fifty, accepted parity in cruiser classes, and conceded lower tonnage in all ship categories. MacDonald sailed from Southampton on September 28, 1929, without military advisers. He and Hoover met at the White House and at the president's rustic summer camp on the Rapidan in Virginia over the course of a week.

The meeting was a considerable success. Although the leaders struck no specific agreements, MacDonald ingratiated himself both with the president and with the American public. The press enthusiastically reported his every move. The prime minister and the president began their discussions on disarmament. They failed to reach further agreements on cruisers, but progressed in other ship categories. Regarding battleships, MacDonald suggested increased ages and reductions in tonnage, with some construction because of the effect on unemployment. Hoover recommended abolishing battleships after 1936, since they seemed obsolete. He hinted that Americans might accept a 25,000-ton maximum displacement if allowed to build one 35,000-ton ship to compensate for the British battleships, *Nelson, Rodney,* and *Hood,* but he refused any reduction of gun calibers. MacDonald conceded that Britain might reduce destroyer tonnage to 150,000 if both nations lowered submarine tonnage. For his part, Hoover allowed that the U.S. might permit Japan more submarines. Both men agreed to reduce the total tonnage for aircraft carriers from 135,000 to 120,000.[97] Many of these topics had been discussed in one form or another by British and American diplomats during the summer.

The president proposed enhancing neutral rights in war by exempting food ships from seizure. But MacDonald feared that Hoover wanted only to protect American shipping during a period of European hostilities. Such an action might create trouble if Britain needed to enforce sanctions as defined by article sixteen of the League covenant.[98] He refused to discuss the issue. He also skirted conversation on armament limits at bases in the Western Hemisphere, pointing out that the arms involved were small.

Despite these minor arguments, agreement on cruisers seemed much more likely, and on October 7, 1929, Whitehall issued invitations to the signatories of the Washington Five-Power Naval Treaty for a conference in London beginning in January 1930. Within weeks the powers, including France and Italy, accepted.

American peace groups applauded this development. If after the Geneva Conference they did not truly "educate" America about peace and disarmament, as Libby had wished—after all, most Americans well remembered the world war and the Washington treaties—the groups did publicize the issues and help harness public fear of war

into support for peace issues. They could not likely gain more influence with the White House during the Coolidge administration because the president paid more heed to conservative business leaders,
many of whom now opposed disarmament. Likewise with the State
Department: Kellogg was hesitant to acknowledge peace groups—he
despised radical pacifists—but he was willing to correspond with
those whom he considered more moderate, such as Shotwell or Levinson, when he needed them. Caution marked his diplomacy, both
in his dealings with domestic peace groups and with advocates of
preparedness, including the navy, to which he had deferred during the
Geneva Conference.[99]

Nevertheless, as has been mentioned, peace groups did enjoy a
measure of success. They helped pressure the State Department to
settle issues in Latin America peacefully and to proceed with the
Kellogg-Briand Pact, for which they supplied initial ideas, impetus,
and persuasion. With regard to passage of the Kellogg-Briand Pact,
they profited from Briand's desire for a military alliance and from
Kellogg's wish to polish his reputation after his much-criticized performance during Geneva. Peace leaders were only partially successful in their campaign against the naval bill, however, helping reduce
spending requests. But this episode hardly constitutes major defeat,
as many politicians, even some favoring further disarmament, recognized that the navy needed appropriations just to maintain current
strength. If peace workers had little to do with actual disarmament
proposals or the direction arms-limitation talks took in late 1929
(they tended to take a wait-and-see attitude toward Herbert Hoover),
they did have an indirect influence on the new national leaders by
lobbying congressmen and State Department and White House officials to pursue negotiations.

It remained to be seen if American peace workers could educate
delegates and governments at the London Conference to use their
power wisely. Significant obstacles to this goal existed. Peace sentiment in other countries did not approach that found in the United
States. Japan had not yet addressed recent Anglo-American cruiser
compromises. France's security threatened to loom large in the equa-
tion of any London agreement. Undaunted, peace groups rallied and
bade farewell to their observers bound for the London conference.

6

THE LONDON NAVAL CONFERENCE

As conferences go, the London Conference of 1930 was not much different from its predecessors concerning naval limitation, except that, unlike those of 1921-22 and 1927, the meeting in London turned into fine technical discussions that then threaded themselves out into political subtleties. The London Conference was far more technical-political than its forebears. In that lies its fascination.

The negotiators at London, one must add, almost certainly did not realize the extent to which their understanding of both the technicalities and the politics was incomplete. In technical issues, for example, the importance of airplanes was not yet fully understood. Aircraft carriers were fairly developed, but the planes that flew onto and off of their platforms were fragile craft, only a bare two decades beyond the time when the Wright brothers had shown the world that flight was possible. Aerial planners of the year 1930 looked to the future uncertainly, and negotiators could not imagine how aircraft would interfere with the technicalities of naval warfare as they had understood it for nearly half a century.

In political matters, negotiators likewise could not know that the coming decade would shatter the neat lines of (essentially) three-power control of the world they had known since the end of World War I. The great nations unrepresented at London would change all that—Germany and the Soviet Union would rise from impotence during the ensuing years and defy the London calculations.

With such limited understanding, however, the men of 1930 had to negotiate, in hope that the world they had known would continue into the indefinite future. They sought to understand and negotiate from the technicalities, in hope that the political understandings they implied would continue.

1930 CALLING.

THE NEW YEAR SUMMONS THE FIVE NATIONS TO THE NAVAL CONFERENCE IN LONDON.

Punch, January 1, 1930.

TECHNICAL TESTIMONY

The cruiser issue that had helped sink the Geneva Conference remained a subject of heated debate during the next few years. Navies sought to skirt the limitations of the Washington Conference by improving the capabilities of unlimited ships—especially the cruiser. It appeared by 1930 that if political leaders in the United States and Britain had come closer to agreement about cruisers, their respective admirals had not. Even at the London Naval Conference, British and American experts remained far apart in their views of this type of warship. They argued at length about whether to rely on a versatile all-around ship for fleet action—a ship not much superior to destroyers—or to develop a cruiser as formidable as possible under the Washington treaty. Neither country, of course, had had any battle experience with either sort of cruiser.

The U.S. Navy's General Board had favored a powerfully armed cruiser since 1927 and held to its position even after the London Naval Conference of 1930. On the one hand, the American navy did not want to increase armor on heavy cruisers at the cost of armament or speed; on the other, it did not want to construct light cruisers fit for general purposes. In a memorandum to the House Naval Affairs Committee written in November 1928, Rear Admiral Andrew Long of the board concluded: "If anyone should ask me why I do not wish to build 10,000-ton cruisers, armed with six-inch guns, my reply is that one of those cruisers might fall in with a 10,000-ton cruiser carrying eight-inch guns, and that in such a case its chances of victory would be zero."[1] In late 1929, the board also overruled recommendations from the Bureau of Construction and Repair and from the Director of Fleet Training for more armor for the 10,000-ton cruisers by sacrificing three eight-inch guns and 3.5 knots of speed.[2]

Board members much disliked the direction the Dawes-MacDonald talks had taken. *Our Navy* magazine in September 1929 expressed their opinion in parody:

> Five little cruisers,
> Sailing close to shore;
> They cut the quota down some
> And then there were four.
>
> Four little cruisers,
> As cute as they could be;
> Along came a conference

And then there were three.

Three little cruisers,
Each with a gallant crew;
Up bobbed a peace pact,
And then there were two.

Two little cruisers,
With men behind each gun;
Then someone suggested
We could get along with one.

One little cruiser,
Only one—no more,
Won't it be the dickens
If someone starts a war![3]

Such was sentiment in American naval circles when President Hoover selected Admiral William V. Pratt, a reserved New Englander, commander in chief of the U.S. Fleet, as technical adviser to the London Conference. Unlike most ranking officers, Pratt supported disarmament for the political gains he believed it offered. He had served as technical adviser at the Versailles and Washington Conferences and at the latter had presented Secretary Hughes much good advice, although this had caused a breach between him and many fellow officers. He consequently did not relish the new assignment but reluctantly accepted it.[4] He also supported the six-inch gun. He knew that Hoover might favor eighteen rather than twenty-one heavy cruisers and that the president believed the U.S. might make up the difference in six-inch-gunned cruisers. This view he approved because he believed the United States would never go to war with Britain. Pratt's arguments helped persuade Hoover that the U.S. could compromise on the cruiser issue.[5]

At the London Conference, the General Board and Pratt and most of his technical advisers differed sharply on the cruiser issue. At the outset, U.S. delegates supported the board's proposal of twenty-one heavy cruisers, but then they began to listen to Pratt and his assistants, many of whom were bureau chiefs who had long disagreed with the board's strong emphasis on ordnance.[6]

The technical arguments for the six-inch-gunned cruiser were complicated. Indeed, Ambassador Dawes described them along with other current technical arguments as being a "technical octopus."[7] When Captain A.H. Van Keuren, chief of design in the Bureau of Construction and Repair, spoke before the American delegates in favor of the six-inch-gunned, or light, cruiser, he argued that the eight-inch-gunned, or heavy, ship was inadequately protected. He suggested eighteen heavy cruisers and more light cruisers, using a new six-inch gun that in many respects could match the eight-inch. He complained that the General Board had refused to issue orders for any new design of the six-inch-gunned cruiser, save for brief summaries comparing the existing six-inch design to the eight-inch.[8]

Captain Harry E. Yarnell, chief of the Bureau of Engineering, supported Van Keuren, agreeing that the heavy cruiser was unbalanced, with a gun too large for effective protection. Using arguments similar to those of the Admiralty, he averred that the U.S. should advocate a 10,000-ton cruiser containing twelve six-inch guns and suggested parity with Britain at 339,000 tons. He supported more tonnage in aircraft carriers than battleships, a position seconded by Pratt.[9]

Pratt's chief of staff, Rear Admiral Arthur J. Hepburn, also favored light cruisers. He recommended construction of the smallest possible number of eight-inch ships to gain Japanese acceptance of a 10-6 ratio. As former director of the Office of Naval Intelligence, he focused on strategy and the threat of Japan and framed the cruiser issue in terms of obligations in the Pacific, especially defense of the Philippines, as outlined by War Plan Orange.[10]

But Captain W.W. Smyth of the Bureau of Ordnance differed. He preferred the heavy cruiser with the eight-inch gun and agreed with a recent study that backed use of the bigger gun, citing "fire-effect tables" of the Naval War College and standard test scores. The study seemed to underscore assertions by the General Board that the eight-inch gun scored better than the six-inch at long ranges and that thin armor on turrets did not pose enough of a threat to forgo use of the gun. Smyth discussed salvo patterns, percentage of hits at various ranges, armor, and tactical questions, but his highly technical remarks likely left little impression on the delegates, save perhaps Stimson and Senator David Reed of Pennsylvania.[11]

Pratt wanted a six-inch-gunned cruiser for fleet work, because he believed a ship with the smaller gun could prevent attack by destroyers and escort cruisers. He desired such a vessel to possess adequate protection against six-inch shells, especially around turrets and guns, and greater speed, permitting better night action. He favored a new design rather than more of the existing Omaha's—which were not protected against six-inch shells—and a ship with four more broadside guns. Pratt considered the General Board's plan inflexible because in effect it ignored the problems encountered at Geneva and did not allow for compromise. He pronounced it "reactionary and not in keeping with the spirit of the present conference."[12]

Rear Admiral Schofield, the veteran of the Geneva Conference and afterward the influential war plans director, estimated that between 70 and 80 percent of the Navy's officers disagreed with Pratt. The General Board had reacted to Pratt's appointment by calling Admiral Jones out of retirement and persuading President Hoover to appoint him as one of the conference advisers. Admiral Charles F. Hughes, chief of naval operations, insulted that he was not selected as a technical adviser and, like Schofield, suspicious of Britain, attacked Pratt's position not only because Pratt opposed the heavy cruiser but also because he dared challenge the board. Hughes had personally signed all the board's recommendations regarding naval limitation during 1929 and tended to rely more on the board than would his successors.[13] Among Pratt's technical assistants in London, Rear Admiral J.R.P. Pringle, president of the Naval War College, Lieutenant-Commander Harold C. Train, and, as mentioned, Captain Smyth opposed their chief on cruiser firepower.[14] All other members of the General Board later testified against Pratt.

The naval experts' disagreements with Pratt went beyond technical differences, of course. Fundamentally, most of them considered disarmament unwise. If they thought at all of political gains, they did not deem them worth any weakening of American maritime security. It is not surprising that most naval officers opposed disarmament, since some had served during the entire era of the naval technical revolution, 1880-1930, from sail to steam to oil. Watching politicians attempt to undo or limit technical progress was beyond their endurance.[15]

Even after the American delegates at London decided to accept a reduction from twenty-one to eighteen heavy cruisers, the board continued its opposition. Jones filed a minority report two days after the delegation changed its mind and then returned home on the *Berengaria*, suffering an attack of ulcers.[16] Pringle wanted to join him, regarding himself as window dressing for the politicians.[17] Rear Admiral Bristol opposed light cruisers before congressional committees. By this time the General Board had in hand a report presenting favorable arguments for the eight-inch gun and playing down advantages of the six-inch gun, such as more-rapid fire.[18]

One should note a special aspect of the case for the eight-inch gun that proved confusing. The General Board compared this weapon with the existing six-inch gun, the 6/53, the bag-loaded gun of the *Omaha* cruisers, whereas Pratt compared it with a newly developed triple-mounted six-inch gun, the 6/47 that fired more rapidly. By 1929-30, many officers in the navy, though not the General Board, acknowledged, however, that the rate of fire of the new six-inch was superior to previous models. Thus the two sides were arguing about different things and often talked past each other.[19]

The British meanwhile appeared to have had a change of heart about heavy cruisers. They had been forced to reevaluate their cruiser position because of their experience at Geneva, recent Staff College studies, Treasury calls for a smaller and less costly ship, and, not least, attacks from the press. Following the Geneva Conference of 1927 and Lord Cecil's resignation, the *New Statesman* had suggested that the prime minister invite the First Lord of the Admiralty, Bridgeman, "to retire into private life and take his ridiculous cruiser programme with him."[20] Sir Charles Madden, the First Sea Lord, agreed with the latest Staff College report that Britain should insist on six-inch cruisers. To do otherwise would be to confess "that our policy at the Coolidge conference was incorrect and has been reversed."[21] Practice results mounting eight six-inch guns against four eight-inch seemed to demonstrate that the eight-inch gun was potentially superior, despite defects. Yet officials recommended the six-inch gun for reasons of economy and because efforts to develop a suitable eight-inch gun had failed. The director of plans noted in late 1928 that a new, lighter cruiser of less than 6,500 tons armed with a six-inch gun might be more convenient and more able to develop a rapid yet sufficient fire than the disappointing eight-inch guns.[22] Admiralty officials also predicted that, cost aside, the navy would be unable to get the number of cruisers it wanted without reducing the displacement of each ship. The director of gunnery development agreed with officers who believed: "If our supporting cruisers are liable to have to fight 10,000-ton cruisers, the proper answer is to have 10,000-ton cruisers ourselves. Omitting this from consideration, the advantage lies in having six-inch cruisers, as we can have more of them for the same outlay."[23] Another well-known naval officer, Admiral Sir Herbert Richmond, the former commandant of the Imperial Defence College, had argued in lead articles in the *Times* that 10,000 tons should be the largest size ship of the navy. He also believed that the government should build to this size unilaterally rather than engage in disarmament agreements with other powers.[24]

But at least one important Admiralty official, the controller, Admiral Ernle Chatfield, objected to the six-inch gun. He agreed that the light cruiser would do for fleet work, as it might fall back

RESTRAINED ENTHUSIASM.

Mr. MacDonald.⎫ "LOUD CHEERS FOR DISARMAMENT! NOW THEN, ALL TOGETHER—
Mr. Hoover. ⎭   HIP! HIP! . . ."
M. Briand. "TRÈS BIEN."
Signor Mussolini. "BRAVO!"

Punch, October 16, 1929.

on support, and the six-inch gun excelled against destroyers; yet, he argued, it would be folly to use an unsupported light cruiser on trade routes, even those considered safe. He proposed parity with the Americans in heavy cruisers and development of a convoy-defense cruiser of 7,200 tons and slower speed, bearing an eight-inch gun.[25]

Japan appeared more flexible concerning cruisers. The Ministry of the Marine did not oppose building a few light ships. The *Furutaka*-class cruiser had proven disappointing, as officers judged the guns too big for displacement. So the navy proposed a new class of heavy cruiser.[26] Japan's strategists would not accept less than a ratio of 70 percent with the other powers in heavy cruisers. Many naval officers remained bitter about Japan's acceptance of the Washington ratios and vowed to improve the empire's position in a future treaty.[27] Ambassador Dawes noted at the conference, in fact, that the Japanese civilian delegates and their technical experts differed over the value of light and heavy cruisers and over how many of each the Imperial fleet could use.[28]

CRUISER RESOLUTION

Despite the misgivings of naval experts over the cruiser, political leaders looked forward to the conference. The Anglo-American cruiser discussions of the previous summer seemed promising, and delegates departed for London optimistic about their ultimate success. Most realized, however, that after agreement on cruisers, they would have to grapple with French desires for security guarantees, a potentially more serious problem.

The Americans had learned from their experience at the Geneva Conference. The delegation to London contained a mixture of prominent political leaders, many of whom were acquainted with the arms question. In fact, half-way through the conference Secretary Stimson would boast to his sister that the delegation was working together like "a well-trained football team." This was certainly of benefit to Stimson, for although he had been well tutored on the naval technical details, he had been nervous and tired on his arrival, knowing little about European politics. He confessed he had since been "cutting or trying to cut many new wisdom teeth in respect to European diplomacy."[29] The delegation included Stimson; Dawes; Secretary of the Navy Charles F. Adams, the great-great grandson of President John Adams; Senator Joseph T. Robinson of Arkansas, a leading Democrat on the Naval Affairs and Foreign Relations committees; Senator David A. Reed of Pennsylvania, a longtime Republican member of the Committee for Military Affairs and a major in the field artillery during the last war; Gibson, delegate to the Geneva Conference; and Dwight W. Morrow, ambassador to Mexico, a quick learner who soon understood the experts' technical data.

Other delegations were also distinguished. MacDonald headed the British delegation, assisted by his imperturbable foreign secretary, Arthur Henderson. Wakatsuki, the agile former premier, led the Japanese delegation, consisting of Admiral Takarabe Takeshi, the Anglophile Minister of the Marine, Matsudaira, ambassador in London and formerly in Washington, who had attended the Washington Conference, and Nagai Matsuzo, Hugh Gibson's counterpart in Belgium. Premier André Tardieu, a forceful orator, headed the French delegation, which included Briand, Georges Leygues, Minister of the Marine and former premier, Joseph de Fleuriau, ambassador at London, and René Massigli, the cabinet's disarmament specialist, who had attended conferences in the past. The young, handsome, and articulate foreign minister, Dino Grandi, led the Italian delegation.

Following the opening of the conference by King George in the Royal Gallery of the House of Lords, the American and British delegates privately opened discussions of the cruiser question. Stimson, Reed, Morrow, and Adams met MacDonald and Henderson on February 3, 1930, to agree on the impossibility of a yardstick. MacDonald then made clear that the Admiralty would not accept twenty-one American heavy cruisers, but would agree to fifteen and any number of smaller ships. Later he conceded eighteen heavy cruisers for the Americans, provided they reduced their total cruiser tonnage from 339,000 tons to 315,000. Discussion of other categories revealed consensus about submarines, destroyers, and battleships. MacDonald's change of heart about battleships was notable—he now accepted a holiday in battleship construction until 1936.[30] The next day, the American delegates, after last-minute testimony from Pratt and Jones, voted to accept the British offer of eighteen heavy cruisers. Actually, most of the delegates had considered the lower figure since hearing from their experts the preceding week.[31] According to Stimson, everyone feared that if they based their figures on twenty-one heavy cruisers, the Japanese would require an increase in their numbers, which would encourage Australia and New Zealand to increase theirs, leaving parity for the U.S. and Britain itself, but not for the British Empire.[32]

The cruiser compromise between the Americans and the British came about only after objections to a new British proposal setting limits on light cruisers and the American demand for a new battleship had been settled. On February 11, the British delegates proposed limiting light cruisers to between 6,000 and 7,000 tons and constructing only fixed percentages of the ratios for them. MacDonald explained to Stimson that he hoped to avoid a new cruiser race in this category but might have to increase British tonnage because of attacks in Parliament and the press. The message found its target, for although Stimson refused to hear of displacement limits under 10,000 tons for light cruisers, he realized he could not press MacDonald to reduce the number or total tonnage of all British cruisers.[33] The British desire to limit light cruisers seemed to contradict their position at the Geneva Conference as well as MacDonald's earlier assurance that if the Americans accepted the light cruiser, they could build as many as they wished. But the British had changed their position because they wished to limit the cruisers of the Japanese and the French. To remove the last obstacle to a cruiser settlement, the Americans gave up their demand to build a battleship before 1936 that would compensate for the extra tonnage the British had enjoyed after the Washington Conference. Stimson and Hoover decided that an agreement was worth sacrificing the battleship tonnage.[34]

Delegates then turned to French and Italian demands. The Americans negotiated with the French during social occasions—where chamois gloves and tails or tuxedos, rather than uniforms as at Geneva, were de rigueur. They also met in rooms adjoining the conference hall in St. James's Palace on small chairs around white tables laden with ash trays and matchbooks. Morrow served as the American spokesman, and Briand described him as "dégourdi comme une pochette de souris"—shrewd as a pocketful of mice.[35] But in spite of Morrow's efforts, the French resisted compromise. As one historian has noted, the French had arrived in London with proposals that emphasized overall security, rendering naval limitation almost "incidental."[36] The French nevertheless resisted parity for Italy, on the grounds that their own interests extended far beyond the Mediterranean, into the North Sea and the waters of the Far East. The Quai d'Orsay was also loath to grant parity for reasons of prestige and, more important, now feared the increasing militancy of Italy.[37] The Italian, Grandi, proved little more conciliatory: he claimed he would be shot at the first station across the border if he returned to Italy agreeing to the terms of the French.

French difficulty with the negotiations involved other factors than the question of Italian parity, of course. Anglo-French relations had recently suffered and the French did not believe that success at London was as politically important as did the British and Americans. French diplomacy also suffered from an essential contradiction. French unhappiness with the British stemmed from events of 1929. Chancellor of the Exchequer Philip Snowden at the Hague Conference discussing the Young Plan for reparations had dismissed French claims and demanded more British reparations. Foreign Secretary Arthur Henderson had also announced British withdrawal from the Rhineland, prompting an especially angry response from Paris. MacDonald's Labour government, finally, gave top priority to Anglo-American relations, seemingly ignoring the French.[38] The French therefore did not feel particularly conciliatory toward the British. At the same time, however, the Quai d'Orsay did not want the Americans to go home angry, because it wished to bring the Americans closer to the League and to European affairs.

The French did not place as much importance in the conference because domestic support for disarmament in France lagged behind that in the Anglo-Saxon countries. In part, this was because the French had engaged in considerable naval building since 1928.[39] But a Quai d'Orsay memo for Tardieu written before the conference also noted that MacDonald, and, to a lesser extent, Hoover had staked much on the outcome of the conference, whereas French leaders had not. The French were also put out by the Rapidan and subsequent naval discussions: "The fate of these auxiliary vessels depends primarily on us, for the English figures assume that we will resign ourselves . . . to the percentage they give us. But politically we do not need success at any price."[40] The French suspected secret agreements between the Anglo-Saxon powers at Rapidan, despite declarations to the contrary by the American ambassador to Paris, Walter Edge. Premier Tardieu had responded before the conference that France might require a security agreement complementing any disarmament agreement.[41] The French did cheerfully note Anglo-American disagreement over freedom of the seas, as the two sides did not discuss it at Rapidan and, when Hoover mentioned it in a speech in November, the British had remained silent. Here possibly was a point to exploit. Finally, Paris disapproved of Anglo-American insistence on using the Kellogg-Briand Pact as the basis for discussion. The French instead preferred using the League covenant (article 8) as the basis of conversation, as it might promote an international security system linking land, air, and sea disarmament. Any such arrangement would hopefully include the Americans.[42]

French foreign policy on the Continent also affected diplomacy at London. Briand favored Franco-German reconciliation, such as he had sought with Premier Gustav Stresemann. But he also supported the principle of equality among states, especially among East European states, that in alliance with France might serve as a collective military counterweight to Germany. But these goals clashed with one another because while Germany demanded to rearm, France's eastern allies never cooperated with each other, leaving France in a difficult spot. The French tended therefore to equivocate, seeking alliances in the west—perhaps with the United States or with Britain, if its current behavior improved—while delaying disarmament.[43]

As Morrow and Tardieu struggled to find a solution, aided by Briand and Grandi, the French continued to put up barriers to agreement. By February 12 they were demanding the right to build ten heavy cruisers and wanted vessels under 600 tons included in fleet tonnage, contrary to the wishes of other delegations. They refused, in addition, to sign an agreement that would punish nations making submarine attacks on commercial shipping.

French-Italian discord appeared almost impossible to resolve. The French would have to augment their fleet to prevent Italian parity, but by so doing they would improve on their ratio with Britain, which would threaten the Anglo-American agreements. A weary Stimson suggested to Hoover that the United States consider a two-power treaty with Britain if the French remained adamant. To Acting Secretary of State Joseph P. Cotton, Jr., he confided that the search for general agreement suffered from Tardieu's frequent absences, due to an unsteady coalition in Paris. On February 18, Tardieu's government fell, and the French delegation returned temporarily to Paris.[44]

PEACE PARTISANS

Looking to the work of peace groups at the time of the London Conference, it is clear that their way was made much easier by the revelation, shortly before the conference, that the so-called journalist, Shearer, had been working for shipbuilding firms at the Geneva Conference in 1927. The Shearer Affair, as it was called, certainly had complicated the task of navy supporters. Just before the conference, the Navy League president, William H. Gardiner, who beamed when friends called him "the admiral" (although he had never served in the navy), had trumpeted recent navy arguments in pamphlets with such titles as *Trade and Navies*, *Parity in Naval Strength*, and *Cost of*

Armaments. Yet these made little impression. Shearer hired Carnegie Hall for a lecture, "Inside of the Geneva Conference of 1927," but attracted only 350 people, half of them with free tickets. Acting Secretary Cotton confirmed to British observers that American navy supporters were much less "potent" than a year or two previously.[45]

Before the conference, such peace groups as the WILPF had decided not to organize an international committee in London, counting instead on the work of members in their own countries. They settled on this course partly because of problems in combining national viewpoints and partly because disarmament had suffered a drop in popularity after the Great Depression brought hard times to shipbuilding and related industries. Nevertheless, cooperation between peace groups did occur. The British Womens' Peace Crusade, representing eighteen organizations, joined the American International Committee on the Cause and Cure of War (ICCCW) in asking delegates to allow a petition. The ICCCW had met in Washington a few days before the conference and passed resolutions for reduction of armament and for entry into the World Court. Prime Minister MacDonald, along with representatives from the U.S. and Japan, received the ICCCW petition early in February.[46]

American groups gradually increased their efforts. Laura Puffer Morgan, reporter and lobbyist for the NCPW, wanted the United States to conform to the Washington ratios and believed a decision on cruisers might smooth the way to the abolition of battleships. She reported from London that "the cruiser proposal is disappointing, but at least it points to a turn toward the six-inch gun cruiser instead of the eight-inch." She distributed pamphlets to American and British correspondents and delegates, interviewed peace groups to ascertain their views, and took tea with Mrs. Dwight Morrow. In the United States, Frederick Libby campaigned to abolish battleships, and wrote a pamphlet entitled "What Has Happened at London?" which he mailed to farm, labor, and religious journals, twenty-four hundred daily newspapers, YWCAs, libraries, social workers, college departments of history, congressmen, and governors.[47] Dorothy Detzer wrote the president every day "as though he were my mother," to protest the American position on parity. The State Department official, Prentiss Gilbert, inquired how long she planned to continue: "In your office, you just turn on a spigot, and the State Department is flooded. . . . We are having to commandeer every typist in the stenographic pool to handle the letters."[48]

Nicholas Murray Butler, Carrie Chapman Catt, Detzer, Shotwell, Libby, and the journalist, Walter Lippmann, met in February in

New York to sign a petition, eventually bearing twelve hundred signatures, that called for arms reduction. The petition (which was sent to Stimson in London) opposed demands of delegates for an American battleship similar to the British *Rodney* and a cruiser tonnage above that of the Naval Act of 1929. It also decried Senator Robinson's speech to American journalists in London in which he characterized the peace movement as a small band of pacifists outside the mainstream of American opinion.[49] The signers agreed with Morgan of the NCPW that "if the American delegation succeeds in negotiating a treaty on the basis of which it is working at present it will mean that the United States will have a navy incomparably the most powerful . . . in the world."[50] Although the signers recognized that a treaty of this sort would set limits on naval construction by all powers, they failed either to mention that the British navy would still be larger for some time than the American or to recognize the unlikelihood of American building.

Peace activists began to call for a consultative pact similar to what Briand had had in mind when proposing his peace pact. In a letter to the *New York Times*, Shotwell wrote: "For almost a month the searchlights of the various delegations [in London] have played upon ships and their equipment; so bright a light, indeed, that almost every bolt in the welding, as well as every gun on the decks, could be counted and measured." The one area left in the dark, he wrote, was a consultative pact. The petition of the twelve hundred signatures echoed Shotwell, calling on the delegates to reestablish the Kellogg-Briand Pact as the conference's foundation.[51]

Cotton warned Stimson that the State Department could not hope to have the support of the navy groups and was quickly losing the support of the peace groups. Tired of the carping criticism of private peace promoters, Cotton had already warned the groups that "this business of shooting at the piano player is an indoor sport I deplore."[52] With Hoover's assent he advised the delegates to take the lead in reducing or limiting armaments, as "it would restore confidence in this country back to the plane of our initial high purposes if such a position of the American delegation is made known." But Stimson defended the American delegation. For the president to call for reductions in arms at that stage, he wrote, would give the impression that he sympathized with the peace press.[53]

Hoover's sympathies did create problems for him. In a September 1929 letter meant for MacDonald's eyes, Hoover wrote about peace and disarmament in words little different from either Detzer or Catt: "It seems to me that there is the most profound outlook for peace today that we have had at anytime since the last half century, more especially if we succeed in our conference of January next, yet in effect we are plunging along building more ships at fabulous expense only with the hope and aspiration that at the end of a period so short as six years we shall be able to sink a considerable portion of them. . . . All this is illogical and is the simple negation of our own aspirations and I believe also of public opinion on both sides of the Atlantic."[54] The president had presented similar sentiments to the British while secretary of commerce during the Geneva Conference.[55] In an Armistice Day speech, Hoover had promised reduction, not just limitation, and peace supporters held him to his promise. At the same time, his political support weakened, for his nomination of Charles Evans Hughes as Chief Justice of the Supreme Court stirred strong protest among members of his own party in the Senate. Even more important, unemployment continued to increase, despite talks with business leaders at the White House. The president's vulnerability encouraged conservative antitreaty workers to block the negotiations. Senator Kenneth McKellar of Tennessee asked that the delegates be recalled, since no other powers were interested in limitation. Congressman Fred Britten scheduled hearings of the House Naval Affairs Committee, calling for ranking naval officers to appear. Judge Advocate General Ernest Lee Jahnke skirted Britten's plans, explaining that the congressman's agenda were under discussion at London and not ready for public consumption.[56]

The president did not ignore public comment over the shape of the negotiations in London. In fact, in contrast to other foreign-policy issues, Hoover took careful note of public opinion when it came to disarmament. During the cruiser negotiations in London the summer before the conference he had had surveys of editorial opinion on the cruiser issue and on the proposed visit of Prime Minister MacDonald conducted. Mindful of his own publicity activities during the Washington and Geneva Conferences, he also attempted to sway public opinion: news releases were to present American proposals and any agreements in a positive light and delegates were to pronounce themselves "satisfied and proud" with conference accomplishments.[57] But the president also realized the problem of image—that most Americans expected parity, or near parity, in cruisers, since that issue had scuttled the Geneva Conference of 1927. In the end, he valued naval limitation over either reduction or lack of accord.

In Britain, MacDonald encountered little agitation from peace groups. The League of Nations Union remained philosophically tied to government approval and financially dependent on government aid. Pacifist groups supported their bolder American cousins but their own appeals to political leaders were infrequent and weak. Badgered by Conservative opposition to the negotiations and still holding a thin margin in Parliament, the prime minister took no lead in discussion but allowed the Americans to deal with the Japanese while he consulted the Cabinet about continuing difficulties with the French.

Premier Hamaguchi also faced political challenges, though not from peace groups. Even though his Minseito party held a substantial majority in the lower house of the Diet, he had little room to maneuver with the United States. As the new American ambassador in Tokyo, William Castle, noted with surprise, the public, press, and government officials all were fascinated by the naval conference and opposed anything less than a 70 percent ratio in cruisers and desired parity in submarines.[58] The Japanese Navy League, composed of several pro-navy organizations, upheld these "fundamental claims." It had organized a campaign under the auspices of the city of Tokyo and the Imperial Marine Association to "educate" the public. The meetings took place in public halls and schools where naval officers spoke about the conference and inculcated the 70 percent demand for heavy cruisers.[59] The naval officers may have been attempting in part to counter the source of most international news in Japan: London's Reuters news agency.[60] At any rate, no group opposed the League except the weak Association for the Realization of Armament Reduction, in part because the government unwittingly aided navy supporters by instituting a restrictive press law that required newspapers reporting on current politics to tender deposits, forfeitable if they incurred government objection. The law forbade reports of the proceedings of governmental departments, reprints of confidential documents, and specific, detailed editorial guesses about government policy.[61]

Despite these restrictions, a small amount of uncensored news was reported, as the police could only confiscate newspapers after publication—not before—newspapers might present material for government review and then change the contents before publication, and editors could use blank type—replacing objectionable words or phrases with the letters x and o.[62] Nevertheless, Japanese editors imposed much self-restraint, as traditionally journalists had not reported government problems or scandals until announced, for fear of bringing disgrace to the government and the nation in the eyes of foreigners. Newspapers in Japan had also become big busi-

"WE NEED MORE SECURITY"

—Rose in the Boston *Herald*.

From *Literary Digest*, March 8, 1930.

ness in the early twentieth century and many publishers had close ties to government officials. This situation substantially reduced the news that peace groups could create, and information about the negotiation in London outside of the Navy League meetings dried up. Censorship was a blow to Japanese organizations interested in internationalism, especially as they had never been as powerful as those in Western countries.[63]

GUARANTEES AND RATIOS

Anglo-American efforts to alloy French fears of security and pro-
tracted American-Japanese negotiations dominated the latter half of
the London Conference. When the French returned in early March,
delegates wearily reassembled. On the eve of the French delegation's return, rumor had circulated in Washington that Secretary
Stimson favored and Senator Robinson opposed a consultative pact
with Paris. Echoing the president, Cotton at the State Department
warned that the U.S. was not inclined to gain French cooperation at
the cost of broadening the Kellogg-Briand Pact, as the Senate would
probably not accept such a treaty. Accordingly Stimson told the
French that the United States would not agree to a pact.

The French, in fact, had gone back and forth about whether they
required a consultative agreement. They feared for their security because they no longer placed much faith in the Locarno agreements,
entertaining strong doubt about British commitment to the Continent. Ambassador Fleuriau told Stimson that the French detected a
"bad case of nerves" in British leaders after the coal strike of 1926.[64]

French diplomats sensed that MacDonald and Henderson differed over the advisability of an Anglo-French consultative pact.
Henderson favored a pact similar to the Geneva Protocol of 1924,
which offered consultation in case of aggression against a signatory,
whereas MacDonald, ever conscious of his minority government
and of American disapproval, did not. The prime minister recognized that most of the British people opposed closer relations with
France, especially any requiring sanctions or alliances, for the burden of such action with Paris—or the League for that matter—
would fall on the British navy, which would have to maintain a
blockade on any aggressor.[65] Many Britons, he feared, would not distinguish between a consultative pact and an alliance.

The French at last showed their hand—a consultative agreement
by itself would not suffice, Paris needed stronger assurances from the
British. Hoping to force concession, the French announced plans to
retain two seven and one-half-inch cruisers, thereby greatly increasing their total tonnage. At the same time, they told Stimson that they
did not rely on a security Pact from the U.S., but did desire American
thoughts on the Kellogg-Briand Pact and European affairs. Although a
consultative pact would be helpful, they slyly added, France needed
even more a treaty of mutual assistance with Britain. If the U.S. entered such a pact it might encourage the British to sign.[66]

British security pledges were not forthcoming, and Briand's departure for Paris on March 21 probably meant the end of any five-power treaty, though his leaving caused a flurry of last-minute Anglo-American hand-wringing. Stimson received a midnight telephone call from an agitated MacDonald and was persuaded to call a meeting between himself, MacDonald, and Henderson to review the American position on a consultative pact and its possible implications. Thrashing about for a last-minute solution, in this meeting Stimson agreed to a limited consultative agreement, whatever that meant, provided the British offered guarantees to the French. He did so without informing Washington. Believing that the conference rested "on the brink of a precipice," he wanted to encourage British discussion with the French.[67]

But Stimson soon tempered his offer of consultation, as he was overruled by Hoover, who, like MacDonald, did not worry about consultation as much as he feared domestic reaction. Hoover suspected Americans might assume that the agreement meant an additional military burden. Given such a scenario, navy allies in the Senate could easily defeat any treaty coming out of the conference. The president announced that the United States would not accept a consultative pact.

Reacting to the agitation of peace groups for a consultative pact, the president sent them a message through James McDonald of the Foreign Policy Association: "Seven of the most eminent men of America are now over there doing their best to secure reduction: let them alone." The State Department attempted to prevent the association from holding a meeting in New York protesting the president's announcement.[68] Cotton reported to Stimson that the president was bothered by agitation of peace groups and that pacifist activity seemed on the increase.[69]

Indeed, Hoover still feared (with good reason) that the Foreign Policy Association and its allies might try to "get out another broadside urging the country to root for" the consultative pact. Therefore, before breakfast on March 25, 1930, the same day that Cotton issued his report, the president telephoned Thomas Lamont, the Morgan partner with whom he maintained regular communication, to ask him to dissuade McDonald from this action. In an illuminating letter that underscores the close informal links between business and government during the New Era, Lamont wrote Dwight Morrow in London of his response to the president's entreaty:

I suggested to Mr. McDonald that he and the others hold their horses for the time being, and I repeated to them President Hoover's statement to me that the question of a Consultative Pact was not the crux of the question and was not the thing that was going to save the conference. . . . I conferred again with the White House, told them that McDonald and his friends would not move ahead any further without consultation and, in fact, arranged for two of them to go over on Friday to have a little further talk. Certainly they ought not to make any move that is not agreeable to the Administration.[70]

In London, a chagrined Stimson announced that the United States had never agreed outright to a consultative pact. He criticized people who spread "peace propaganda" supporting the French position and limited the press room to bona fide journalists who made daily reports home. This action shut out representatives of the NCPW, the American Committee for the Outlawry of War, the Carnegie Endowment for International Peace, and the Foreign Policy Association, who had been using the State Department's press facilities to serve the cause of peace.[71]

Without American support, Prime Minister MacDonald could not convince his cabinet to consider the consultative pact, and negotiation with the French ended. The best diplomats could now hope for was a three-power treaty between the United States, Britain, and Japan. France's demand for security had proved insurmountable when combined with the inability of Britain to define its relation to the Continent.[72]

In contrast to the Anglo-American talks with France, American conversations with Japan eventually brought a positive result. The American desire for a ratio of 10-10-6 in cruisers was almost impossible to obtain because Japan had already built up its navy. In effect, the U.S. was asking Japan to halt building while it caught up. But when Japan called for an improvement in the Washington Treaty ratio from 10-10-6 to 10-10-7 it got its way.

Assuming the Japanese might be coerced by the Anglo-American cruiser agreement, Stimson and MacDonald had informed Wakatsuki of the agreement's details. Their belief that the Japanese might agree to the status quo had some foundation, for Premier Hamaguchi, Shidehara, and Wakatsuki himself had advocated a pro-Western policy. In addition, Stimson judged Wakatsuki a man who might make an unpopular decision, but not until after the Japanese elections, scheduled for February 20.[73] Yet Stimson failed to realize that the ratio could not be a Japanese bargaining point for several reasons: economic hard times in Japan, a press and public convinced that a higher auxiliary ratio was a patriotic necessity, and the navy's real need for small vessels to patrol Chinese waters.

It is interesting that American naval men partly corroborated Japan's claim that it must have a 10-7 ratio. Pratt, Hepburn, Bristol, Coontz, and Pringle later testified that this ratio would allow the American fleet to protect the Hawaiian Islands without operating in Japanese waters.[74]

Stimson designated Senator Reed as the chief negotiator with the Japanese. A sticking point seemed resolved by a suggestion made by Saito Hiroshi to Sir Robert Craigie that since the Americans demanded eighteen heavy cruisers and the Japanese favored fifteen, the Americans should delay laying down the three in dispute until 1935. This would give the Japanese a de facto 10-7 ratio in cruisers until that year. In practical terms, the Japanese could not build another cruiser until 1936, since they already had twelve, whereas the U.S. could build nine heavy cruisers in that time.[75]

On February 27, Reed and Ambassador Matsudaira finally agreed upon a formula that delayed American cruiser construction and granted Japan a de facto 10-7 ratio in heavy cruisers until 1936. During the next weeks the two men struggled to fit numbers into their compromise and finally altered it so the Americans could lay down one of the three delayed cruisers in 1933, another in 1934, and the last in 1935. Wakatsuki and Stimson also conferred; on behalf of the Americans, Stinson agreed to an outright 10-7 ratio for light cruisers and destroyers and parity in submarines. In 1936, the Japanese could decide if they wanted to replace their *Furutaka*-class cruisers with 10,000-ton ships, provided the Americans had laid down their final three cruisers.

This completed the American-Japanese negotiations and the delegations recommended acceptance to their governments.[76] A weary Wakatsuki believed that the agreements were the best that Tokyo could hope to achieve, as he cabled his superiors. He recorded in his memoirs: "If the government had not sent its approval or if it had sent its approval with substantial amendments or demands appended, I was absolutely resolved, quietly and without threats, to resign from the delegation."[77] Hoover readily agreed to these concessions, probably because he still regarded Japan as a force for peace: at Washington the Japanese had made concessions to China, and Japanese leaders in 1930 were clearly pro-Western.[78]

In Tokyo, the newspapers, supported by the navy, opened a barrage of criticism. In an opening salvo, the influential Tokyo *Nichi Nichi* called the Reed-Matsudaira compromise the "American proposal" because it did not offer a permanent 70 percent ratio in heavy cruisers; the newspaper likened it to a "beautiful gold lacquer lunch box containing gruel."[79] The *Japanese Advertiser* published a statement from naval authorities that the proposal was not acceptable. Although the Foreign Office insisted the next day that this statement was unofficial, it was clear at the time that the government had divided on the issue. Hamaguchi and Admiral Kato Kanji met at the premier's residence to discuss the proposal, and Kato told the premier the navy opposed the compromise. Kato asked for an agreement like the Locarno treaties, defining national aims in the Pacific, especially toward China. Shidehara meanwhile weakly explained to Ambassador Castle that the cabinet needed time to study the proposal, as it lacked records of the negotiation.[80] More likely, Hamaguchi, Shidehara, and their allies needed time to deal with Kato and his supporters.[81]

The politicians were eventually victorious, aided by a minority of naval officers. No happier about the vessel numbers than his American and British naval counterparts, Admiral Takarabe, the chief naval expert, kept quiet because he feared blame if the conference failed. He did not command the attention and loyalty either among the public or navy officers, that Navy Minister Kato Tomosaburo, the chief navy expert at Washington, had enjoyed, and so could not repress discontent among his colleagues in the navy.[82] Nevertheless, Vice Minister of the Marine Yamanashi Katsunoshin and Admiral Okada Keisuke, now the powerful secretary of the Supreme War Council, took Takarabe's silence as approval. Yamanashi said Japan accepted the arrangement because it provided what amounted to a 10-7 ratio for heavy cruisers, even if the Americans would not admit it. He noted that Japan could minimize any limit on ship numbers by technological improvement on individual ships and an increase of the naval air force, and could try for a higher ratio in 1936.[83] At length, the Japanese delegation announced acceptance on April 2 and straightened out final points by April 10.

Japan's acceptance made possible an expansion of the Anglo-American arrangement, and when France and Italy agreed to sign the general articles of the proposed pact, a five-power treaty became possible. This treaty contained five parts, of which all nations signed four. Part one extended the holiday in capital ships until 1936 and prohibited cruisers over 10,000 tons. Part two restricted submarines and special vessels. Part four limited submarine warfare. Part five specified that the treaty would remain in effect until December 3, 1936, except for part four, which was permanent. Part three dealt with naval agreements concerning only the United States, Britain, and Japan. An escalator clause that had made up part of the original

Anglo-American cruiser agreement formed a preface to this section. (The escalator clause permitted building by a signatory if nonsignatories engaged in significant naval construction.) Amid much pomp, the delegates signed the London Treaty on April 22, 1930.

IN RETROSPECT

In the end, peace groups were disappointed in some of the results of the treaty. They had publicized the conference and continually met with journalists and administration members to push for lower ratios and the consultative pact. Their pressure worried the president and the State Department, leading to an attempt to limit peace-group influence in New York and London. Despite their visibility, peace promoters found themselves unable to sway decisions once the conference began. Part of their trouble was that pacifists wanted arms reduction, not just arms limitation, and internationalists supporting the consultative pact could not understand why Hoover would oppose such an action. The peace groups came closest to affecting policy when they took advantage of the split in elite opinion over the consultative pact to make their case to the public and to the government. But when the elites closed ranks, adopted some of the peace groups' own rhetoric, and urged the cancellation of the New York rally, the peace groups complied, not wishing to engage in civil disobedience or disloyalty. As a result, their influence diminished and their policy wishes were partially assimilated or dismissed. Their enthusiasm for the final treaty was therefore less than wholehearted.

In fact, the London Treaty offered its signatories mixed blessings. Resolution of the cruiser question represented a gain, together with the improvement in Anglo-American relations. Stimson always considered the goal of the meeting to be better relations with London, which had been strained since the Geneva Conference. In this limited way the treaty was successful. But the arrangement provided little restriction, and it even permitted Americans to increase auxiliary vessels. It also brought to light, as if more evidence were needed, France's fears for its security. An arms-control agreement, naval or otherwise, that would include the Continental powers seemed impossible so long as the French believed themselves threatened by Germany and Italy. To the Quai d'Orsay, the Maginot Line and numbers of submarines were more reassuring than a disarmament pact that lacked British or American pledges of protection. If observers had thought that France had altered its position on this point before the London Conference, they could harbor no such illusions by the time conference delegates departed London. Further, one may argue that any gains of the treaty were outweighed by the resentment it caused in Japan, where the military refused to accept limits on Japan's colonial aims. Premier Hamaguchi was assassinated in 1931 and his was the last civilian government until 1945.

Could the treaty's weaknesses be blamed on inadequate negotiators or technical experts?

President Hoover showed less interest in the political benefits of disarmament than had Coolidge or Harding. This inattention to political implication is not surprising, for Hoover faced other problems of his presidency, such as the Depression, with the same strongly moral approach that he brought to the disarmament issue. Yet he recognized some political imperatives well enough. It is difficult, for example, to criticize him for refusing the guarantees that might have soothed the French in 1930: he knew that no chief executive could have faced down Congress, ignored the worsening depression, and persuaded a distracted public that involvement in European affairs were in their interest. But agreement with Japan was not so clearly desirable as to grant the 10-7 ratio, especially given conditions in China that threatened the political guarantees of the Four- and Nine-Power Treaties of 1922.

As for Hoover's lack of understanding of Japan's needs, perhaps the trouble was American representation in Tokyo. Ambassadors in Tokyo had usually been political appointees, who bothered Hoover more with requests for greater allowances for better housing than with complete accounts of the political scene. Also, Tokyo was regarded as a less desirous post than one of the European capitals. Before Castle's arrival, the State Department received little accurate reporting on press opinion regarding naval ratios. Still, if the president had had a clearer vision of the Japanese public's view toward Japan's rights in Manchuria and their determination to remain there despite Western disapproval, he may have hesitated in granting naval concessions.

One may criticize Stimson for not keeping Washington informed during the discouraging period of negotiation that occurred in mid-March—the period when he told Briand "no" to a consultative pact and MacDonald "maybe," thereby confusing the issue, as Hoover had already refused such an agreement. The secretary had little room for maneuver, however,—the French would not sign a naval agreement without a guarantee and the British, unsure of policy vis-à-vis the Continent, could not be pushed.[84] Then he overreacted. After all, Americans and Britons had considered a three-power treaty even before the conference, should France or Italy or both refuse concession.[85] At one point, Stimson himself had even suggested an Anglo-American two-power treaty. He seemed willing to offer more concessions than Hoover, who had yielded only in the cruiser category. Perhaps Stimson's Anglophilia or ill health caused this lapse in judgment. He may also have failed to keep the president abreast of developments because he distrusted the president's judgment.

As for Admiral Pratt, his advice proved of mixed value. In one respect, his misgivings about heavy cruisers, were later justified when American heavy cruisers constructed under the London Treaty came down the ways: the first four cracked their steering gears during their shakedown cruises.[86] But in other ways he proved less than prescient, failing to realize that the navy did not have much support within the Hoover administration. The president was no friend of the navy, and indeed was more concerned with the national budget, especially after the Great Depression began.[87] Within Congress the navy had few friends, for congressmen were mainly concerned about the cost of a fleet "second to none." To them the theory of parity with Great Britain was more important than the actuality. Pratt had been out of Washington for most of the late 1920s—at the Naval War College and at sea with the U.S. Fleet—and appears to have been out of touch with national politics.

Prime Minister MacDonald was, like Hoover, more committed than his domestic opponents to disarmament as a moral issue, but his position in Parliament was weak. As Cecil and others of the LNU noted, he was torn between support for disarmament and the desire to defend the empire. Even if he had been stronger, he likely would not have veered far from the Admiralty's position. As with the American president, it is hard to criticize MacDonald for failing to accommodate the French, for Parliament would not have permitted broad guarantees. But he and the Cabinet never stopped to consider just what their country's position in relation to the Continent should be. By 1930, it was clear that France needed support.

As with Hoover, it is easier to criticize MacDonald for his position toward the Japanese. During negotiations with the United States, the British had kept their eye on Japan's heavy cruisers, yet allowed the Americans to urge concessions on the Japanese. Faced with a united Anglo-American front, Japan might have agreed more readily to compromise or, more likely, left the conference without agreement, thereby taking the blame for its failure.

Hamaguchi negotiated for political and economic reasons, perhaps believing that success at London would solidify his support at home. He supported Shidehara's commitment to accommodation. Once convinced that Japan had received adequate concessions, he maneuvered his domestic foes to gain acceptance of the Reed-Matsudaira compromise. He and the delegates also gained more from the conference than the other participants, if one compares their goals before the conference with results obtained. They did, after all, force the Americans to capitulate on the 10-7 ratio.

Negotiators at London recognized that the achievements of the conference depended on those of the preceding conferences. The Washington Conference had set up a model of collective security based on arms limitation and political reconciliation. Signatories regarded it as a success. The Geneva Conference carried on the tradition of Washington, at least in American eyes, as the powers sought to extend the 5-5-3 ratio to auxiliary ships, especially cruisers. Discussions there flagged areas of disagreement about cruisers that could be discussed at a later conference. Failure at Geneva contributed to actions—the Kellogg-Briand Pact, the Anglo-French naval compromise, and the American Naval Act of 1929—sufficiently inspiring or disturbing to justify another attempt at halting the cruiser race and extending the Washington ratios. The change of leadership in London and Washington brought opportunity to begin discussions anew. In the end, the treaty's weaknesses did not result from errors in judgment of the participants as much as from suspicion remaining from the war years, especially between France and its neighbors, the shortcomings of the Treaty of Versailles, and the strain of the Great Depression. Leaders in 1930 had little inkling that the deepening depression would invite totalitarian governments to bring about another world war. Statesmen at the time believed that they had produced a new age in international security.

When the conference delegates at London left the Great Hall of St. James's Palace for the last time, an era of cooperation had ended and a new and darker era was about to begin.

7
DISARMAMENT IN THE GREAT DEPRESSION

The years after the London Naval Conference, so far as they concerned naval disarmament and general limitation of armaments, were a disappointing time for arms control advocates, for not much came of this once-heralded idea. Indeed, the apogee of arms limitation turned out to be the meetings in London. Thereafter the industrial nations of the world found themselves forced to deal with the Great Depression, the economic debacle that began with the crash of the New York stock market in 1929. Production worldwide dropped in bewildering ways, accompanied by increasing unemployment. By the time economics began to turn up a little, indicating that troubles might be over, the Hitler regime in Germany, which came to power in 1933, had embarked on an increasingly assertive foreign policy that soon disturbed the politics of Europe and turned thoughts of peace into those of war.

In retrospect, and even at the time, the early 1930s constituted a tremendously disillusioning era, for those years proved a final dashing of belief that the peace of the world, seemingly so assured in the late nineteenth century, might now be coupled with economic prosperity—that the twentieth century could come into its own as an enlightened time when the troubles of preceding centuries no longer would intrude. The First World War had shaken trust in all sorts of principles, and probably more than any other event in our present century disarranged the hopes of peoples everywhere, ending any real possibility that the philosophy of the nineteenth century, "onward and upward," would prevail. The 1920s and momentary prosperity had briefly banished thoughts of the world war, and confidence had returned. But with the coming of the Great Depression the old uncertainties arose again.

The years between the London Conference of 1930 and the Sec-

Original publication unknown. Courtesy of the Naval Historical Center.

ond London Conference of 1935-36 marked the final downturn of
hope, and form a cheerless subject for analysis. The period began
with ratification of the naval treaty in the United States and elsewhere, followed by its proclamation; it ended with a conference
that did little more than confirm the chaos into which the peace of
the world was disappearing.

TREATY RATIFICATION

Because he had pinned so many hopes on naval disarmament—indeed believing that it would ensure peace both in Europe and Asia—President Hoover naturally desired approval of the London Treaty as soon as possible. Any delay would broadcast to the world that the United States was not really in favor of the treaty and would also raise the specter of more serious opposition, for only a decade earlier the Senate had refused to approve the Treaty of Versailles, at least in a form acceptable to President Woodrow Wilson.

To Hoover's consternation, some of his supporters in the Senate began to advise waiting until autumn to submit the treaty for ratification. Senator David Reed, returning from London, so suggested because recent speeches of some senators, such as those made by Kenneth McKellar of Tennessee and Frederick Hale of Maine, suggested that the immediate Senate reaction might be negative. Sufficient uncertainty existed, so Reed sensed, that it would be possible in the interim for the president to speak privately with his more timid supporters and persuade them gradually to back the treaty.

Still, there appeared to be supporters of immediate submission—believers in action, Hoover might have called them. The majority leader, James E. Watson of Indiana, favored voting immediately, because Claude Swanson of Virginia, a key navy supporter, and William E. Borah, head of the powerful Committee for Foreign Relations, seemed ready. The Old Man of the Republican party, Elihu Root, apparently also favored the expansion of Washington limits at London, in part because he believed that Congress would not likely augment the navy much, and because he trusted the Japanese from his days as a diplomat before World War I.[1]

Hoover himself seized the moment and sent in the treaty. Quite apart from its merits, he may have thought that it would divert attention from his recent veto of benefits for veterans of the Spanish-American War, an increasing sentiment against Prohibition, and the rising unemployment.[2]

The London Naval Treaty of course did not have unanimous public support. Not surprisingly, conservative groups opposed it; the Daughters of the American Revolution, for example, passed a hostile resolution at their annual convention. The *Chicago Tribune* and the *Journal of Commerce* (New York) attacked it. But most organizations and publications gave moderate approval, and a few major newspapers, such as the *Christian Science Monitor*, waxed enthusiastic. The labor and farm press remained mostly quiet on the issue, being more concerned with economic problems.[3]

As noted, businessmen were generally less enthusiastic about disarmament than they had been before the Washington Conference, largely because tax reduction, the issue they cared most about, had been achieved. But many nevertheless supported the president and the London Treaty, because additional tax savings appeared possible and international security concerns did not seem to warrant a larger navy. One writer advocating passage of the treaty even depicted the ratification debate in Washington in business terms, as "the interplay of forces representing on the one hand the desire for adequate insurance and on the other the desire to reduce the premium as much as possible."[4] *Business Week* had suggested before the conference that naval limitation might mean that "purchasing power [would] be released for the benefit of domestic business and international trade." The president of the U.S. Chamber of Commerce wrote Hoover that his organization had concluded the treaty did not "jeopardize adequate defense" and thus the Chamber would support it. He perhaps did so because the chairman of the Chamber's Committee on National Defense, although offering lukewarm support for the Kellogg-Briand Pact and naval limitation, had testified in favor of industrial preparedness in congressional hearings and had urged the same in the Chamber's magazine, *Nation's Business*.[5] *The Commercial and Financial Chronicle*, more sympathetic to disarmament than many other business journals, remarked when the terms of the treaty had been disclosed that there appeared "nothing brilliant about the London outcome. Nevertheless . . . there seems to be no good reason why the treaty, as far as the United States is concerned, should not be promptly ratified."[6]

Hearings before the Senate Foreign Relations Committee opened on May 12 and before the Naval Affairs Committee two days later. Secretary Stimson served as the administration's leading witness and displayed a grasp of the issues. He explained that the United States had agreed at London merely to divide cruisers into two equal types, both being necessary for a fleet. He did not want, he said, to put all the navy's eggs in one basket. Seeking to counter charges that limitation rather than reduction had been achieved, he went on:

The very fact that a nation is willing to agree that it shall not exceed a limit fixed by agreement with other nations, and that the amount of the navy shall be known, produces confidence by terminating rivalry. Then as that confidence grows, it produces more limitation and more reduction, and so on. It is a beneficent circle, working from limitation to confidence and from confidence back to limitation. In that way, I think, it is one of the most practical measures for producing international good will upon which, more than anything else, the preservation of peace depends.[7]

Stimson repeated this theme in a radio address of June 12, attacking "warriors" who did not understand the political benefits of the treaty but insisted on belittling its achievements: "They are likely to be blindfolded to one-half of the horizon, a very important half." By implication, of course, he was censuring Admiral Jones and the General Board. His remarks prompted an angry memorandum from Jones, who saucily suggested that the secretary was overstepping the bounds of his office.[8]

Senator Hiram Johnson of California subjected Stimson to stiff questioning in hearings of the Foreign Relations Committee. Privately, Johnson groused about the administration's rush tactics; he feared senators would not take time to inspect the details of a treaty he believed flawed. Dismissing as "veriest twaddle" the assertion that the treaty was a step toward peace, he insisted that it did not grant parity with Britain, permitted the United States to build only as many cruisers as Britain desired, and gratuitously raised Japan's ratio. Although he realized that the Senate would probably pass the treaty by a large margin, he did his best to defeat it, questioning administration officials and calling witnesses he knew opposed the treaty.[9]

Captain Harry Yarnell went far to counteract Senator Johnson's obstructionism and convince the committee of the treaty's merits. In a statement to the committee, he backed Admiral Pratt's position that the navy could design a six-inch cruiser as good as a heavy cruiser. Reacting to testimony that the Philippines would be vulnerable because of the higher Japanese cruiser ratio, he stressed the political importance of the treaty.[10]

Rear Admiral Mark L. Bristol, head of the General Board, disputed Yarnell's statement, writing Johnson that Yarnell had disregarded the principles of national defense to such an extent as to make his conclusions "valueless."[11] Admiral Schofield estimated that seven or eight out of ten ranking officers agreed. Admiral Wiley summed up the attitude of many navy officers in testifying that he had opposed the 5-3 ratio of the Washington treaty and considered the new concessions equally ill-advised. He said that the navy would have to "go out of business" if the United States had too many conferences.[12]

The committee nevertheless approved the treaty with no report, only four members, Johnson, Robinson of Indiana, George Moses of Vermont, and Henrik Shipstead of Minnesota, voting against it.[13]

With these Senate preliminaries, passage was assured. Senator Reed led the administration's fight on the floor. By careful and cagey questioning of naval personnel in earlier hearings, he had managed to demonstrate that the range of the eight-inch gun, described by many witnesses as over 20,000 yards, remained unproved because splashes of shells were difficult to see. He drew particular attention to the treaty's proviso that Japan, beginning in 1934, would build no more cruisers while the U.S. caught up. When the Senate failed to act before the session ended in early July, Hoover called a special session.[14] In a masterful speech on July 15, Reed coolly compared the fleets of each major navy and declared that ratification of the London treaty would end the cruiser race and balance the American fleet. When the Senate passed a resolution sponsored by McKellar, demanding cables, memoranda, and other particulars of the treaty negotiations, Senator Robinson of Arkansas helped Reed with a clause making compliance unnecessary if judged not in the public interest. The matter blew over. The Senate consented to the treaty on July 21, 58 to 9, attaching a reservation by George Norris of Nebraska that there were no secret agreements. Everyone thereupon departed steamy Washington.[15]

In Britain, the public paid scant attention to the treaty. The press focused on the budget, Anglo-Egyptian negotiations, and the situation in India, where masses of protesters were calling for independence. What little comment the treaty aroused was optimistic. The *Manchester Guardian* urged approval, acknowledging that much work remained before 1936. J.L. Garvin of the *London Observer* wrote that talks between the British and French governments might continue. The *Daily Herald* (Labour) admitted that on balance the treaty was good.[16]

Debate began in the House of Lords on May 8. Interestingly, both delegates of the Geneva Conference of 1927, Viscounts Cecil and Bridgeman, opposed the London Treaty, Cecil because it did not go far enough, and Bridgeman because it went too far. Hoping for delay, Bridgeman called for the negotiation papers and received the backing of Admirals Beatty and Jellicoe and Lord Carson. But support for the motion died, and opposition ended.

In the House of Commons, Churchill led the attack on the treaty for reasons similar to those he had advanced in Cabinet against concessions at Geneva in 1927. He saw no connection between the

Washington treaties and the London Treaty, as the instruments of 1921-22 established Anglo-American battleship parity, whereas that of 1930 promoted British inferiority because the few cruisers allowed Britain would be spread over a large part of the world. He especially disliked the increased ratio for Japan. Stanley Baldwin endorsed Churchill's stance and moved to appoint a committee to examine the treaty, in the hope of defeating it. In particular, he questioned the decision to accept fewer than seventy cruisers. But he fared no better than Bridgeman had in the House of Lords. Prime Minister MacDonald defended the results of the conference, describing them as but "a little nibble at the cherry" of disarmament, and he observed that the treaty did not represent the last word on arms control because it looked to more Anglo-French conversations and to talks at the Preparatory Commission. He urged quick passage.[17] Baldwin's motion was defeated, and on July 24 the House approved the treaty.[18]

Acceptance proved more difficult in Japan. Conservatives encouraged antitreaty demonstrations, while some newspapers complained that the delegates had not struck a good bargain. Admiral Takarabe wisely visited Viscount Saito in Korea to allow emotions to cool, but on his belated return to Japan a junior naval officer presented him with a dagger and denounced him as a traitor. Admiral Kato, chief of the Navy General Staff, described the treaty as "offering us the crumbs and telling us to eat them."[19] Still, most newspapers, including many of the largest and most influential, accepted the treaty, and delegate Wakatsuki received a suitable welcome in the capital. The emperor even praised him in a rare political statement.[20]

The Meiji Constitution did not specify how treaties were to be confirmed, although by custom the Privy Council advised the emperor on his proper course. The question arose about who had authority to limit the navy—the emperor, as advised by the navy, or the cabinet. Premier Hamaguchi knew that if the cabinet simply presented the controversial measure to the emperor, the minister of war would almost certainly resign, forcing the fall of the cabinet. The naval staff argued that the cabinet had overstepped its bounds in advising the delegation at London; the government countered that, because the treaty dealt with politics and economics, its handling of the delegation had been proper. The opposition Seiyukai party attacked the treaty but stopped short of agreeing with the navy staff, lest the latter use the same argument against a future Seiyukai government. Public opinion generally followed the government.[21]

There followed an involved negotiation. Hamaguchi decided not to claim that the cabinet possessed the right to approve the treaty, but allowed the Diet and House of Peers to debate the issue. A veritable battle ensued between the government and its opponents in the Diet and War Council. Hamaguchi insisted that the treaty did not impair Japan's defense, that the empire had gained much international good will and could present its case again in another conference, and that failure to sign probably meant another cruiser race. He submitted the treaty to the Privy Council on July 24, and that body appointed an investigative committee. After long weeks of examination and sharp debate it could not reach a conclusion, so Hamaguchi argued his case before the emperor, attended by the council. At length the council voted unanimously to ratify.

Opponents outside the council remained intransigent. The navy was wracked by resignations. Admiral Kato resigned as chief of the naval staff, helping force the resignations of Vice Admiral Suetsugu Nobumasa, vice chief of staff, Vice Admiral Yamanashi of the Ministry of the Marine, and Navy Minister Admiral Takarabe. Senior army officials were also angry that Hamaguchi had served as acting navy minister for Takarabe while the latter was in London attending the conference. They had not forgotten budget cuts in 1925 that had rendered the army more technologically efficient but at the cost of size. They also feared Hamaguchi might act as army minister as well. For his troubles Hamaguchi was assassinated in early 1931.[22]

TECHNOLOGICAL INNOVATIONS

Following the exchange of ratifications of the London Treaty, naval officers in the United States, Britain, and Japan concentrated on designing ships that conformed to treaty standards and on influencing their political superiors to expand their respective fleets.

Aware that the administration had failed in the past to authorize construction, American officers hoped that the president might finally now consider enlarging the fleet.[23] But they hoped in vain. Serious expansion began only when the chairman of the House Committee for Naval Affairs, Carl Vinson, introduced a bill to strengthen what he described as the nation's dangerously weak position vis-à-vis the Japanese. When the House defeated the bill, the indefatigable Vinson argued that shipbuilding would furnish a source of employment and managed to convince Hoover's successor, Franklin D. Roosevelt, to allocate $238 million from the National Industrial Recovery Administration to the fleet. Isolationists and disarmament defenders protested, but Roosevelt accepted Vinson's logic that new construction was necessary, as many of the ships built during the First World War were becoming obsolete. The Vinson-Trammel Act of 1934 authorized building the navy to treaty limits by 1942 (an increase of 102 ships) and appropriated money to begin the program. The administration carefully announced that a treaty navy was the goal and that the president planned only moderate construction during the first year.[24]

Meanwhile, the General Board began planning for adapting its cruisers to the London Treaty. In Washington, Admiral Pratt testified before the Senate Foreign Relations Committee that the treaty gave the navy a building schedule, a goal for which to aim, that would help eliminate the construction bulges of 1916 (battleships) and 1917-18 (destroyers). Captain Johnson, director of Naval Intelligence, seconded Pratt's contention and added that the treaty's construction timetable furnished the navy with something to "hang its hat on." Pratt and the bureaus of Engineering, Construction and Repair, and Ordnance initially spent much time designing and modifying the heavy cruisers authorized by the Naval Act of 1929. In building the first cruisers, designers had underestimated their displacement; the first eight heavy cruisers displaced far less than 10,000 tons. The first two, the *Pensacola* and *Salt Lake City*, also possessed inadequate armor, and officers described them as "eggshells with hammers." A dissatisfied Pratt and the General Board ordered enhanced protection, particularly around vulnerable magazines, machinery, and gun turrets.[25] In March 1933, however, the board reversed itself and ordered more gunpower, from an improved gun, at the expense of protection. Tests had demonstrated flaws in the eight-inch gun, such as inaccuracy at long range, insufficient rate of fire, and problems with ammunition-loading. Naval intelligence had received descriptions of the Japanese *Mogami*-class cruisers, which featured high speed and fifteen six-inch guns. Ordnance experts also set to work ameliorating the deficiencies of the eight-inch gun. Too, there were problems with torpedoes. The last American heavy cruiser built under the Washington Five-Power Treaty, the *Wichita*, laid down in 1934, carried no torpedoes because the board saw them as secondary weapons to main batteries and antiaircraft guns. Only in 1936 did the director of fleet maintenance recommend that future cruisers carry torpedoes, presumably because the latest Japanese cruisers possessed them.[26] Because they lacked the torpedoes of their Japanese opponents, American treaty cruisers would suffer from the board's decision during the Solomons campaign of the Second World War.

Pratt supervised the designs of four other ship types—a conventional six-inch cruiser, a gunboat, a flight-deck cruiser, and a battle cruiser—but the navy built only conventional six-inch cruisers and the gunboats.

Designers spent much time wrestling with the problem of putting airplanes on cruisers. The correspondence between the chief of naval operations, the bureaus, and the secretary of the navy between 1930 and 1934 reveals a multiplicity of plans, proposals, and recommendations. Pratt, Rear Admiral William A. Moffett, chief of the Bureau of Aeronautics, and Rear Admiral Harris Lanning, the president of the Naval War College from 1930 to 1933, favored a landing deck so as to use planes in the scouting that cruisers often did for convoys and carriers. The General Board recommended designs for a such a cruiser. But many officers harbored doubts about the project. Schofield feared the fire hazard of aviation fuel in aircraft and in fueling stations. Deck piping for the fuel also might interfere with gunfire. He believed that such a cruiser, rather than being able to serve as a screen, would require its own screen of cruisers or destroyers to protect its aircraft.[27] Many members of the board agreed with War College studies maintaining that such a ship constituted neither cruiser nor carrier. The ship's advocates, Pratt, Moffett, and Lanning, however, retired in 1933. After developing the Brooklyn-class cruisers authorized by the Vinson-Trammel Act, the Bureau of Construction and Repair attended to designs for a flight deck cruiser, but the General Board ended by stressing fleet action over aircraft. It decided to forego a prototype because the navy was short of conventional cruisers. A report from the director of war plans in 1936 suggested that aircraft should rank behind armament.[28]

Similar thoughts encouraged the board to emphasize battleships and cruisers over aircraft carriers after the London Conference. The board still favored battleships. Most officers continued to think in terms of gunnery battles at sea and did not fully sense the importance of air battles, especially involving ship-launched planes.[29] It is true that during exercises in 1929, planes from the carriers Lexington and Saratoga had evaded fleet forces and theoretically bombed the locks of the Panama Canal. And based on this experience and on the prodding of Admiral Moffett, planners by the late 1920s had designated various tasks to carriers, including leading landings in the Philippines, attacking the Mandates, and patrolling.[30] But little evidence existed pointing to carriers as the capital ship of the future: fleet maneuvers had demonstrated the vulnerability of carriers, especially of flammable planes exposed on decks; carriers and planes encountered difficulties in bad weather and at night; and exercises hinted that carriers might be used early in battle, leaving the battle line only as last recourse. The navy conducted few exercises testing carriers, in part because General Board members were not convinced of their importance and because those few officers who did appreciate carriers debated about the proper size—Moffett wanted small carriers instead of large ones like the *Saratoga* and *Lexington*. He and others in the Bureau of Aeronautics noted that the new smaller carrier, *Ranger*, could launch almost as many planes as the larger carriers. The goal of carriers, as he saw it, was to put as many planes as possible into the sky.[31]

In addition, battleship technology changed in 1933 34, when engineers designed a battleship that could travel twenty-eight knots, rather than twenty or twenty-one, with adequate armor and arms within the treaty limits of 35,000 tons. The faster battleships required faster screen and scout vessels, eating up more developmental money per ship. Progress in battleship design, doubts about carriers, treaty limits, and funding problems combined to prevent more thorough investigation into carriers.[32] The navy's top brass still favored battleships, and the assumptions of the strategy of Alfred Thayer Mahan, at the time the Washington treaties expired in 1936.[33]

In London, the Admiralty succeeded in convincing political leaders that Britain needed to increase the fleet. Naval officers succeeded less because of their persuasive talents than because of a worsening international political climate that seemed to threaten the empire at several points. In the Far East, there was the Japanese occupation of Manchuria in 1931-33, when the Japanese Kwantung Army used the pretexts of Chinese boycotts and an alleged plot to blow up the Japanese-controlled South Manchurian Railway to seize the province. British intelligence detected Japanese naval building in 1932-33 and reported that cruisers of the *Mogami* class displaced at least 8,500 tons.[34] The Admiralty felt compelled either to resort to the escalator clause of the London Treaty and build an unlimited number of cruisers or to increase the displacement of the cruisers permitted by the treaty. Despite a preference for smaller cruisers, it increased the displacement of new six-inch-gunned cruisers from 7,000 to 7,500 tons, with guns in triple mountings.[35] Admiral Chatfield, the First Sea Lord, approved these recommendations for the *Leander* class, reversing his position of 1928 when he had argued for eight-inch-gunned cruisers. The Admiralty also drew up plans for an even heavier six-inch cruiser, and the prime minister told a group of officers in October 1933 that he approved of a proposed "M" cruiser of 8,900 tons, carrying twelve six-inch guns.[36]

The British paid even less attention to aircraft carriers than did the Americans. They carried out few carrier exercises and were concerned more about protecting trade routes because of the threat posed by the new German pocket battleship, the *Deutschland*. In November 1928, the Admiralty had recommended converting old battleships into carriers to permit two carriers, rather than one, to accompany each fleet. But it delayed construction of a new carrier. Like their American counterparts, most officers favored armament over aircraft.[37]

In Japan during these years the navy virtually dominated the civil government. After the London Conference, the Navy General Staff exerted control over the more moderate Ministry of the Marine. Staff leaders used maneuver and even threats to purge admirals who had supported the London Treaty, for after 1930 many officers lost what little confidence they had had in Shidehara's program of cooperation with the Western powers. They recommended scrapping the Washington agreements. They doubted the strength of the Western economies because of the expanding depression, and resented what they considered acts of economic warfare by the West, especially the Smoot-Hawley Act of 1930, which closed American trade to many Japanese goods.[38] The London Treaty came in for a barrage of criticism from officers and the press during the "May 15 Incident" trial—the court-martial of Premier Inukai's assassins in August 1933. The American attaché reported:

The widest possible publicity is being given to the trial—obviously intended as a warning to the civilian authorities that unless the economic and social evils of the capitalistic democracy are corrected further use of 'direct action' may be necessary. The criticism of the government and the naval authorities as incompetent, weak-kneed and corrupt for accepting an inferior ratio under the London Naval Treaty, and the publicity which is being given this phase of politics, is clearly directed toward preventing the Japanese nation from ever accepting any treaty which does not give Japan practical parity with the United States and Great Britain.[39]

Japan, many junior naval officers concluded, would decide for itself the proper policy to pursue in the Far East, and it would not include disarmament.

Admiral Okada, no friend of arms control, replaced the more conciliatory Admiral Saito as premier in July 1934, following publication of a communiqué by junior officers asking abrogation of the

Washington treaties and a new cabinet that could halt political unrest.[40] Although some prominent politicians, including former premier Wakatsuki, lead delegate to the London Conference of 1930, had defended the London Treaty in a speech in October 1933, they soon desisted. Wakatsuki did so because he realized he was probably marked for assassination and that public opinion seemed to favor the navy's antidisarmament stand.[41] In 1934, liaison committees of civilians and military personnel, dominated by the navy, began to form policy for the foreign office. Under these circumstances the navy had little trouble gaining political approval of increased construction.[42]

When designed, the *Mogami*-class cruisers that so worried British planners displaced 9,500 tons, but when launched they displaced 11,200 tons. After refitting in 1937-38, they reached 12,400 tons. They carried increased armor, six-inch guns with reinforced barbettes refittable with eight-inch guns (later done), and possessed stronger hulls.[43] In short, the Japanese proved unable to handle their treaty cruiser requirements within the prescribed 10,000 tons. Rather than sacrifice what they considered essentials, they simply refused to confine themselves to treaty limits. This decision may have had something to do with the mysterious capsizing of the torpedo ship *Tomotsuru* in March 1934. Investigation afterward pointed to poor design, based on treaty restrictions.[44] Although the Americans and British suspected what was going on, they do not appear to have realized the extent to which the Japanese had gone over the limits. The diplomats at London had not discussed verification, preferring to rely on national good will.

As for carriers, the Japanese by 1928 had completed their first two, by converting battleships. They finished two more by 1933, which placed them on a par with the United States Navy.[45] They experimented with ship-launched aircraft and with planes armed with torpedoes considerably more than did the American or British navies, yet battleship advocates continued to overshadow those officers who desired carriers. Like the Americans, Japanese officers could not decide whether a bigger or smaller carrier was preferable or how many to attach to the fleet. Their deliberations continued as the war in China expanded, beginning in 1937.

PRESSURE GROUP ACTIVITY IN THE 1930S

After the London Conference, economic dislocation hampered the efforts of civilian navy supporters who sought construction to treaty limits while it aided, at least for a short time, those of peace groups calling for naval limitation. In the depths of the Great Depression it was difficult to support expenditures for navies. In the United States the depression was acute: the gross national product slid by a third, the banking system teetered, farm prices dove, and gold reserves dropped, as Americans feared that the United States might follow Britain off the gold standard. Circumstances in Britain, although alarming, were not as dire: for a while the economy even enjoyed a mild upswing.[46] Increased naval construction in both the United States and Britain, however, seemed out of the question. For a time it appeared that the disarmament process that Secretary Hughes had begun in 1921-22 would be completed by the economic cataclysm that began in 1929.

At the outset of the depression years, the London Treaty had seemed acceptable to large-navy enthusiasts in the United States, if only because they believed that it constituted the ultimate limitation; it was assumed that there could not possibly be more limitations to come. In its first comment on the London Conference of 1930, the Navy League had recommended ratification of the treaty, but with amendments and reservations. The president of the league, William Howard Gardiner, naturally disapproved of the treaty, warning that "naval power is not like a fire department, to be called upon only when the conflagration of war appears." But his efforts were halfhearted. The league suffered weakened relations with the Navy Department after Pratt's appointment as chief of naval operations.[47]

Under such circumstances, the Navy League did what it could. It berated President Hoover for not building up to treaty limits. Navy League supporter Henry Cabot Lodge, an editorial writer for the *New York Tribune*, wrote in support of a navy built to treaty limits. Following the administration's announcement that it would build only five of the eleven destroyers for which Congress had appropriated money, Gardiner wrote speeches for admirals highly critical of the London Treaty. One such speech, in draft, found its way to the White House, where President Hoover ordered offending passages cut.

But then the league went too far—Gardiner produced a vitriolic pamphlet, "The President and the Navy," so critical of Hoover that the president, stung by the attack, took measures against it. The FBI conducted an investigation that revealed the small size of the league—it had no branch offices outside Washington—and provided information about a few of its members. Hoover appointed a committee to investigate the league and forbade navy officers to belong to it. To serve on his committee the president shrewdly selected administration officials including Navy League men currently in the administration. Ironically, the committee and the Navy League executive board lunched in neighboring rooms at the Metropolitan Club in Washington the same day the committee tentatively agreed on its findings. Not surprisingly, the committee report criticized the league in strong terms. League membership plummeted, and Gardiner was forced to resign. The journalist William Allen White wrote that "the entire country applauds as President Hoover smashes back in Rooseveltian manner at the insolence of the Navy League."[48]

Peace groups continued to endorse the London Treaty. Sidney Gulick of the Federal Council of Churches had urged that the U.S. ratify the treaty because not doing so would foster a belief that naval conferences were worthless. He suggested that the U.S. reduce arms by example and continue to cooperate with the Preparatory Commission for the forthcoming World Disarmament Conference at Geneva. He also proposed that the nation join the World Court, ratify the Pan-American arbitration treaty, and assure other nations that the United States would not aid any aggressor. To make certain that prominent members of the Senate favored naval disarmament, the NCPW sent Jeannette Rankin to interview members of the Foreign Relations Committee. The Council also persuaded Felix Morley of the Brookings Institution to rebut Henry Cabot Lodge's editorial in its *International Disarmament Notes*.[49] Dorothy Detzer of the WILPF meanwhile made the most of her "picnic and dinner party relationship" with influential people, including the secretary of Senator Borah's staff.[50]

Peace organizations continued to group themselves roughly in two blocs. James McDonald of the Foreign Policy Association formed a new conservative group, known as 99 Park Avenue, which sought disarmament but also collective security, even at the risk of American involvement in European or Asian affairs. The Carnegie Endowment for International Peace, ICCCW, and League of Nations Association, the latter headed by Clark Eichelberger, adhered to this bloc. The other grouping, led by Clarence Pickett of the American Friends Service Committee attracted pacifists, members of the Socialist party, the NCPW, and faculty members from the Union Theological Seminary in New York.[51]

In preparation for the World Disarmament Conference of 1932, both blocs publicized the cause of disarmament. The 99 Park Avenue group sponsored disarmament institutes in six Midwestern cities, and the Carnegie Endowment appropriately arranged disarmament meetings for Armistice Day 1931. The radical bloc displayed much more enthusiasm. Detzer blamed armament races on "masculine insecurity nurtured by a selfish patriotism" and urged the appointment of Dr. Mary E. Woolley, president of Mount Holyoke, to the delegation scheduled to go to Geneva. Detzer helped organize a transcontinental peace caravan of 150 automobiles that started from California in 1931, traversed the nation collecting signatures on a petition asking for women delegates to Geneva and for complete disarmament, and ended at the White House, ironically escorted by the Navy Band. To publicize her cause she also met with congressmen and the press. All the while eleven international groups, including the ICCCW and the WILPF, formed the Disarmament Committee of the Women's International Organizations and established headquarters at Geneva. Pierre Boal of the State Department told Navy Department officials that, judging from previous conferences, the navy should expect a remarkable pressure at Geneva.[52]

With the opening of the new conference in 1932, peace groups engaged in a flurry of activity. The International Committee arranged to produce news reports, consultative groups to interview delegates, members to lecture in the United States and in the Netherlands, France, Germany, and, of course, Switzerland. The WILPF collected signatures for a "No More War" petition and organized mass meetings. Captain T. Kinkaid, a naval aide at the Geneva Conference, noted that peace groups at the Geneva Conference printed a daily *Conference Journal* which provided communications from peace groups around the world, secured a special Plenary session of the conference at which they addressed delegates, and showered delegates and the president of the conference (Arthur Henderson) with telegrams.[53]

In Britain, private peace organizations also promoted the cause. British groups circulated a petition that by May 1931 obtained almost a half million signatures. The Trade Union Congress passed a resolution that the Geneva Conference could not succeed unless disarmament treaties covered one fourth of the arms expenditures of governments. A demonstration at the Royal Albert Hall drew an audience of 20,000 that listened to MacDonald, Baldwin, and Lloyd George.[54]

Japanese advocates of peace through disarmament similarly held meetings, sent delegations to the ministries of foreign affairs and education, and circulated literature. Yet, as a Japanese WILPF member reported to Detzer, the disarmament message did not attract a wide audience.[55] Censorship restricted communication in Japan. Economically speaking, the times were not right for talk of disarmament: the silk, rice, and bond markets were slumping and foreign trade had fallen 40 percent. The depression dramatically affected Japanese farmers and tended increasingly to radicalize the army, many members of which came from the segments of society hardest hit by the country's economic difficulties—small landowning families and the peasantry.[56] The largest Japanese peace organization, the League of Nations Association of Japan, remained preoccupied with China. It published *International Gleanings from Japan*, a monthly journal that focused almost exclusively on Japanese-Chinese relations, describing anti-Japanese propaganda in Nationalist Chinese schoolbooks, listing anti-Japanese groups in Shanghai, and explaining new restrictions on Japanese businessmen in China. It also put out a pamphlet by Viscount Ishii in which he defended in strong terms Japan's rights in Manchuria. Naval disarmament seemed nearly forgotten in Japan.[57]

DISARMAMENT AFTER THE LONDON TREATY OF 1930

For a while after the London Conference of 1930, the attention of the naval powers shifted to the efforts of the French and Italian governments to agree on limitation of their navies. Hope had followed hope. The statesmen first had expected that a Franco-Italian accord might come before the Preparatory Commission meeting in late 1930. It was not to be: the French and Italian delegates achieved little. Gibson visited Premier Mussolini but did not obtain any sort of compromise. When Foreign Secretary Henderson and First Lord of the Admiralty Alexander met with Il Duce in February 1931, they seemed on the verge of success, but nothing came of the conversation that month. Italian claims for parity with France were incompatible with the ratios of the other powers at London.

Delegates at last gathered in Geneva for the World Disarmament Conference, the conference toward which the Preparatory Commission had labored for nearly six years. Hoover appointed Stimson as chairman of the American delegation to the Geneva Conference, with Gibson as acting head.[58] The Americans planned no naval initiatives; they essentially wanted to continue the Washington and London treaties and forestall capital-ship reduction. As Gibson had observed not long after the London Conference, the United States had less interest in the new conference because treaties already limited its navy, its army was so small that reduction was ludicrous, and the proposed measures of air limitation were so vague that they meant little.[59] He also incidentally provided a remarkably prescient estimate of the length and achievement of the coming conference at this time. He wrote that the conference would "probably meet in February or March 1932 and, discouraging as it may sound, it will probably go on and on."[60] He had come to believe that armaments would never be abolished completely but that treaties could perhaps maintain military balances.[61] Secretary Stimson later wrote that Americans regarded the Geneva Conference as really "a European peace conference with European political questions to be settled. . . . The necessary work of settling them must be done by the leaders of Europe." He realized that Germany's position in European affairs could not be ignored as it had at Geneva in 1927 or at London in 1930, but he did not know how to reconcile German military ambition with French fear of its neighbor. Stimson therefore hoped the Europeans might find a solution. The secretary also hesitated over further naval disarmament because of the Manchurian crisis; in particular he worried whether the navy possessed enough carriers for possible action in the Far East.[62]

Britons were no more optimistic. Mindful of Geneva in 1927, Austen Chamberlain believed that although the U.S. would "push strongly for disarmament *by others*, their own attitude in this and other international questions of the moment will not, I fear, lend much weight to their arguments."[63] MacDonald had also wondered about the amount of disarmament the Empire could afford. He had written privately to Cecil:

There is a fundamental weakness in all our international transactions, and that is a lowering of the position which this country has held for so long in the eyes of the world. I feel it to be a problem to which we ought primarily to address ourselves. Its influence upon the minds of other people was shown by a remark that was made to me by one of the French Delegates to the Naval Conference, when he said that the only reason why we wanted to reduce our Navy was that we could not afford to build up to old standards. We shall have to be very careful not to allow our peace determination to be interpreted by unfriendly people to mean that we have got flabby and useless—that it is spirit going out of us, rather than wisdom going into us.[64]

France and Italy had negotiated settlement in March 1931, but the measure failed of ratification because the problem of parity between the two remained unsolved; the Italians demanding it and the French refusing it. The French came to Geneva resolved to bolster their security by linking any disarmament of land, air, and sea.[65] They also sought guarantees from other countries, even Italy if need be, against German rearmament. French diplomats' heads had been turned by Mussolini's proposal of a four-power arms limitation meeting should the disarmament talks at Geneva flounder.[66]

Britain also debated its future stand on disarmament. Although London would concentrate on land and air reduction at Geneva, the Admiralty nevertheless demanded seventy cruisers and wanted to limit capital ships drastically. It desired abolition of the heavy cruiser and restricted numbers of aircraft carriers and six-inch cruisers. In short, the British planned no new initiative, preferring to make their wishes known when the Americans approached them.[67] Malcolm MacDonald, secretary to his father, remarked to Cecil that at the new Geneva Conference the government simply wanted to establish the London Treaty as the international standard until 1936 and otherwise hoped that the conference would pass a resolution asking the French and Italians to adhere to the limitation clauses of the London Treaty.[68]

Meanwhile Whitehall's opinion of Japan began to change in early 1932 because of events in China. The British had reacted less strongly to the Manchurian Incident of 1931 than had the United States, and continued to refuse to join Secretary of State Stimson's call for a combined naval mission to China after the Shanghai Incident began on January 28, 1932. But in the months following Shanghai, London began to move closer to the American position, criticizing Tokyo more strongly and frequently and sponsoring a League resolution that called for the maintenance of the military status quo in the Far East. The British, of course, had greater economic interests in the Yangtse valley than they had in Manchuria.[69] Under such circumstances naval disarmament began to look less attractive to many British leaders.

The Japanese proposed to ask parity in auxiliary ships and would brook no discussion of political matters. Because of the nation's new position in Manchuria and an increasing Japanese presence in North China, disarmament seemed of no avail; discussing it, one Japanese critic observed, was like sailing a small boat on "a turbulent sea against contrary winds."[70]

As for disarmament on land or in the air, the many delegates at Geneva had to contend with the grand series of disarmament projects identified over several years by the Preparatory Commission. On land the conferees could examine the advisability of trained reserves, which constituted the strength of the French and Italian armies, or they could consider limitation of land armaments according to either numbers of troops or expenditures. Because of the clash between China and Japan in Manchuria, most nations leaned toward supervision of any treaty—the Preparatory Commission had established a Permanent Disarmament Commission to oversee possible agreements at Geneva. The question remained how much power this commission would hold.

Conference delegates encountered serious obstacles from the start. Proposals were almost innumerable and, of course, too ambitious, especially considering the deteriorating international situation. On the very day when the conference opened, it was necessary to delay the ceremonies for a short time because of an emergency meeting of the League of Nations Council, summoned to consider the Manchurian crisis. Thereafter, delegates did what they could in the face of increasing trouble in the Far East. During the first phase of the conference, from February to June 1932, the missions studied all categories to determine what weapons were defensive and what offensive (that is, threatening to civil populations). The conference's naval commission found this task impossible. The British members presented proposals for the abolition of naval aircraft. In desperation, or perhaps inadvertence, President Hoover suggested limiting the numbers of battleships and submarines by one third and carriers, destroyers, and cruisers by one fourth. He also sought to trim land armies by one third and limit troop numbers to a ratio equal to that of the German army as established by the Treaty of Versailles. Finally he wanted to abolish chemical warfare, bombers, and large mobile guns.[71]

The president perhaps offered these proposals to draw attention from the impasse over war debts and reparations at the Lausanne Conference sessions, which opened in June 1932. He was backed in this instance by the influential financier and perennial presidential adviser, Bernard Baruch, who, though he had long supported a strong navy, had come to believe that a disarmament of all nations would be more useful than a moratorium on war debts.[72] In short, Hoover may have wished to achieve a bold foreign-policy initiative that would deflect criticism of his economic measures. He was, after all, a candidate for reelection in November.

A British observer carefully noted the difficulty of American proposals at Geneva, so far as they concerned limitation of naval arms: the United States wanted Britain to accept a reduction nearly double its own, to a level of parity lower than Britain was willing to go. London would have had to scrap ships whereas American treaty tonnage was largely unbuilt—"phantom vessels sailing on the seas of fancy."[73] Another drawback to the American plan: British naval reductions would have encouraged the Dominions to build.

Norman Davis, a member of the American delegation, shrewdly observed that only accompanying diplomatic arrangements would put Hoover's disarmament plan across, such as a land-arms agreement between France and Germany or a naval accord between France and Italy.[74] Japan also rejected Hoover's naval suggestions, as the Foreign Office, Navy, and War Ministry adamantly opposed them. The Japanese press condemned them, citing Japan's special interests in Manchuria and the need for security. The weak cabinet dared not accept the proposals.

Despite MacDonald's forecast to Baldwin that "a month's steady work of a delicate and difficult kind is required to bring Geneva near to an end," the conference, unable to agree, recessed on July 23, planning to meet again in September.[75] Americans were not as optimistic. State Department officials complained that so much of the work at Geneva did not concern disarmament per se that the department could not build a staff under the disarmament budget. Hugh Wilson wrote in December that unless the French received a guarantee of security from the British and Americans, which was not likely, the conference would fail. By March 1933, Pierrepont Moffat was having trouble getting the army and the navy to retain concessions offered at the start of the conference. In addition, the new secretary of state, Cordell Hull, was less concerned with disarmament than with debts and the Far East.[76] At the same time, important businessmen such as Owen Young, who had much to do with European financial restructuring during the 1920s, began to doubt that disarmament was wise given the world economic situation. Young, for one, believed that the Disarmament Conference in Geneva should recess until western leaders had reached agreement at an economic summit in London. He believed that the one depended on the successful conclusion of the other.[77]

The rise of militaristic governments in Germany and Japan eventually rendered the work of the Geneva Conference impossible. In Berlin, the Bruening cabinet fell; Franz von Papen and General Kurt von Schleicher followed, and then Adolf Hitler. Germany withdrew its delegates from Geneva in September 1932, only to return there in December. In October 1933, the Germans withdrew again. Japanese politics similarly entered a stormy period. After Prime Minister Inukai, whose party had won an election in February 1932, was assassinated in August, Admiral Saito formed a cabinet that tried to keep peace between factions in the navy. In March 1933, after the League of Nations adopted the so-called Lytton Report, chaired by Lord Lytton of Britain, which was critical of Japan's actions in Manchuria, Japan withdrew its delegation from the League of Nations, never to return.[78] After drifting for months, the World Disarmament Conference mercifully adjourned sine die in June 1934, never to reassemble.

Few held out any hope for what would be the last naval disarmament conference of the interwar years, which met in London between December 1935 and March 1936. Talks during the summer and autumn of 1934 concerned the Americans, for the Admiralty, worried about Japan and Germany's effect on France, recommended seventy cruisers and building to limits in its memorandum for the Second London Conference, without compensation to the U.S.[79] But the U.S. had already been angered by Whitehall's request that it postpone laying down four six-inch cruisers in September 1933. Moffat wrote that the request "has created so much resentment here that more detailed publicity would, I fear, needlessly embitter Anglo-American relations at the moment."[80] Whitehall also wanted to explore a naval compromise with the Japanese. But during subsequent talks between Chatfield, the First Sea Lord, and Admiral Yamamoto, the Japanese insisted on a 10-7 ratio in capital ships, 10-8 in heavy cruisers, and parity in submarines, destroyers, and light cruisers. Chatfield gloomily reckoned that "we shall have no treaty. . . . The Japanese proposals are likely to be unacceptable to the USA. I think the sparks will be flying in a fortnight's time."[81] Meanwhile, the Japanese government announced in December 1934 that it would abrogate the Five-Power Treaty in two years. Britain's weakness in regard to naval limitation reflected the tenuous leadership of MacDonald. Still prime minister but a broken figure, he had left the Labour party to head a coalition government but enjoyed little support in Parliament, and suffered from deteriorating health. Neville Chamberlain, chancellor of the Exchequer, soon to be prime minister, forthrightly asked that Britain limit its worldwide obligations and concentrate on European problems.

On the eve of the Second London Conference, the American attitude toward naval limitation was glum. The General Board proposed compensating the United States in other classes of ships for increases in British cruisers and opposed reduction in the numbers or size of capital ships. Much as Admiral Pratt had believed of the London Treaty, so Pratt's successor, Admiral William H. Standley, judged that a new treaty offered the best chance that Congress would provide appropriations for the navy to build to treaty limits. President Roosevelt quixotically pressed the board to accept a plan that would permit some limitation but allow building to treaty limits. He instructed the delegation to the Second London Conference, headed by Admiral Standley and Norman Davis, to ask for tonnage limits, unless the Japanese delegation withdrew, in which case the Americans might accept the British position for qualitative limits, albeit with an escape clause.[82]

The Second London Conference opened on December 9, 1935, and reached a stalemate within a week. The Japanese delegation refused to back down on its ratio demands, set out earlier by Admiral Yamamoto, and quickly retired from the conference, as the other powers had expected. The British and Americans signed a treaty on March 25, 1936, that maintained the sixteen-inch limit on guns of capital ships, set a 35,000-ton limit on battleship displacement, and established a five-year building holiday for heavy cruisers. But the Americans could finish some of their heavy cruisers, as the U.S. Navy had fallen below current treaty limits. The treaty limited displacement of light cruisers to 8,000 tons, that for carriers to 22,000 tons, and guns for each to 6.1 inches.[83]

The era of naval disarmament thus ended. Many nations signed the new treaty, but it hardly achieved naval limitation. In the later 1930s, the Japanese furiously built their navy toward parity with the Americans and British and by 1941 would have a clear superiority in carriers—the capital ships, as it turned out, of World War II. As international tension mounted, cheating on treaty limits became common, and powers could rely only on inadequate intelligence reports. Japanese cruisers, as mentioned, had passed beyond the restrictions of the Washington and London treaties, even while those treaties remained nominally in effect. The Americans and the British eventually sensed what was happening, but public opinion in these countries, nurtured by the peace movement, supported by financial constraints, bolstered by the hope that what had not happened would not happen, made it impossible to seize the moment and build beyond the Japanese.[84]

And so the time of decision passed, and with it the chance for world peace.

8
CONCLUSION

In one of his last speeches during the presidential campaign of 1932, Herbert Hoover listed the accomplishments of his administration and emphasized disarmament—he had sought it, he said, because of his experiences in the world war. Having been so involved with the war, he beheld a personal responsibility to prevent another such cataclysm. Surely here was one of the primary reasons, perhaps even the sole reason, for the fascination of statesmen and publics with the limitation of naval armaments during the 1920s.

There was in addition the economic reason for taking interest in disarmament. At the outset of the 1920s, observers showed concern over national budgets, burdened by large debt because of the war. At the end of the decade and during the 1930s, many thoughtful individuals feared what the Wall Street crash and then the Great Depression itself could mean for budgets, and they saw the intense difficulty of naval construction during a time of economic trouble.

Political leaders in the United States, Britain, and Japan showed interest in disarmament partly because they could gain politically from it. A success in foreign affairs that had broad public approval, helped balance the budget, and deflected interest from troubling domestic problems could bolster their positions within their parties and with the electorate. Presidents and premiers after the Washington Conference carefully noted how Harding, Lloyd George, and Hara had profited from their participation in that conference, and they hoped to equal those successes when timing proved auspicious. They initially hoped that politics internationally had entered a period of lessening tension. Hoover wished for better Anglo-American relations. In Britain, parties hoped to better relations with the Continent, especially after the assurances that Britain had given at Locarno. In Tokyo, political leaders at first sought naval adjustments through disarmament. When the situation in China turned down, and governing became difficult because of pressure from the military, the government's position began to shift. Stability in the Far East became more important than arms control.

As a causal variable in affecting disarmament, nongovernmental pressure groups influenced public opinion but were less important than such other variables as public memory of the world war and the desire for economy, especially in the United States with its traditional congressional frugality in maintaining the navy. Yet social groups in the three naval powers contributed to the disarmament process and, as mentioned, their efforts are easily comparable until the London Naval Conference of 1930. After the depression deepened, conditions changed and analysis becomes more difficult. But during the late 1920s, social groups in the United States, Britain, and Japan largely benefited from common sociopolitical controls: a relatively calm international situation, democratic governments, stable economies, and governments that sought naval disarmament.

The domestic structure of each country most affected the achievement of their social groups. In the United States, the open, weak structure permitted social groups the greatest impact. They could easily interact with legislators, government bureaucrats, and the media because an independent Congress featuring weak parties publicly discussed policy, providing a forum for individual actors to make their views heard. Social groups enjoyed windows of opportunity during the late 1920s and early in 1930 that afforded them chances to influence policy: the failure of the Geneva Conference of 1927, Hoover's election in 1928, and elite disagreement about a consultative pact during the London Conference of 1930. Social groups won only partial victories because their coalitions often shifted and because elites often assimilated their messages and diluted their original demands. British social groups operating within an open, strong structure found fewer opportunities to affect policy. True, these groups also had access to politicians and the media and also beheld political opportunities following the Geneva Conference and MacDonald's election. But powerful political parties dominating the executive hampered the efforts of social groups to alter policy. Japan's closed, strong domestic structure granted social groups—at least the peace groups—the least room for maneuver. Individual citizens had little input into political affairs. A weak legislature allowed little public debate on policy while a small number of established interest groups maintained their hold on policy. Increasing suppression of radical political groups after 1925 did not encourage nongovernmental actors to attempt political work that ran counter to elite views.

Working within the above domestic parameters, preparedness groups sought to convince their fellow citizens to build navies and to reject arms control. Navy leagues in the United States, Britain, and Japan were particularly active in this work. Composed of business leaders, politicians, and navy officers, the leagues worked to counteract the propaganda of groups supporting disarmament. The Navy League in Japan was the most important, for it assumed quasi-governmental authority by 1930 in disseminating its message to a variety of business groups, schools, and community centers. It benefited from a censorship imposed on its opponents that did not extend to its own activities. In the United States, publicists such as William Shearer encouraged building but encountered little success and much derision. Patriotic groups had the greatest success in the United States with the large naval bill of 1929, for which they made numerous appearances before business and civic groups. But it was the memory of the recent Geneva Conference and the obsolescence of the navy more than their efforts that brought passage of the bill.

By publicizing disarmament, peace groups hoped to bring public opinion to favor conferences. In the United States, conservative and radical peace workers circulated petitions, wrote editorials, engaged in countless meetings with each other and with congressmen, and donated funds to international peace organizations. British groups persuaded clergymen, such as the archbishop of Canterbury, to participate in prayer meetings for the cause. They also occasionally held huge peace rallies in London and in other cities. In Japan, peace workers focused on better Japanese-American relations, believing that disarmament would follow.

But the effectiveness of peace groups varied. Those in the United States proved the most energetic, independent, and useful in spreading their message, not only because of the more auspicious domestic structure but because they controlled their mobilization resources and did not rely on government support as did British and Japanese peace societies. In Britain, the League of Nations Union, the largest peace group, preferred naval budget and manpower restrictions overseen by an international body (for instance, the League of Nations) to disarmament conferences limiting types of ships. Japanese groups, much smaller than their Western counterparts, had only recently organized and had to contend with a censorship unknown in the West.

What difference did peace groups make in the campaign for disarmament? They held out a vision of a more peaceful world and encouraged leaders to reach for it. They focused attention on naval disarmament, but they could not translate this awareness of the issue into international agreement. Part of their problem was inherent: the idealistic outlook of many groups, especially that of church and women's organizations in the United States, ignored international security needs. Peace workers argued in general terms for disarmament and rarely pushed their governments to modify specific technical positions, in part because few if any of them really understood the detailed issues. Too, their demands for public sessions and open diplomacy at the conferences demonstrated an ignorance toward the need for privacy in diplomatic conversation. Peace workers, along with some political leaders, also placed extraordinary faith in the political power of world sentiment to enforce disarmament agreements. When James Shotwell or Dorothy Detzer or Salmon Levinson spoke of enabling public opinion to "function with a vengeance" for disarmament, they failed to account for the effects of nationalism, and they assumed that world opinion would move as a single entity in a rational manner.[1] Part of their problem was environmental: by 1936, memories of the world war, a major motivating force for peace, had faded with the maturity of a new generation. In addition, peace groups lost the prestige the League had formerly afforded them when it appeared powerless to prevent aggression in Manchuria and Ethiopia. The international tension, finally, prevented even those making more limited appeals for disarmament from attaining their goal by the mid-1930s.

The Washington treaties actually were a remarkable combination of arms limitation and political settlement. They succeeded because delegates had not attempted too much. Charles Evans Hughes and the other delegates settled for agreement on capital ships. They resolved questions regarding China and the mandated Pacific islands by tacitly accepting geographic areas of dominance for each of the naval powers. Coolidge, Baldwin, and Wakatsuki could hardly have avoided being seduced by the popular success of the first disarmament conference when they considered participation in subsequent efforts. They hoped that the Geneva Conference of 1927 would come to represent a high point of naval disarmament by extending the limits of the Washington treaties to auxiliary ships.

The Geneva Conference of 1927 served as an introduction to the London Conference. Diplomats laid out their disagreement on cruisers, the thorny problem that had defied solution during and after the

Washington Conference. The Americans and British could not agree on the size of gun, and consequently on the size of cruiser necessary to carry it, to implement their naval strategies. A related issue was parity. After the British blockade experience of World War I, American leaders and naval officers insisted that the United States required a navy second to none in order to guard its commercial routes. Britain equivocated on the point, its delegates accurately pointing out that their country had worldwide imperial commitments, whereas the United States did not. They conceded parity at some meetings and denied it at others. By the end of the conference they would not grant it. Exasperated, the Americans suggested that the British and Japanese fashion a compromise, then rejected it when offered. Neither government could enter another conference confused about the position of the other. Participants at the conference did reach tentative agreements on ships in categories other than cruisers, however, which served as benchmarks for similar agreements at London.

Geneva ironically helped raise interest in future meetings. The Kellogg-Briand Pact became possible in large part because of alarm over the failure of the naval conference; it encouraged political leaders and peace activists to new efforts. Geneva encouraged the British to pursue bilateral naval conversations with the French, resulting in a compromise that so angered the United States that statesmen quickly sought an improved relationship. Finally, the American government reacted to the failure of the conference by passing the largest naval construction bill in a decade. The choice seemed to be disarmament or naval construction.

Delegates at London in 1930 completed the task begun at Geneva. Led by new leaders more enthusiastic about disarmament, the United States and Britain fashioned the outline of a cruiser compromise before the conference out of the remnants of arguments pressed at Geneva. The Americans suggested a yardstick, and it prompted renewed talks, even though the yardstick was never used. President Hoover overrode his navy board, which MacDonald could not and would not do, and accepted fewer cruisers with eight-inch guns and more with six-inch. He did not overly concern himself with which guns were preferable. He accepted a de facto 10-7 ratio for Japan in auxiliary ships because he regarded the Hamaguchi government as a force for peace in the Far East. Delegates also reached accord on ship categories that had presented little problem three years earlier—destroyers, submarines, and smaller vessels. All parties signed the agreement, and to observers it appeared to extend the Washington system.

But by 1935, when President Roosevelt sent his delegates to the Second London Conference on what he believed was a treasure hunt, the agreements of Geneva and London had already begun to unravel.[2] Roosevelt viewed disarmament quite differently than had Secretary Hughes in 1921-22 when he remarked that the Washington treaties had ended competition in naval arms.

Failure to disarm in the 1930s came partly because of changing technology. During most of the life of the Five-Power Treaty, battleship technology did not change much. But diplomats at the London Conference virtually ignored the ship type that would prove most important during the 1940s—aircraft carriers. Along with carriers, strategists by the mid-1930s had to contend with rapid changes in the types of planes, which planners had not foreseen in 1930. The rising importance of carriers cast doubt on agreements that emphasized surface ships, which no longer necessarily represented the most important weapons of a nation's arsenal. Meanwhile, the addition of torpedo tubes to the Japanese cruisers helped end the debate about cruiser guns. In World War II fire support became important in landing operations, but ship logs from battles of the Solomon Islands campaign—where cruiser fire was important—such as Savo Island, Guadalcanal, and Kula Gulf, do not distinguish enough between the six-inch and the eight-inch gun to measure which one performed better. After the Solomons campaign, air torpedo attack and radar became important, fire power less so.[3]

Statesmen needed to contend with verification. The issue had been a problem since the Versailles Conference, when Americans had spurned French proposals for League verification and enforcement of disarmament measures.[4] Intelligence could observe adherence to restrictions governing size and numbers of battleships, but enforcement of the London Treaty was more difficult. True, one could explain limitation in terms of numbers, but one could not readily monitor compliance because of the several categories of ships, each with varying displacement.

Not surprisingly, lack of enforcement led to cheating. At Geneva in 1933, American and British delegates harbored enough suspicion about Japanese activities to discuss compliance. Although they tentatively agreed to a plan proposed by Prime Minister MacDonald, nothing came of it because they could not agree on punishment if a violator were apprehended.[5] The problem loomed ever larger during the mid and late 1930s as nations began to rearm. Leaders could not expect help from the League of Nations, as its prestige plummeted after 1932-34, when the Geneva Conference broke up and the League refused to take action against aggressors.

Domestic support for disarmament, strong in the 1920s, dwindled in the 1930s. After the Washington Conference, the peoples of the naval powers still remembered the war and desired reductions in navies to reassure themselves about avoiding another war. But after 1930, people in the United States did not think much about disarmament because of worsening economic conditions. President Hoover supported arms control, but his delegates to Geneva in 1932 and most of the American public did not. President Roosevelt only went through the motions of discussing disarmament. Disarmament fell from favor in Britain because the public and politicians beheld shipyards as important for employment in a period of economic and political uncertainty. As MacDonald suffered from poor health and a weak political base, executive leadership on this and other issues flagged. In Tokyo, the battle over the London Treaty did not end with the Privy Council's belated acceptance of the treaty. Unrest in China encouraged Japanese expansion of foreign markets. The second round of disarmament conferences in Geneva and London in the mid-1930s could not allay Japan's uneasiness about the situation in China.

A final difference between the Washington treaties and the London treaty involved the increasing level of international anxiety. Before London, nothing had proved dangerous enough to upset the Washington system. The Dawes Plan and the Locarno pact in Europe had seemed to guarantee European stability. The civil war in China, though troubling, had not prevented Hamaguchi and Shidehara from pursuing arms control. After the London Treaty, circumstances changed, as the weaknesses of the Treaty of Versailles began to appear. The rise of fascist regimes led to one crisis after another—in Manchuria, Ethiopia, the Rhineland, and Spain—and made disarmament seem increasingly unwise.

Today the problem of arms control is far more complicated. American specialists couch their proposals in language that does not appear to give much away because public sentiment has swung from fear of the former Soviet Union to hope for peace. Negotiating has changed in our time, for officials sign agreements at summit meetings, preceded by low-profile conversations lasting several years. These discussions contrast with the Preparatory Commission meetings and high-profile disarmament conferences of the 1920s and 1930s. Attention, too, has focused on nuclear weapons (land, air, and sea) because they are the first-use weapons of our day. Peace groups in the United States, Europe, and Japan have urged their reduction or elimination because of the high danger of accidental use. Unlike their counterparts in the interwar years, present-day statesmen usually emphasize the international political gains of any agreement over the economic gains: nuclear arms have sometimes seemed a less expensive deterrent than conventional forces.

Contemporary arms-control conversations nonetheless resemble in many ways the discussions of the interwar years. As in that time, there is now public demand for arms control. The United Nations, as did the League, maintains a Disarmament Council. Like negotiators between the wars, today's diplomats engage in bean counting—listing numbers of weapons that may be quite dissimilar. There are good reasons for doing so, such as the ability to explain the cuts politically, but such actions should be reexamined periodically to determine if they still make strategic sense. The dissolution of the Soviet Union, for instance, has demanded such reevaluation. Participants in arms control today also have encountered problems of enforcement—verification, how much each side is willing to let the other see, what schedule for on-site verification is satisfactory, and so on.

Arms control, one may conclude, is an issue that will be with us for years to come. Because it is popular in the United States, Europe, Russia, and Japan, political leaders will find themselves under pressure to negotiate a plan to reduce arms. Leaders should take advantage of the situation and participate in discussions. But they must remember what their predecessors in the early twentieth century sometimes ignored—that arms control is no substitute for military planning or arms procurement. Peoples must see arms control as part of preparedness; limitation should conform above all to political realities, but also to strategy, war plans, and development of weapons. These are important elements of national security. At best, arms limitation can provide predictability in defense planning, slow the spread of weapons, and present political gains to leaders. But it cannot, by itself, prevent war.

NOTES

Abbreviations Used

ADM   U.K. Admiralty, files, Public Record Office, London.
Balch MSS   Emily Greene Balch, papers, Swarthmore College Peace Collection, Swarthmore, Pa.
Bristol MSS   Mark L. Bristol, papers, Naval Historical Foundation Collection, Library of Congress, Washington, D.C.
CAB   U.K. Cabinet Papers, Public Record Office, London.
Castle MSS   William R. Castle, papers, Herbert Hoover Presidential Library, West Branch, Iowa.
Cecil MSS   Robert Cecil, Viscount of Chelwood, papers, British Library, London.
CDPR   U.S. Department of State, Confidential Diplomatic Post Reports, Japan, 1930-1935, Frederick, Md., 1982 (microfilm).
CFR   U.S. Congress, Senate Committee on Foreign Relations.
CID   Committee of Imperial Defence, minutes, Public Record Office, London.
CMD   U.K. Parliament, Command Papers, Public Record Office, London.
CNO   Chief of Naval Operations.
Cong. Rec.   Congressional Record, Washington, D.C., 1922-1930.
CSDN   Conseil Supérieur de la Défense Nationale.
DBFP   Documents on British Foreign Policy, 1919-1939.
DPCDC   League of Nations, Documents of the Preparatory Commission for the Disarmament Conference.
FCCC   Federated Council of Churches of Christ.
FO   U.K. Foreign Office, records, Public Record Office, London.
FOR   Fellowship of Reconciliation.
FRUS   Papers Relating to the Foreign Relations of the United States, 1921-1936.
GB   U.S. Department of the Navy, Records of the Navy General Board, National Archives, Washington, D.C.

Gibson letters	Hugh S. Gibson, diaries, letters, and notes, 1922-1930, Herbert Hoover Presidential Library, West Branch, Iowa.
Gibson papers	Hugh S. Gibson, papers, Hoover Institution on War, Revolution, and Peace, Stanford, Calif.
Hoover Miscellaneous MSS	Herbert C. Hoover, miscellaneous papers, Hoover Institution on War, Revolution, and Peace, Stanford, Calif.
Hoover Presidential MSS	Herbert C. Hoover, papers, presidential series, Herbert Hoover Presidential Library, West Branch, Iowa.
Hornbeck MSS	Stanley K. Hornbeck, papers, Hoover Institution on War, Revolution, and Peace, Stanford, Calif.
Hull MSS	Hannah Clothier Hull, papers, Swarthmore College Peace Collection, Swarthmore, Pa.
ICCCW	International Committee on the Cause and Cure of War.
JB	General Records of the Joint Army and Navy Board, 1903-1947, National Archives, Washington, D.C.
JPS	Japanese Peace Society.
Jones MSS	Hilary P. Jones, papers, Naval Historical Foundation Collection, Library of Congress, Washington, D.C.
Kellogg MSS	Frank B. Kellogg Papers, Minnesota Historical Society, St. Paul, Minn.
LNA	League of Nations Association.
LNAJ	League of Nations Association of Japan.
LNA MSS	League of Nations Association, papers, Swarthmore College Peace Collection, Swarthmore, Pa.
LNU	League of Nations Union.
MacDonald MSS	J. Ramsay MacDonald, papers, Public Record Office, London.
Mayer MSS	Ferdinand Mayer, papers, Herbert Hoover Presidential Library, West Branch, Iowa.
Morley MSS	Felix Morley, papers, Herbert Hoover Presidential Library, West Branch, Iowa.
NCCCW	National Committee on the Cause and Cure of War papers, Swarthmore College Peace Collection, Swarthmore, Pa.
NCPW	National Council for the Prevention of War.
NCPW MSS	National Council for the Prevention of War, papers, Swarthmore College Peace Collection, Swarthmore, Pa.
NSL	National Security League.
NYT	*New York Times.*
ONI	U.S. Department of the Navy, Office of Naval Intelligence Files, RG 39, Naval Attache Reports, Tokyo, 1887-1939, National Archives, Washington, D.C.
Parl. Deb.	U.K. *Parliamentary Debates.*
Pratt MSS	William V. Pratt, papers, Naval Historical Center, Washington Navy Yard, Washington, D.C.
Roosevelt MSS	Theodore Roosevelt, Jr., papers, Library of Congress, Washington, D.C.

SD   U.S. Department of State.
SecNavy   U.S. Department of the Navy, Secret and Confidential Cor-
              respondence of the Office of the Secretary of the Navy,
              1927-1930, National Archives, Washington, D.C.
Stimson MSS   Henry L. Stimson, diary and papers, Yale University Li-
              brary, New Haven, Conn.
Train log,   Harold C. Train, Log of the Third Session of the Preparatory
1927   Commission for the Reduction and Limitation of Arma-
              ments, General Board Disarmament Conference Records,
              National Archives, Washington, D.C.
Train log,   Log of the London Naval Conference, 1930, General Board
1930   Disarmament Conference Records, National Archives,
              Washington, D.C.
WILPF   Women's International League for Peace and Freedom.
WILPF MSS   Women's International League for Peace and Freedom, pa-
              pers Swarthmore College Peace Collection, Swarthmore,
              Pa.
Wilson MSS   Hugh R. Wilson, papers, Herbert Hoover Presidential Li-
              brary, West Branch, Iowa.

Introduction

1. For a similar bureaucratic-politics approach for an earlier period, see Roger Dingman, *Power in the Pacific: The Origins of Naval Arms Limitation, 1914-1922* (Chicago, 1976).

2. For Realist arguments see: Gabriel Almond, *The American People and Foreign Policy* (New York, 1960); James Rosenau, *Public Opinion and Foreign Policy: An Operational Formulation* (New York, 1961); Philip E. Converse, "The Nature of Belief Systems in Mass Publics," in *Ideology and Discontent*, ed. D.E. Apter (New York, 1964), 206-61; Barry Hughes, *The Domestic Context of American Foreign Policy* (San Francisco, 1979); and Bernard Cohen, *The Public's Impact on Foreign Policy* (Boston, 1973). For dissenting views, see Eugene R. Wittkopf, *Faces of Internationalism: Public Opinion and American Foreign Policy* (Durham, N.C., 1990); Thomas Risse-Kappen, "Public Opinion, Domestic Structure, and Foreign Policy in Liberal Democracies," *World Politics* 43 (July 1991): 479-512; Benjamin I. Page and Robert Y. Shapiro, "Effects of Public Opinion on Policy," *American Political Science Review* 77 (1983): 175-90; and Robert Dallek, *The American Style of Foreign Policy: Cultural Politics and Foreign Affairs* (New York, 1983), 93-99.

3. For more on controlled comparable-cases methodology, see Arend Lijphart, "The Comparable-Case Strategy in Comparative Research," *Comparative Political Studies* 8 (July 1975): 158-77; and Alexander L. George, "Case Studies and Theory Development: The Method of Structured, Focused Comparison," in *Diplomacy: New Approaches in History, Theory, and Policy*, ed. Paul Gordon Lauren (New York, 1979), 43-68.

4. Catt to David Starr Jordan, September 21, 1928, David Starr Jordan

Papers, in John D. Crummy Peace Collection, Hoover Institution on War, Revolution, and Peace, Stanford, Calif.; Knox transcript, no date (circa 1932), Dudley W. Knox Papers, Naval Historical Foundation Collection, Library of Congress, Washington, D.C.

5. B.J.C. McKercher, *The Second Baldwin Government and the United States, 1924-1929* (New York, 1984); Christopher Hall, *Britain, America, and Arms Control, 1921-1937* (New York, 1987); John Robert Ferris, *The Evolution of British Strategic Policy, 1919-1926* (New York, 1989); Dick Richardson, *The Evolution of British Disarmament Policy in the 1920s* (New York, 1989).

1. The Politics of Disarmament

1. Hosoya Chihiro, "Britain and the United States in Japan's View of the International System, 1919-1937," in *Anglo-Japanese Alienation, 1919-1952: Papers of the Anglo-Japanese Conference on the History of the Second World War*, ed. Ian H. Nish (New York, 1982), 4.

2. Lloyd George, for example, linked German disarmament to general disarmament in the Fountainbleau Memorandum during negotiations. See Lorna Jaffe, "Abolishing War? Military Disarmament at the Paris Peace Conference, 1919," in *Arms Limitation and Disarmament: Restraints on War, 1899-1939*, ed., B.J.C. McKercher (New York, 1992), 43, 52.

3. Maurice Vaisse, *Sécurité D'Abord: La politique française en matière de désarmement, 9 décembre 1930-17 avril 1934* (Paris, 1981), 2.

4. This discussion is based on Dick Richardson, *The Evolution of British Disarmament Policy in the 1920s* (New York, 1989), 4-9; Christopher Hall, *Britain, America, and Arms Control, 1921-1937* (New York, 1987), 16-19; Roger Dingman, *Power in the Pacific: The Origins of Naval Arms Limitation, 1914-1922* (Chicago, 1976), 70-79; and William Reynolds Braisted, *The United States Navy in the Pacific, 1909-1922* (Austin, Tex., 1971), 410-19.

5. Hosoya, "Britain and the United States," 6; Ian H. Nish, *Japanese Foreign Policy, 1869-1942: Kasumigaseki to Miyakezaka* (London, 1977), 118-25.

6. Michael S. Sherry, *The Rise of American Air Power: The Creation of Armageddon* (New Haven, Conn., 1987), 35. Sherry provides a fine discussion of the interplay between air power and naval disarmament, 34-38.

7. Dingman, *Power in the Pacific*, 148.

8. Ibid., 162, 165, 172-77; Ferris, *Evolution of British Strategic Policy*, 96-100; Frank Costigliola, *Awkward Dominion: American Political, Economic, and Cultural Relations with Europe, 1919-1933* (Ithaca, N.Y., 1984), 81-84.

9. Dingman, *Power in the Pacific*, 182-89.

10. Hosoya, "Britain and the United States," 7-8. Also see Ian H. Nish, *Alliance in Decline: A Study in Anglo-Japanese Relations, 1908-1923* (London, 1972).

11. Dingman, *Power in the Pacific*, 216.

12. Ernest Andrade, Jr., "United States Naval Policy in the Disarmament Era, 1921-1937" (Ph.D. diss., Michigan State University, 1966), 37. For naval expenditures, see Raymond Leslie Buell, *The Washington Conference* (New York, 1922), 139; and U.S. Navy General Board (hereafter, GB), 438, Serial (hereafter ser.) 1088, September 27, 1921, both cited in Raymond G. O'Connor, *Perilous Equilibrium: The United States and the London Naval Conference of 1930* (Lawrence, Kans., 1962), 145, n. 13. Appropriations for the fiscal year 1922 (July 1, 1921 through June 30, 1922) amounted to 32 percent of Japan's total budget as compared to 12 percent for the U.S. and 9 percent for Britain.

13. Braisted, *The United States Navy in the Pacific*, 580-81, 588.

14. O'Connor, *Perilous Equilibrium*, 12-13. O'Connor believes that these episodes demonstrate how Hughes ignored military factors in the diplomacy of the conference, to the detriment of the navy. Thomas Buckley, in contrast, writes that Hughes properly emphasized political factors in accepting only some of the recommendations of his naval advisers. Hughes, he concludes, correctly maintained the power of the State Department to conduct diplomacy without interference from the navy. Buckley acknowledges, however, that problems did arise from Hughes's failure to achieve limitation of auxiliary vessels and airplanes. See Thomas H. Buckley, *The United States and the Washington Conference, 1921-1922* (Knoxville, Tenn., 1970), 71, 185. Also see Ernest R. May, "The Development of Political-Military Consultation in the United States," *Political Science Quarterly* 70 (1955): 167-69.

15. Buckley, *Washington Conference*, 118, 126.

16. Ibid., 89, 155; Braisted, *The United States Navy in the Pacific*, 595.

17. Buckley, *Washington Conference*, 185; O'Connor, *Perilous Equilibrium*, 7.

18. Dudley W. Knox, *The Eclipse of American Sea Power* (New York, 1922); Harold Sprout and Margaret Sprout, *Toward a New Order of Sea Power* (Princeton, 1943), 269-70.

19. Gerald E. Wheeler, *Prelude to Pearl Harbor: The United States Navy and the Far East, 1921-1931* (Columbia, Mo., 1963), 58.

20. Braisted, *The United States Navy in the Pacific*, 582-83.

21. Andrade, "Naval Policy," 75; Sprout and Sprout, *Sea Power*, 270.

22. Roger Dingman, *Power in the Pacific*, 206.

23. Ibid., 213.

24. C. Leonard Hoag, *Preface to Preparedness: The Washington Disarmament Conference and Public Opinion* (Washington, D.C., 1941), 74-79; Joan Hoff-Wilson, *American Business and Foreign Policy, 1920-1933* (Lexington, Ky., 1971), 37-40.

25. Hoag, *Preface to Preparedness*, chapter 6; Sprout and Sprout, *Sea Power*, 116; *Gazette de Hollande*, November 11, 1922, in Department of State General Records, Record Group 59, (hereafter, SD), 500 A15/1, National Archives, Washington, D.C.; Hector C. Bywater, *Navies and Nations* (Boston and New York, 1927), 159.

26. Much of this paragraph is based on Frank Costigliola, *Awkward Dominion*, 83-84, and Hoag, *Preface to Preparedness*, chapter 7.

27. Herbert Hoover, *The Memoirs of Herbert Hoover*, vol. 2, *The Cabinet and the Presidency, 1920-1933* (New York, 1952), 179.

28. Sprout and Sprout, *Sea Power*, 213, 161; Ferris, *Evolution of British Strategic Policy*, 100-102.

29. Dingman, *Power in the Pacific*, 172-73.

30. Martin Ceadel, *Pacifism in Britain, 1914-1941: The Defining of a Faith* (New York, 1980), 62-63; Donald S. Birn, *The League of Nations Union, 1918-1945* (New York, 1981), 49, 54.

31. Sadako Ogata, "The Role of Liberal Nongovernmental Organizations in Japan," in *Pearl Harbor as History: Japanese-American Relations, 1931-1941*, ed. Dorothy Borg and Shumpei Okamoto (New York, 1973), 460, 463. The two peace groups became one in 1925 when the Japanese Peace Society merged into the League of Nations Association of Japan. The LNAJ then took over the JPS's role as coordinator of peace groups in Japan, excluding Christian groups, which tended to concentrate on spiritual values rather than on international affairs.

32. Nish, *Alliance*, 385; Hosoya, "Britain and the United States," 8.

33. Hosoya, "Britain and the United States," 9-10; Asada Sadao, "The Japanese Navy and the United States," in *Pearl Harbor as History*, ed. Borg and Okamoto, 225-60.

34. Braisted, *The United States Navy in the Pacific*, 482; Lester A. Brune, *The Origins of American National Security: Sea Power, Air Power, and Foreign Policy, 1900-1941* (Manhattan, Kans., 1981), 69-70, 74; Stephen Roskill, *Naval Policy between the Wars*, vol. 1, *The Period of Anglo-American Antagonism, 1919-1929* (London, 1968), 352; Bywater, *Navies and Nations*, 166; Louis Morton, "War Plan Orange: Evolution of a Strategy," *World Politics* 11 (1959): 226; Russell F. Weigley, *The American Way of War: A History of United States Military Strategy and Policy* (Bloomington, Ind., 1973), 245-47, 254. An updated version of the 1919 Plan Orange may be found in General Records of the Joint Army and Navy Board, 1903-1947 (hereafter J.B.), 325, "General Correspondence of the War Plans Division, 1921-1942," serial 228, March 12, 1924, National Archives, Washington, D.C., microfilm. Annual reports of the Office of Naval Intelligence from 1922 to 1926 emphasize Japan as the potential enemy rather than Britain. The reports provide much information about the Japanese merchant fleet and the fuel oil situation in Japan. U.S. Department of the Navy, Secret and Confidential Correspondence between the Office of the Chief of Naval Operations and the Secretary of the Navy, 1919-1927, Record Group 80, plate 212, National Archives, Washington, D.C., microfilm.

35. For detail on the plan of 1922, see Edward S. Miller, *War Plan Orange: The U.S. Strategy to Defeat Japan, 1897-1945* (Annapolis, Md., 1991), 121.

36. For an example of General Board sentiment, see Admiral Hilary Jones testimony, March 3, 1924, U.S. Senate Committee on Territories and Insular Possessions, J.B. 305 (Philippines), ser. 227, National Archives, Washington, D.C., microfilm. Braisted, *The United States Navy in the Pacific*, 506.

37. See Waldo H. Heinrichs, "The Role of the U.S. Navy," in *Pearl Harbor as History*, ed. Borg and Okamoto, 200-5; Wheeler, Prelude to Pearl Harbor, 89.

38. George T. Davis, *A Navy Second to None* (New York, 1940), 315.

39. Braisted, *United States Navy in the Pacific*, 540; *Daily Telegraph*, January 26, 1927, in SD 841.342/2.

40. GB 420-2, ser. 890.

41. Commander W.S. Pye to Chief of Naval Operations, January 28, 1921, Op 12, "Secret and Confidential Correspondence."

42. October 10, 1919, GB 420-2, ser. 928, cited in Roskill, *Naval Policy between the Wars*, 213.

43. Rolland A. Chaput, *Disarmament in British Foreign Policy* (London, 1935), 45; Norman Friedman, *U.S. Cruisers: An Illustrated Design History* (Annapolis, Md., 1984), 105-6. As Americans became more interested in the *Hawkins*-class cruisers, Britons turned toward smaller cruisers with five- or six-inch guns.

44. Memorandum for the Chief of Naval Operations, January 26, 1921, Op 11-HU "Secret and Confidential Correspondence"; William F. Trimble, "The United States Navy and the Geneva Conference for the Limitation of Naval Armament, 1927" (Ph.D. diss., University of Colorado, 1974), 39.

45. W.S. Pye to Chief of Naval Operations, January 28, 1921, Op 12, "Secret and Confidential Correspondence."

46. W.C. Cole, Assistant for Material, to Chief of Naval Operations, January 27, 1921, Op 23-EE, "Secret and Confidential Correspondence"; General Board to Secretary of the Navy, April 29, 1921, GB 420-8, ser. 1033-C; Trimble, "Geneva Conference," 40. Naval yarn cited in Memorandum for Captain Cole, January 25, 1921, Op 25-HA 1/25, "Secret and Confidential Correspondence."

47. Ferris, *Evolution of British Strategic Policy*, 20, 80-82; Historical report, "Cruiser Building Policy," May 6, 1937, Plans Division, Admiralty Papers (hereafter, ADM) 1/9427, Public Record Office, London. For more on this point, see Wheeler, *Prelude to Pearl Harbor*, 89.

48. ADM 1/9272/G.D. 3280/26; Roskill, *Naval Policy between the Wars*, 1, 353.

49. Admiral Earl John Jellicoe, *The Grand Fleet, 1914-1916: Its Creation, Development, and Work* (New York, 1919), 306.

50. ADM 1/9272/G.D. 3260/26; ADM 1/8694.

51. Robert A. Hoover, *Arms Control: The Interwar Naval Limitation Agreements*, vol. 17, book 3, Monograph Series in World Affairs, (Denver, 1980), 62-66, 72.

52. Dingman, *Power in the Pacific*, 123.

53. The General Board normally sent its building proposal to the secretary of the Navy two years before each fiscal year (July 1 to June 30). For more details, see Roskill, *Naval Policy between the Wars*, 1, 209.

54. *New York Times* (hereafter, *NYT*), April 9, 1922, and April 12, 1922. Assistant Secretary Roosevelt turned back the more stringent demands of the Kelley committee, especially on personnel, receiving help from Hughes.

Braisted, *The United States Navy*, 676. For the fate of the bill for fiscal 1923, see *NYT*, April 12, 1922, April 20, 1922, and June 11, 1922.

55. *NYT*, March 22, 1924, April 27, 1924.

56. Joseph H. Kitchens, Jr., "The Shearer Scandal and Its Origins: Big Navy Politics and Diplomacy in the 1920s" (Ph.D. diss., University of Georgia, 1968), 3, 4, 10; *NYT*, April 27, 1924.

57. Armin Rappaport, *The Navy League of the United States* (Detroit, 1962), 92-93, 97, 99.

58. Braisted, *United States Navy*, 675. Unbeknownst to most congressmen, significant disagreement existed among strategists whether War Plan Orange would succeed even with the desired number of ships. For more on this point, see Morton, "War Plan Orange," 230-31, and Braisted, "On the American Red and Red-Orange Plans, 1919-1939," in *Naval Warfare in the Twentieth Century, 1900-1945: Essays in Honor of Arthur J. Marder*, ed. Gerald Jordan (New York, 1977), 272.

59. For more detail, see Roger K. Heller, "Curtis Dwight Wilbur, 19 March 1924-4 March 1929," in *American Secretaries of the Navy*, vol. 2, *1913-1972*, ed. Paolo E. Coletta (Annapolis, Md., 1980), 606-10

60. *NYT*, May 4, 1924, May 24, 1924, Kitchens, "Shearer Scandal," 17.

61. *Congressional Record* (hereafter, *Cong. Rec.*), 68th Cong., 1st sess., 1924, 65, pt. 5: 4254-65.

62. Frederick Lewis Allen, *Only Yesterday. An Informal History of the 1920s* (New York, 1932), 183.

63. *NYT*, May 21, 1924; Rappaport, *Navy League*, 101; Calvin Coolidge, "Promoting Peace through Limitations of Armaments," *Ladies Home Journal* 48 (May 1929): 3-4.

64. *NYT*, May 29, 1924, December 12, 1924; *Cong. Rec.*, 68th Cong., 1st sess., 1924, 65, pt. 5: 4730; *Cong. Rec.*, 68th Cong., 1st sess., 1924, 65, pt. 10: 6782-83.

65. *Parliamentary Debates* (hereafter, *Parl. Deb.*), (Commons), 5th ser., 176 (1924): 2298. For a more complete discussion of this point, see Dingman, *Power in the Pacific*, 161.

66. Keith Middlemas and John Barnes, *Baldwin: A Biography* (London, 1969), 323-24; *Times* (London), October 26, 1923; James H. Mannock, "Anglo-American Relations, 1921-1928" (Ph.D. diss., Princeton University, 1962), 235. John Robert Ferris presents a persuasive argument that Britain was not disarming during the early 1920s, despite the Washington accords, but was building its largest peacetime naval force. Ferris, *Evolution of British Strategic Policy*, chapter 1.

67. Christina Newton, "Anglo-American Relations and Bureacratic Rivalry, 1927-1930," (Ph.D. diss., University of Illinois, 1975), 19-20.

68. Quoted in Sir Robert Vansittart, *The Mist Procession: The Autobiography of Lord Vansittart* (London, 1958), 353. Vansittart served as Baldwin's principal personal secretary in the mid-1920s, and one of his main tasks was to interest Baldwin in foreign affairs. For further discussion of Baldwin's character, see Stuart Ball, *Baldwin and the Conservative Party: The Crisis of 1929-1931* (New Haven, Conn., 1988), 7-17.

69. Kenneth Young, *Stanley Baldwin* (London, 1976), 70.

70. Middlemas and Barnes, *Baldwin*, 328, 334, 338.

71. Peter Duus, *Party Rivalry and Political Change in Taisho Japan* (Cambridge, 1968), 194-95; James B. Crowley, *Japan's Quest for Autonomy: National Security and Foreign Policy, 1930-1938* (Princeton, 1966), 30.

72. Marius Jansen, "Introduction to the Manchurian Incident," in *Japan Erupts: The London Naval Conference and the Manchurian Incident, 1928-1932*, ed. James William Morley (New York, 1984), 123.

73. Hosoya, "Britain and the United States," 12; Nish, *Japanese Foreign Policy*, 126-28, 131-45.

74. See James Neidpath, *The Singapore Naval Base and the Defence of Britain's Eastern Empire, 1919-1941* (London, 1981); and W. David McIntyre, *The Rise and Fall of the Singapore Naval Base, 1919-1942* (London, 1979).

75. Chaput, *Disarmament in British Foreign Policy*, 130-34.

76. B.J.C. McKercher, *The Second Baldwin Government and the United States, 1924-1929* (New York, 1984), 58.

2. The Preparatory Commission

Portions of this chapter and chapters 5 and 6 appeared in altered form in "Peace Groups and the Campaign for Naval Disarmament, 1927-1936," *Peace and Change* 15, no. 1 (January 1990): 26-45.

1. For more detail on peace leaders' links to progressivism, see Dallek, *American Style of Foreign Policy*, 93-99. Also see Thomas Ferguson, "The Right Consensus: Holsti and Rosenau's New Foreign Policy Belief Surveys," *International Studies Quarterly* 30 (1986): 422.

2. Hoag, *Preface to Preparedness*; John Chalmers Vinson, *The Parchment Peace: The United States Senate and the Washington Conference, 1921-1922* (Athens, Ga., 1955); Charles DeBenedetti, *Origins of the Modern American Peace Movement, 1915-1929* (Millwood, N.Y., 1978); Charles Chatfield, *For Peace and Justice: Pacifists in America, 1914-1941* (Knoxville, Tenn., 1971).

3. See, for example, Rosenau, *Public Opinion and Foreign Policy*, Bernard Cohen, *Public's Impact on Foreign Policy*, and Hughes, *Domestic Context of American Foreign Policy*.

4. See, for example, Page and Shapiro, "Effects of Public Opinion on Policy," and Bruce Russett, *Controlling the Sword* (Cambridge, 1990).

5. Much of this discussion of theory is drawn from Risse-Kappen, "Public Opinion," 480-84.

6. For a fine summary of these arguments, see Melvin Small, "Public Opinion," in *Explaining the History of American Foreign Relations*, ed. Michael J. Hogan and Thomas G. Paterson (New York, 1991).

7. Peter K. Eisinger, "The Conditions of Protest Behavior in American Cities," *American Political Science Review* 67 (1973): 11-28; Herbert P. Kitschelt, "Political Opportunity Structures and Political Protest: Anti-Nuclear Movements in Four Democracies," *British Journal of Political Sci-*

ence 16 (January 1986): 57-85; Sidney Tarrow, *Struggling to Reform: Social Movements and Change: Policy Change during Cycles of Protest* (Ithaca, N.Y., 1983), 3; Risse-Kappen, "Political Opinion," 484.

8. Kitschelt, "Political Opportunity Structures," 63; Risse-Kappen, "Public Opinion," 486.

9. Risse-Kappen, "Public Opinion," 484-86; David S. Meyer, *A Winter of Discontent: The Nuclear Freeze and American Politics* (New York, 1990), 5.

10. Meyer, *Winter of Discontent*, xv.

11. Most domestic-structure theory describes the post-1945 era, but it offers the scholar comparative possiblity for the pre-1945 period as well.

12. For a description of "windows of opportunity," an idea much discussed recently in peace research, see Meyer, *Winter of Discontent*, 5.

13. Rosenau, *Public Opinion and Foreign Policy*, chapter 4; Ralph Levering, *The Public and American Foreign Policy, 1918-1978* (New York, 1978), 20-21. Rosenau and Levering describe an attentive public as constituting about 20 percent of the population, with about 5 percent making up the influential public. Recently, however, these numbers have been challenged by R.W. Neuman, who argues convincingly that elite or influential opinion constitutes about five percent of the population, a "middle mass," 75 percent, and the apolitical, 20 percent. R.W. Neuman, *The Paradox of Mass Politics: Knowledge and Opinion in the American Electorate* (Cambridge, 1986); Ole Holsti and James N. Rosenau, "The Domestic and Foreign Policy Beliefs of American Leaders," *Journal of Conflict Resolution* 32, no. 2 (June 1988): 251; Russett, *Controlling the Sword*, 88. Eugene R. Wittkopf argues that despite its ignorance, the mass public still forms opinions and participates in the foreign policy process. Wittkopf, *Faces of Internationalism*, 15.

14. This paragraph is based on Small, "Public Opinion," 171-73; idem, *Johnson, Nixon, and the Doves* (New Brunswick, N.J., 1988); and Levering, *Public and American Foreign Policy*, chapter 2.

15. See Robert C. Hilderbrand, *Power and the People: Executive Management of Public Opinion in Foreign Affairs, 1897-1921* (Chapel Hill, N.C., 1981); and George I. Juergens, *News from the White House: The Presidential-Press Relationship in the Progressive Era* (Chicago, 1981) for the ways that Progressive presidents, especially Theodore Roosevelt and Woodrow Wilson, increasingly monitored and attempted to mold public opinion through the media.

16. Sondra Herman describes these internationalists as "political" in her important study, *Eleven against War: Studies in American Internationalist Thought, 1898-1921* (Stanford, 1969), chapter 1.

17. Charles DeBenedetti, "The American Peace Movement and the State Department in the Age of Locarno," in *Doves and Diplomats: Foreign Offices and Peace Movements in Europe and America in the Twentieth Century*, ed. Solomon Wank (Westport, Conn., 1978), 208-9.

18. Harold Josephson, "The Search for Lasting Peace: Internationalism and American Foreign Policy, 1920-1950," in *Peace Movements and Politi-*

cal Cultures, ed. Charles Chatfield and Peter van den Dungen (Knoxville, Tenn., 1988), 206-7; Gary B. Ostrower, *Collective Insecurity: The United States and the League of Nations during the Early Thirties* (Cranbury, N.J., 1979), 31.

19. Ostrower, *Collective Insecurity*, 28-30.

20. Robert D. Schulzinger, *The Wise Men of Foreign Affairs: The History of the Council on Foreign Relations* (New York, 1984), 14-17.

21. See Herman, *Eleven Against War*, chapter 1, for an in-depth discussion of community internationalists.

22. Robert H. Ferrell, *Peace in Their Time: The Origins of the Kellogg-Briand Pact* (New Haven, Conn., 1952), 15, 26-28.

23. Peter Karsten, *The Naval Aristocracy: The Golden Age of Annapolis and the Emergence of Modern American Navalism* (New York, 1972), 368-71. Also see Rappaport, *Navy League*.

24. This paragraph is based on John Carver Edwards, *Patriots in Pinstripe: Men of the National Security League* (Lanham, Md., 1982), 6-8, 133-34, 142.

25. This paragraph is based on William Pencak, *For God and Country: The American Legion, 1919-1941* (Boston, 1989), 162-63.

26. Ibid., 163

27. Birn, *The League of Nations Union*, 65-66. *Times* (London), May 12, 1927.

28. Ogata, "Liberal Non-Governmental Groups," 465-66.

29. Merlo J. Pusey, *Charles Evans Hughes* (New York, 1952), vol. 2, 454.

30. *NYT*, December 8, 9, 13, and 16, 1926.

31. *Cong. Rec.*, 69th Cong. 2d sess., 1927, 69, pt. 1: 1091.

32. *The Economist* 54 (March 19, 1927): 568-69, *Parl. Deb.* (Commons), 5th ser., 204 (1927): 81-84.

33. *Parl. Deb.*, 5th ser., 205 (1927): 474-75; ibid., 5th ser., 204 (1927): 66, 95, 103-6.

34. Vaisse, *Sécurité D'abord*, 66.

35. *Parl. Deb.*, 5th ser., 205 (1927): 511-12.

36. *Japan Times*, (Toyko), February 16, 1927. For comparisons of each power's number of cruisers, see: *Cong. Rec.*, 69th Cong., 2d sess., 1927, 68, pt. 2: 2066-80.

37. *Japan Times*, March 26, March 27, 1927.

38. This paragraph is based on Nish, *Japanese Foreign Policy*, Chapter 8, especially 152-54, 173.

39. Coolidge Message to Congress, January 4, 1926, *Papers Relating to the Foreign Relations of the United States 1926* (hereafter, *FRUS 1926*) (Washington, D.C., 1941), 1: xxviii.

40. A.C. Temperley, *The Whispering Gallery of Europe* (London, 1938), 58; *NYT*, May 9, 1926.

41. *NYT*, July 14, 1927. Gibson was most famous for attempting to save the life of Edith Cavell during the war. Harold C. Train, "Reminiscences," Columbia University Oral History Project (Annapolis, 1965-66),

oral interviews with John T. Mason, Jr., Library of Congress, Washington, D.C. Microfilm.

42. Kellogg to Houghton, February 11, 1926; *FRUS, 1926*, 1: 51.

43. Hilary P. Jones to Admiral E.W. Eberle, Chief of Naval Operations, August 14, 1926, Hilary P. Jones Papers (hereafter, Jones MSS), Naval Historical Foundation Collection, Library of Congress, Washington, D.C.

44. Chaput, *Disarmament in British Foreign Policy*, 134-37.

45. League of Nations, *Documents of the Preparatory Commission for the Disarmament Conference* (hereafter, *DPCDC*), series 2, 14; Chaput, 138.

46. Vaisse, *Sécurité D'abord*, 32; Jacques Bariety, *Les relations franco-allemandes après la première guerre mondiale* (Paris, 1976), 76.

47. This paragraph is largely based on Vaisse, *Sécurité D'abord*, 29-31, 35-42.

48. Robert Cecil to Austen Chamberlain, May 22, 1926 in *Documents on British Foreign Policy, 1919-1939* (hereafter, *DBFP*), edited by W.L. Medlicott et al., (London, 1968), ser. 1a, 2: 26; Cecil to Chamberlain, May 20, 1926, ibid., 15. Jones thought a deal could be struck with Whitehall. Jones to Admiral Pratt, February 1, 1926, Jones MSS.

49. Chamberlain to Marquess of Crewe, May 31, 1926, *DBFP*, ser. 1a, 2: 53. Edouard Benes of Czechoslovakia confided to Allen Dulles that he thought there would be no progress in disarmament discussions until Germany had entered the League of Nations (negotiation was ongoing) and the Locarno pacts had been tested and found effective; cited in Gibson to Kellogg, June 11, 1926, *FRUS, 1926*, 1: 108-9.

50. Roberts to Chamberlain, July 2, 1926, *DBFP*, ser. 1a, 2: 130.

51. Jones to Secretary of the Navy (Curtis Wilbur), July 13, 1926, Jones MSS.

52. Roberts to Chamberlain, August 13, 1926, *DBFP* ser. 1a, 2, 255; Ibid., Roberts to Chamberlain, August 21, 1926, 297.

53. Jones to Wilbur, September 10, 1926, Jones MSS.

54. Cecil memorandum, September 24, 1926, *DBFP*, ser. 1a, 2: 396.

55. Jones memorandum, November 10, 1926, Jones MSS.

56. Kellogg to Porter, January 11, 1927, *FRUS, 1927*, 1: 163.

57. Harold C. Train, *Log of the Third Session of the Preparatory Commission for the Reduction and Limitation of Armaments*, (hereafter, Train log, 1927) General Board Disarmament Conference Records, National Archives, Washington, D.C., series 5: 3, 6.

58. Gibson to Kellogg, March 24, 1927; Kellogg to Gibson, March 27, 1927, both in *FRUS, 1927*, 1: 183, 188.

59. Gibson to Kellogg, April 4, 1927, *FRUS, 1927*, 1: 190-91; Train log, 1927, 39.

60. Chamberlain to Howard, August 10, 1927, *DBFP*, ser. 1a, 3: 218.

61. Gibson to Kellogg, April 11, 1927; Houghton to Kellogg, April 9, 1927, both in *FRUS, 1927*, 1: 196-97, 199; Train log, 1927, 35; Cecil to Chamberlain, April 12, 1927, *DBFP*, ser. 1a, 3: 220.

62. Train log, 1927, 65.

63. Cecil to Chamberlain, April 12, 1927, *DBFP*, ser. 1a, 3: 220.

64. Gibson to Mary Gibson, February 11, 1927, Hugh S. Gibson letters, (hereafter, Gibson letters) Herbert Hoover Presidential Library, West Branch, Iowa.

65. Gibson to Mary Gibson, January 13, 1927, Gibson letters; *Japan Times*, February 13, 1927.

66. L. Ethan Ellis, *Frank B. Kellogg and American Foreign Relations, 1925-1929* (New Brunswick, N.J., 1961), 164.

67. SD 500 A15 a1/20; *Japan Times*, February 22, 1927; Ellis, *Frank B. Kellogg*, 165.

68. Castle to Gibson, March 9, 1927, Hugh S. Gibson Papers, (hereafter, Gibson MSS), Hoover Institution on War, Revolution, and Peace, Stanford, Calif.

69. Marc Epstein, "The Historians and the Geneva Naval Conference," in *Arms Limitation and Disarmament*, ed. McKercher, 134.

70. Kellogg to Lord Astor, November 2, 1926, Frank B. Kellogg Papers, (hereafter, Kellogg MSS), Minnesota Historical Society, St. Paul, Minnesota. In a remarkably prescient letter, Lord Astor cautioned his friend, the secretary, about the danger of entering too hastily into a naval disarmament conference, observing that conditions had changed since the Washington Conference. Lloyd George, Astor noted, fell from power because of poor preparations for the Genoa Conference. Lord Astor to Kellogg, September 16, 1926, Kellogg MSS.

71. Kellogg to Houghton, May 2, 1927, Kellogg MSS.

72. Kellogg to Coolidge, May 27, 1927, Calvin Coolidge Papers, Library of Congress, Washington, D.C.; Gibson to Mary Gibson, May 14, 20, 25, 1927, Gibson letters. Castle wrote Gibson that he had hoped that Gibson would suggest to Secretary Kellogg Rear Admiral William V. Pratt as a naval delegate instead of Jones. Castle thought that Pratt was a "real negotiator" and took "a broader view" of policy than Jones. Castle to Gibson, May 11, 1927, Gibson MSS.

73. Gibson to Castle, April 15, 1927, Gibson MSS.

74. Esme Howard, *Theatre of Life*, vol. 2, 531.

75. Adolph Berle Clemenson, "The Geneva Tripartite Conference of 1927 in Japanese-American Relations" (Ph.D. diss., University of Arizona, 1975), 151.

76. Ellis, *Frank B. Kellogg*, 166-67;

77. Gibson to Mary Gibson, June 1, 1927, Gibson letters.

78. *The Economist* 104 (April 23, 1927); Toyko *Nichi Nichi*, cited in: *Japan Times*, March 2, 1927.

3. Opening Gambits

Portions of this chapter and chapters 4 and 5 appeared in an altered form in "The Coolidge Conference of 1927: Disarmament in Disarray," in *Arms Limitation and Disarmament*, ed. McKercher, 83-104.

1. William C. Bridgeman, diary, June to August 1927, 143, Shropshire

County Record Office, Shrewsbury, England; Miller, *War Plan Orange*, 135-36.

2. Frank H. Schofield, diary, June 18, 1927, Naval Historical Center, Washington Navy Yard, Washington, D.C.

3. Cecil to Austen Chamberlain, June 17, 1927, Robert Cecil Viscount of Chelwood, Papers, British Library, London.

4. "General Board Report for Delegates to Geneva," June 1, 1927, in notebook, "General Board Reports and Studies re: Geneva Three Power Conference, March 1927-July 1927," 138-39, General Board Disarmament Conference Records, Series 5, Box 12 National Archives, Washington, D.C.

5. Cruiser Report, November 16, 1926, ADM 1/9272/G.D. 3260/26; Report Comparing Forces of Three Naval Powers, February 1, 1927, Command Papers (hereafter, CMD) 2809, Public Record Office, London, microprint; July 23, 1926, October 8, 1926, ADM 1/9267.

6. May 20, 1927, Cabinet Papers (hereafter, CAB) 2 (Committee of Imperial Defence minutes) /5/227; June 1927, CAB 4 (Committee of Imperial Defence Miscellaneous Memorandum) /16/808, Public Record Office, London.

7. *Japan Times*, May 17, 1927.

8. Attaché interview with Kobayashi, April 26, 1927, C-9-b, 18608, Record Group 38, Naval Attaché Reports, 1887-1939, Office of Naval Intelligence files (hereafter, ONI), National Archives, Washington D.C.

9. News summary of *Japanese Advertiser*, Norman Armour to Washington, June 23, 1927, C-9-b, 18608A, ONI.

10. *Japan Times*, June 13, 18, 1927.

11. Ibid., May 5, 1927; Malcolm D. Kennedy, *The Estrangement of Great Britain and Japan, 1917-1935* (Berkeley and Los Angeles, 1969), 108.

12. Gibson to Castle, April 19, 1927, William R. Castle Papers, Herbert Hoover Presidential Library, West Branch, Iowa (hereafter, Castle MSS).

13. Castle to Houghton, May 2, 1927, Castle MSS.

14. Castle to Gibson, May 3, 1927, Castle MSS.

15. Bridgeman to Chamberlain, June 3, 1927, Austen Chamberlain Papers, Foreign Office Records (hereafter, FO) 800/261/38, Public Record Office, London.

16. *Japan Times*, June 7, 1927.

17. Beatty memorandum, April 13, 1927, ADM 1/8715/188.

18. *NYT*, May 28, 1927;1 Esme Howard to Chamberlain, June 3, 1927, *DBFP*, ser. 1a, 3: 602.

19. Schofield diary, June 20, 1927.

20. League of Nations, *Records of the Conference for the Limitation of Naval Armament; Held at Geneva from June 20 to August 4, 1927* (Geneva, 1927).

21. Nish, *Japanese Foreign Policy*, 141.

22. Gibson to Kellogg, June 22, 1927, *FRUS, 1927*, 1: 48; Wheeler, *Prelude to Pearl Harbor*, 145.

23. Jones to Wilbur, June 25, 1927, Jones MSS.

24. Notes on British Empire Proposals, June 20, 1927, Mr. London to Chamberlain, June 22, 1927, *DBFP*, ser. 1a, 3: 606, 611; Gibson to Kellogg, June 23, 1927, *FRUS, 1927*, 1: 51.

25. Schofield diary, June 24, 1927.

26. Kellogg to Gibson, June 24, 1927, *FRUS, 1927*, 1: 55-56.

27. *Japan Times*, June 22, 24, 25, 29, 1927.

28. Sir John Tilley to Chamberlain, June 27, 1927, *DBFP*, ser. 1a, 3: 618.

29. Simonds, in *Review of Reviews*, cited in *Japan Times*, June 23, 1927.

30. Bridgeman to Chamberlain, June 28, 1927, *DBFP*, ser. 1a, 3: 621-23; Cecil to Tyrrell, June 24, 1927, Cecil Papers, British Library, London.

31. Kellogg to Gibson, June 24, 1927; Coolidge to Kellogg, June 30, 1927, both in *FRUS, 1927*, 1: 56, 64. Coolidge was not in close touch with the day-to-day negotiations—his summer home in the Black Hills was sixty-four miles from Rapid City, where his executive office had been established. *Literary Digest* 93, no. 12, (June 11, 1927): 10.

32. Gibson to Kellogg, June 30, 1927, *FRUS, 1927*, 1: 65-66.

33. June 29, 1927, CAB 23 (Cabinet Conclusions) /55/37(27)10, Public Record Office, London. Although the secretary to the Cabinet, Sir Maurice Hankey, an opponent of disarmament, told Baldwin on July 1 that Bridgeman had made a statement about parity of which the Cabinet had no knowledge, the Cabinet had realized on June 29 that its opposition to parity contradicted Chamberlain's and Bridgeman's previous statements. Baldwin sent a message to Geneva directing the delegates to announce that the British would build to their needs and would set no lower limits on other powers. Stephen Roskill, *Hankey, Man of Secrets*, Vol. 2, *1919-1931* (London, 1977), 439; Newton, "Anglo-American Relations," 29. Churchill continued his attack, backed by Beatty, against parity at a meeting of Cabinet on July 4. July 4, 1927, CAB 23/55/38(27)5.

34. Gibson to Kellogg, July 2, 1927, *FRUS, 1927*, 1: 67-68.

35. Schofield diary, June 29, July 2-5; London to Chamberlain, July 5, 1927, FO 412/115/51.

36. Schofield diary, July 5, 1927; Bridgeman to Chamberlain, July 5, 1927, CAB 4/16/814; Hall, *Britain, America, and Arms Control*, 45-46; McKercher, *Second Baldwin Government*, 71-73.

37. Chamberlain to Cecil, July 5, 1927, Cecil MSS; McKercher, *Second Baldwin Government*, 66. Chamberlain had spent most of the spring dealing more with the Egyptian crisis and sour Anglo-Soviet relations than with disarmament.

38. July 7, 1927, CAB 2/5/228; Hall, *Britain, America, and Arms Control*, 46.

39. Gibson to Kellogg, July 5, 1927, *FRUS, 1927*, 1: 72, Schofield diary, July 6, 1927.

40. Gibson to Kellogg, July 6, 1927, *FRUS, 1927*, 1: 77-78; Minutes of British delegates' meeting, July 7, 1927, ADM 116/2609; Howard to Chamberlain, July 6, 1927, *DBFP*, ser. 1a, 3: 641-42.

41. Kellogg to Gibson, July 8, 1927, Coolidge to Kellogg, July 9, 1927, *FRUS, 1927*, 1: 82-83, 89.

4. A Diplomatic Impasse

1. London to Chamberlain, July 2, 1927, found in: ADM 116/2609.

2. Howard to Chamberlain, July 13, 1927, FO 800/261/109.

3. Quoted in Morris Robert Werner, *Privileged Characters* (New York, 1935), 344.

4. Kitchens, "The Shearer Scandal and Its Origins," 134.

5. Ibid., 129, 141.

6. Schofield diary, June 30, 1927; Kitchens, "The Shearer Scandal and Its Origins," 142.

7. Kellogg to Gibson, July 11, 1927, *FRUS, 1927*, 1: 93.

8. Howard to Chamberlain, July 13, 1927, FO 800/261/110; Kellogg to Gibson, July 12, 1927, Gibson to Kellogg, July 14, 1927, both in *FRUS, 1927*, 1: 96, 106.

9. Schofield diary, July 20, 1927; Kitchens, "The Shearer Scandal and Its Origins," 151; Jones memorandum, July 13, 1927, Jones MSS.

10. *NYT*, July 7, 1927.

11. Arnold J. Toynbee, *Survey of International Relations, 1927* (London, 1929), 55-56.

12. Ibid., 56-57; Schofield diary, July 8, 1927, Bridgeman diary, 153.

13. Schofield diary, July 9, 1927; *NYT*, July 10, 1927.

14. *NYT*, July 10, 1927; Sir Reginald H.S. Bacon, *The Life of John Rushmore Earl Jellicoe* (London, 1936), 495.

15. *NYT*, July 9, 1927; Gibson to Kellogg, July 9, 1927, *FRUS, 1927*, 1: 89.

16. Gibson to Kellogg, July 9, 1927, *FRUS, 1927*, 1: 89; Bridgeman to Baldwin, July 12, 1927, *DBFP*, ser. 1a, 3: 675.

17. Chamberlain memorandum on conversation with Houghton, July 11, 1927, *DBFP*, ser. 1a, 3: 656; memorandum presented to Cabinet, July 13, 1927, CAB 23/55/40(27)4a.

18. *Parl. Deb.*, 5th ser., 208 (1927): 1786.

19. Jellicoe speech reprinted in the *Times* (London), July 15, 1927, cited in Toynbee, *Survey of International Relations, 1927*, 57.

20. Ibid., 59, 76-77; P.J. Noel-Baker, *Disarmament and the Coolidge Conference* (London, 1927), 32, 34; *Parl. Deb.*, 5th ser., 210 (1927): 2101-6; Beatty, Balfour, and Churchill arguments against parity with the United States, July 14, 1927, CAB 2/5/229.

21. Cabinet meeting, July 13, 1927, CAB 23/55/40(27)4a.

22. Jones later reiterated his argument in a speech to the veterans of World War I. Jones speech, October 5, 1927, Jones MSS. Dudley Knox, editor of the Naval Institute *Proceedings*, informed Jones during the conference of his error: Jones could not compare the coastal trade of the United States and the foreign trade of Britain. Knox to Jones, July 6, 1927, Dudley Knox Papers, Naval Historical Foundation Collection, Library of Congress, Washington, D.C.

23. Hugh R. Wilson, *Diplomat between the Wars* (New York, 1941), 218;

clipping, Tokyo *Nichi Nichi*, September 22, 1927, in ADM 1/8715/188. Admiral Beatty and Ambassador Howard also cited Jones as an obstacle to agreement. Beatty comments, July 14, 1927, CAB 2/5/229(4); Howard to Chamberlain, July 13, 1927, FO 800/261/108.

24. Minutes of British Delegates' meeting, July 19, 1927, ADM 116/2609; Schofield diary, July 15, 1927; Baldwin to Bridgeman, July 15, 1927, *DBFP*, ser. 1a, 3: 682.

25. Richardson, *British Disarmament Policy*, 128-29; McKercher, *Second Baldwin Government*, 73-74.

26. Gibson to Kellogg, July 18, 1927, *FRUS, 1927*, 1: 109; Schofield diary, July 18, 1927. British discussion of American actions found in: British delegates' meeting, July 19, 1927, ADM 116/2609.

27. Robert Cecil, *A Great Experiment: An Autobiography* (New York, 1941), 358-63; Bridgeman diary, 155, 145; Bridgeman to Cecil, November 21, 1927, Chamberlain to Cecil, August 14, 1927, Cecil MSS.

28. *NYT*, July 19, 1927; CAB 2/5/229; Baldwin to Bridgeman, July 19, 1927, *DBFP*, ser. 1a, 3: 698.

29. *NYT*, July 20, 1927. The Cabinet worried about its delegates' resolve—recent dispatches had hinted at concessions in parity, tonnage, and even gun caliber. Roskill, *Hankey, Man of Secrets*, 2: 439-40.

30. *Times* (London), July 23, 1927; Cabinet meeting, July 22, 1927, CAB 23/55/42(27)1; Cabinet meeting, July 26, 1927, CAB 23/55/42(27)1, CAB 23/55/44(27)1; *Parl. Deb.*, 5th ser., 209 (1927): 1246-49; McKercher, *Second Baldwin Government*, 74.

31. Hugh Gibson to Mary Gibson, July 23, 1927, Gibson letters.

32. Kellogg to Coolidge, July 22, 1927, *FRUS, 1927*, 1: 124.

33. Coolidge to Kellogg, July 25, 1927, *FRUS, 1927*, 1: 133.

34. Hall, *Britain, America, and Arms Control*, 47-48.

35. Tilley to Chamberlain, July 21, 1927, FO 412/115/75; Schofield diary, July 20, 1927.

36. Bridgeman diary, 145; Ishii Kikujiro, *Diplomatic Commentaries* (Baltimore, 1936), 196; Gibson to Kellogg, July 22, 1927, *FRUS*, 1927, 1:123.

37. Bridgeman diary, 157.

38. Cabinet meeting, July 29, 1927, CAB 23/55/46(27)1.

39. McKercher, *Second Baldwin Government*, 84; Epstein, "Historians and the Geneva Naval Conference," 137.

40. *NYT*, July 30, 1927; Schofield diary, August 2-3, 1927.

41. Wilson to Kellogg, August 5, 1927, Hugh R. Wilson, papers (hereafter, Wilson MSS), Herbert Hoover Presidential Library, West Branch, Iowa.

42. Madden memorandum, CAB 4/16/808, Appendix 1; Hall, *Britain, America, and Arms Control*, 49-50; McKercher, *Second Baldwin Government*, 75-76.

43. Cecil to Col. Edward M. House, September 15, 1927, Cecil MSS. In response to Cecil's resignation and charges that Churchill had sabotaged the conference, Churchill drily noted that "the Cecils are always ill or resigning." Kenneth Rose, *The Later Cecils* (London, 1975), 172; Cecil charges, Cecil to Chamberlain, August 10, 1927, FO 800/261/192.

44. Interestingly, as Mark Epstein has pointed out to me, Theodore Roosevelt, Jr., claimed that Coolidge had remarked to Roosevelt and to Frank Stearns (a key adviser to the president) in 1924 that the election of that year would be his last. Roosevelt wrote the president that after the announcement from South Dakota, he had been "assuring various public leaders that from my judgment of your character, you meant exactly what you said." Roosevelt to Coolidge, August 3, 1927, Theodore Roosevelt, Jr., papers, (hereafter, Roosevelt MSS), Library of Congress, Washington, D.C. But Stearns, for one, was shocked by the announcement, as he wrote the president, and Roosevelt may not have been the best judge of character vis-à-vis political action: he also predicted that Franklin Roosevelt would not run for a third term in 1940, based in part on his estimation of FDR's character. Stearns to Coolidge, August 1927, in Claude M. Fuess, *Calvin Coolidge: The Man from Vermont* (Boston, 1940), 399; T. Roosevelt to Hugh Gibson, May 31, 1939, Roosevelt MSS.

45. Dawes statement, *NYT*, August 8, 1927; MacDonald statement, *Parl. Deb.*, 5th ser., 210 (1927): 2089-95. A cartoon in the *Chicago Daily Journal* probably best sums up Dawes's presidential motive in depicting a ring of naval vessels with a big top hat flying into their midst inscribed: "No competitive naval building—Dawes." *Chicago Daily Journal*, August 15, 1927, in Charles G. Dawes Papers, Northwestern University, Evanston, Illinois.

46. Villard, *Prophets True and False* (New York, 1928), 47.

47. For more on this point, see Dingman, *Power in the Pacific*, 217.

48. Kellogg to Simonds, August 17, 1927, Kellogg MSS.

49. Chamberlain to Howard, August 10, 1927, *DBFP*, ser. 1a, 3: 729.

50. Cecil, *A Great Experiment*, 186.

51. Churchill to Bridgeman, August 18, 1927, FO 800/261/281.

52. Berthelot to Aime-Joseph de Fleuriau (ambassador to London), November 17, 1927, Fleuriau MSS, quoted in Vaisse, *Sécurité D'abord*, 42.

53. Briand to Paul Claudel (ambassador to Washington), December 31, 1927, Ministère des affaires étrangères, *Limitation des armements navals: Trente-cinq pièces relative aux travaux préparatoires du désarmement et à la limitation des armements navals, 21 mars 1927-6 octobre 1928* (Paris, 1928), 33-35.

54. Bridgeman diary, 159; Kellogg to Coolidge, October 24?, 27?, 1927, Kellogg MSS.

5. Recriminations and Rapprochement

1. Frederick J. Libby, "Why an American Peace Movement?" National Council for the Prevention of War *News Bulletin*, July 1, 1928, in Knox MSS; Ferrell, *Peace in Their Time*, 111.

2. Ferrell, *Peace in Their Time*, 64, 68-69, 77, 86. Also see Harold Josephson, *James T. Shotwell and the Rise of Internationalism in America*, (Cranbury, N.J., 1974), 156-60.

3. Vaisse, *Sécurité D'abord*, 33.

4. For a fine discussion of the World Court battle, see Michael Dunne, *The United States and the World Court, 1920-1935* (London, 1988), chapter 3, 122-56.

5. Pamphlets, Box 1, League of Nations Association Papers (hereafter, LNA), Swarthmore College Peace Collection, Swarthmore, Pa. In fact, the League would pay little attention to disarmament until 1929-30. Minutes of the committee for the Tenth anniversary of the League of Nations meeting, October 7, 1929, LNA MSS. The League of Nations Non-Partisan Association changed its name to the League of Nations Association in December 1928.

6. DeBenedetti, "American Peace Movement," 210.

7. Dorothy Detzer correspondence, Folder: England, 1925-1929, Women's International League for Peace and Freedom Papers (hereafter, WILPF), Swarthmore College Peace Collection, Swarthmore, Pa.; DeBenedetti, *Modern American Peace Movement*, 190-91.

8. Emily G. Balch to Hannah Clothier Hull, November 3, 1927, Hannah Clothier Hull, papers (hereafter, Hull MSS), Swarthmore College Peace Collection, Swarthmore, Pa.; Ferrell, *Peace in Their Time*, 155-56; program, Third Annual Conference on the Cause and Cure of War, National Committee on the Cause and Cure of War Papers (hereafter, NCCCW MSS), Swarthmore College Peace Collection, Swarthmore, Pa. Although disarmament was discussed at the 1928 NCCCW conference, the bulk of the organization's efforts, particularly as reflected in Catt's favored project, the public reading education courses, was directed toward such subjects as arbitration, internationalism, and information about Asia and Latin America. See, for instance, NCCCW *Bulletin*, November 3, 1927, March 15, 1928, NCCCW MSS.

9. Chatfield, *For Peace and Justice*, 99; Ferrell, *Peace in Their Time*, 99.

10. Capper Resolution text, December 9, 1927, *Cong. Rec.*, December 9, 1927, 70th Cong., 1st sess., 1927, 69, pt. 1: 351; Burton Resolution, ibid., January 25, 1928, 70th Cong., 1st sess., 1928, 69, pt. 2: 2045.

11. Ferrell writes that the Capper Resolution demonstrated western interest in the peace campaign and caught the attention of the administration, whereas DeBenedetti believes that it did not attract wide interest in the West, judging from the amount of coverage it received from newspapers there. The administration did begin to notice the campaign with the Capper Resolution, even if peace workers were never able to gain as many converts to their cause in the West as in the East and Old Northwest. Ferrell, *Peace in Their Time*, 117; DeBenedetti, *Modern American Peace Movement*, 200-1.

12. Kellogg to Elihu Root, December 23, 1927, Kellogg MSS.

13. Kellogg to Clara Kellogg, May 5, 1928, Kellogg MSS.

14. The Foreign Service School, established in 1925 to train foreign service officers, stressed in lectures and courses that disarmament had no place in modern diplomacy. Robert D. Schulzinger, *The Making of the Diplomatic Mind: The Training, Outlook, and Style of United States Foreign*

Service Officers, 1908-1931 (Middletown, Conn., 1975), 83, 97-99; De-Benedetti, "American Peace Movement," 205-6.

15. Melvyn P. Leffler, *The Elusive Quest: America's Pursuit of European Stability and French Security, 1919-1933* (Chapel Hill, N.C., 1979), 161.

16. Ibid.

17. Howard to Chamberlain, April 20, 1928, *DBFP.*, ser. 1a, 5: 605-6; Newton, "Anglo-American Relations," 125.

18. Kellogg to George W. Wickersham, May 19, 1928; Kellogg to Borah, July 19, 1928; Levinson to Kellogg, October 29, 1928; all in Kellogg MSS.

19. DeBenedetti, "American Peace Movement," 213. For a recapitulation of Shotwell's position, see Pratt to Shotwell, January 26, 1928, William V. Pratt Papers, Naval Historical Center, Washington Navy Yard, Washington, D.C.

20. Detzer to Dorothy Woodman, June 22, 1928, WILPF MSS; De-Benedetti, *Modern American Peace Movement*, 188.

21. Quoted in *Women's Journal*, February 1930, p. 19, as cited in Jacqueline Van Voris, *Carrie Chapman Catt: A Public Life* (New York, 1987), 211.

22. Detzer to Kathleen Courtney, March 5, 1928, WILPF MSS; Harrison speech in Kathleen Whitaker (Sayre) file, Emily G. Balch Papers (hereafter, Balch MSS), Swarthmore College Peace Collection, Swarthmore, Pa.

23. Kellogg to George W. Wickersham, December 24, 1928, Kellogg MSS.

24. Birn, *League of Nations Union*, 82-84; series of letters between Cecil, MacDonald, and Lloyd George, March, 1928, J. Ramsay MacDonald Papers, (hereafter, MacDonald MSS), Public Record Office, London.

25. Cabinet Conclusions, June 22, 1928, CAB 23/58/34(28)2; Untitled manuscript on disarmament, Container 67, Mark L. Bristol Papers, Naval Historical Foundation Collection, Library of Congress, Washington, D.C.

26. Lord Salisbury to Chamberlain, May 3, 1928, FO 800/262/374-75. For evidence that the French may have deliberately been trying to play the British off the Americans to gain more concessions from Whitehall, see Richardson, *British Disarmament Policy*, 169.

27. Cabinet memorandum, November 17, 1927, CAB 24/189/C.P. 292(27). Disarmament Report, November 24, 1927, CAB 24/189/58(27)3.

28. "Report on current naval discussions," March 28, 1928, ADM 1/8724/56; Report: "General History of Disarmament" (undated), CAB 4/19/998b; Cabinet Conclusions, June 6, 1928, CAB 23/58/31(28)1; Cabinet Conclusions, June 22, 1928, CAB 23/58/34(28)2; Richardson, *British Disarmament Policy*, 177.

29. Cabinet Conclusions, July 4, 1928, CAB 23/58/36(28)2; Jon Jacobson, *Locarno Diplomacy: Germany and the West, 1925-1929* (Princeton, 1972), 190; David Carlton, "The Anglo-French Compromise on Arms Limitation, 1928," *The Journal of British Studies* 8 (1969): 151. Carlton argues correctly that the British gave in to the French on most crucial points.

Among other concessions, Whitehall withdrew objection to the abolition of submarines to gain French acceptance of Anglo-French parity in two classes of cruisers. Also see Richardson, *British Disarmament Policy*, 179.

30. Crewe to Chamberlain, July 19, 1928, FO 800/263/15; Untitled manuscript on disarmament, Bristol MSS.

31. Newton, "Anglo-American Relations," 140-41.

32. British chargé (Chilton) to Kellogg, July 31, 1928, *FRUS, 1928*, 1: 264.

33. Telegram, Coolidge to Kellogg, August 2, 1928, *FRUS 1928*, 1: 267; letter, Coolidge to Kellogg, August 3, 1928, ibid., 270; Kellogg to Coolidge, August 4, 1928, Kellogg MSS.

34. Jones memorandum on Anglo-French agreement, August 4, 1928, Jones MSS.

35. Kellogg to Coolidge, September 22, 1928, Kellogg MSS.

36. Cushenden to Chamberlain, November 22, 1928, FO 800/263/60; McKercher, *Second Baldwin Government*, 175; Richardson, *British Disarmament Policy*, 179; Cabinet Conclusions, September 24, 1928, CAB 23/58/44(28); Cabinet Conclusions, October 1, 1928, CAB 23/58/45(28)2; "General History of Disarmament," CAB 4/19/998b.

37. Briand to M. de Sartignes, July 23, 1928, September 1, 1928, France, Ministère des étrangères, *Limitation des armements navals*, 50-52, 59.

38. Kellogg to Coolidge, August 9, 1928, SD 500.A15 3 1/2; Memorandum, Division of West European Affairs, November 21, 1928, SD RG 43, Entry E161, 200.5/1.

39. Gibson to Castle, November 17, 1928; Castle to Gibson, December 19, 1928, Gibson MSS.

40. Middlemas and Barnes, *Baldwin*, 374; Cabinet Conclusions, December 19, 1928, CAB 23/59/57(28)6. Ramsay MacDonald later acknowledged the American contribution to the death of the compromise in a speech to Parliament during the debate over ratification of the London Treaty. Speech transcript, June 20, 1930, MacDonald MSS.

41. Morgan to George A. Innes, September 13, 1928, Morgan to Wilson Harris, December 9, 1927, National Council for the Prevention of War Papers (hereafter, NCPW MSS), Swarthmore College Peace Collection, Swarthmore, Pa.

42. Foreign Policy *Bulletin* 7, no. 48 (October 4, 1928), quoted in Frank Abbott, "The Foreign Policy Association," (Ph.D. diss., Texas Tech University, 1972), 72.

43. Quoted in David Marquand, *Ramsay MacDonald* (London, 1977), 473.

44. Heller, "Curtis Dwight Wilbur," 612; Giovanni Engely, *The Politics of Naval Disarmament* (London, 1932), 45.

45. Britten speech, March 15, 1928, *Cong. Rec.*, 70th Cong., 1st sess. 1928, 69, pt. 5; 4846.

46. Report on campaign against naval construction bill, February 15, 1928, Whitaker file, Balch MSS; NCPW *Bulletin*, July 1, 1928, in Knox MSS; Detzer to Hull, February 18, 1928, pamphlet of the American Legion, "Save Our Navy," February 24, 1928, both in Hull MSS.

47. Britten speech, March 15, 1928, *Cong. Rec.*, 70th Cong., 1st sess. 1928, 69, pt. 5; 4846-48.

48. Abernathy remarks, March 15, 1928, *Cong. Rec.*, 70th Cong., 1st sess., 1928, 69, pt. 5; 4856; Treadway quote, February 21, 1928, ibid., 1928, 69, pt. 3; 3387.

49. Armin Rappaport, *Navy League*, 113-14, 123; Navy League pamphlets, in Knox MSS. For perhaps the best summary of both the navy and peace forces arguments, see the series of letters and rebuttals by Laura Puffer Morgan and Adm. Frank H. Schofield, introduced into the *Congressional Record* during the Senate debate by Senator David I. Walsh (Mass.), *Cong. Rec.*, January 30, 1929, 70th Cong., 2d sess., 1929, 70, pt. 3; 2435-37.

50. Hoff-Wilson, *American Business and Foreign Policy*, 51-53.

51. Lamont, "What Will Europe Renewed Mean to the United States?" *Nation's Business* 125 (May 20, 1927): 17. At the time, Lamont was much more interested in extending a loan to the Japanese government for Manchurian development—and securing State Department approval for it— than he was with disarmament. For more on this episode, see *FRUS 1927*, 2: 482-92; Herbert Feis, *The Diplomacy of the Dollar: First Era, 1919-1932* (Baltimore, 1950), 36-38; and Warren Cohen, *Chinese Connection: Roger S. Greene, Thomas W. Lamont, George E. Sokolsky and American-East Asian Relations* (New York, 1978), 148-53.

52. Detzer to International Branch of WILPF (undated, early 1929), WILPF MSS; DeBenedetti, *Modern American Peace Movement*, 214.

53. Detzer report to Board of International WILPF (undated, early 1929), WILPF MSS; DeBenedetti, *Modern American Peace Movement*, 211.

54. Chaput, *Disarmament in British Naval Policy*, 166.

55. Courtney to Detzer, November 15, 1929, WILPF MSS.

56. Chamberlain to Murray, January 28, 1928, FO 800/261, cited in Cecelia Lynch, "A Matter of Controversy: The Peace Movement and British Arms Policy," in *Arms Limitation and Disarmament*, ed. McKercher, 70 n. 43.

57. League of Nations Union *Annual Report, 1928* (London, 1928), 18; Birn, *League of Nations Union*, 85. For a different view on the effectiveness of British peace groups, see Lynch, "A Matter of Controversy," 61-82.

58. Ogata, "Liberal Nongovernmental Groups," 465; Akira Iriye, *After Imperialism, The Search for a New Order in the Far East, 1921-1931* (Cambridge, 1965), 262.

59. Gibson wrote his mother that the meeting in 1928 was "not an encouraging session. Most of the time was spent in broadcasting Soviet propaganda and the remainder in airing Franco-German rows." Gibson to Mary Gibson, March 27, 1928, Gibson letters. For the official State Department attitude, see Kellogg to Hugh Wilson, February 28, 1928, *FRUS, 1928*, 1: 242-43.

60. Howard to Cushenden, November 7, 1928, *DBFP*, ser. 1a, 5: 851-54; Newton, "Anglo-American Relations," 152.

61. Castle to Gibson, January 17, 1929, Gibson MSS.

62. Quoted in Newton, "Anglo-American Relations," 158.

63. For more on the changing views of the Conservative government,

see Newton, "Anglo-American Relations, 152-64, 184-87, and McKercher, *Second Baldwin Government*, chapter 8.

64. Joan Hoff-Wilson correctly argues that most Hoover biographers, for instance, David Burner, in his study *Herbert Hoover: A Public Life* (New York, 1979), place too much emphasis on Hoover's Quaker background. She notes that his disrupted childhood, progressivism, and career in engineering were more important in creating his mind set than was Quakerism. Joan Hoff-Wilson, "Herbert Hoover: The Popular Image of an Unpopular President," in *Understanding Herbert Hoover: Ten Perspectives*, ed. Lee Nash (Stanford, 1987), 7 n. 9.

65. Stimson to Levinson, November 12, 1929, Henry L. Stimson, Diary and Papers, (hereafter, Stimson MSS), Yale University Library, New Haven, Conn. Microfilm.

66. Castle to Gibson, June 11, 1929, Gibson MSS.

67. Coolidge to Hoover, March 30, 1929, Herbert Hoover Papers (hereafter, Hoover MSS), Herbert Hoover Presidential Library, West Branch, Iowa; Kellogg to Hugh Wilson, December 15, 1928, *FRUS, 1928*, 1: 262.

68. Gibson had served as liaison between Hoover and the Belgian government for the postwar Commission of Relief in Belgium and later coauthored a book with Hoover, *The Problems of Lasting Peace* (New York, 1942).

69. For more on this meeting, see Newton, "Anglo-American Relations," 168-69.

70. Ronald E. Swerczeck, "The Diplomatic Career of Hugh Gibson, 1908-1938" (Ph.D. diss., University of Iowa, 1972), 225; Stephen Roskill, *Naval Policy between the Wars*, vol. 2, *The Period of Reluctant Rearmament, 1930-1939* (London, 1976), 38.

71. Jones to Gleaves, April 28, 1929, Jones MSS.; O'Connor, *Perilous Equilibrium*, 27.

72. Newton, "Anglo-American Relations," 181-82; *Baltimore Sun*, April 23, 1929, in Felix M. Morley Papers, Herbert Hoover Presidential Library, West Branch, Iowa. Former Secretary Kellogg conferred with MacDonald, whose Labour party was favored in the upcoming elections, after Gibson's speech and reported him enthusiastic. Kellogg to Stimson, April 24, 1929, Hoover MSS.

73. MacDonald to Thomas, February 25, 1929, MacDonald MSS.

74. Marquand, *Ramsay MacDonald*, 504-6.

75. Boston *Daily Globe*, January 25, 1929, in Balch MSS; O'Connor, *Perilous Equilibrium*, 27, 30-31.

76. McKercher ably traces the second Baldwin government's emphasis on this theme, pointing out that Whitehall paid close attention to Senator Borah's tirades about neutral rights. But the American government and public did not. Further, Borah belatedly supported the American claim for cruiser parity, and he called for Britain to scrap cruisers to achieve it, as Americans had with battleships at Washington. McKercher, *Second Baldwin Government*, 178-82. Borah statement, *Japan Times*, August 3, 1929.

77. Stimson to Atherton (chargé in London), May 14, 1929, *FRUS, 1929*, 1: 112.

78. Dawes, Gibson, and MacDonald, mindful of the experiences at the Geneva Conference, soon established that if a five-power conference faltered, the United States, Britain, and Japan would break off into a three-power conference. MacDonald memorandum, June 25, 1929, CAB 23/61/24(29).

79. Gibson to Stimson, June 20, 1929, *FRUS, 1929*, 1: 128.

80. Gibson to Mary Gibson, June 29, July 7, November 16, 1929, Gibson letters.

81. Gibson, Dawes to Stimson, July 29, 1929, *FRUS, 1929*, 1: 164-66.

82. Roskill, *Naval Policy between the Wars* 2; 41-42.

83. MacDonald to Dawes, n.d. (1929), Cecil MSS; Dawes to Stimson, July 10, 1929, Hoover MSS; Raymond G. O'Connor, "The 'Yardstick' and Naval Disarmament in the 1920s," *Mississippi Valley Historical Review* 45 (1958-59): 457.

84. Kobayashi Tatsuo, "The London Naval Treaty, 1930," in *Japan Erupts: The London Naval Conference and the Manchurian Incident, 1928-1932*, ed. James William Morley (New York, 1984), 21; Eric Lacroix, "The Development of the A Class Cruisers in the Japanese Imperial Navy, Part Four," *Warship International* 18, no. 1 (1981): 75.

85. Akira Iriye, "Japan's Policies toward the United States," in *Japan's Foreign Policy, 1868-1941: A Research Guide*, ed. James W. Morley (New York, 1974), 436, 440.

86. Kobayashi, "London Naval Treaty," 21-22.

87. Crowley, *Japan's Quest for Autonomy*, 33, 38, 40; MacDonald, "Memorandum on Current Status of Naval Discussions," July 25, 1929, CAB 2/5/444; Dawes to Stimson, August, 12, 1929, *FRUS, 1929*, 1: 189.

88. General Board to Secretary of the Navy, July 13, 1929, GB 438-1, ser. 1437; Report, "General History of Disarmament" (undated), CAB 4/19/998b. The Admiralty had foreshadowed the U.S. Navy's objections to a yardstick. Sir Charles Madden, Beatty's replacement as First Sea Lord, testified to the Baldwin Cabinet that it was not possible to devise a precise formula applying equally to all navies. Madden testimony to Cabinet, June 6, 1928, CAB 23/58/31(28)1.

89. O'Connor, *Perilous Equilibrium*, 41-43; General Board recommendations for disarmament conference, September 11, 1929, GB 438.1, ser. 1444a; Gerald E. Wheeler, *Admiral William V. Pratt, U.S. Navy: A Sailor's Life* (Annapolis, 1974), 295. Hoover was confused about the General Board's disagreement on the yardstick and requested clarification using the *Omaha*s as examples. Hoover to Captain (Ret.) Allen Buchanan, September 24, 1929, GB 438-1, ser. 1449.

90. Hoover to Stimson, August 30, 1929, Hoover MSS.

91. *Cong. Rec.*, September 13, 1929, 71st Cong., 1st sess., 1929, 71, pt. 3; 3582; also see *Washington Star*, September 9, 1929, in Hoover MSS.

92. Kitchens, "Shearer Scandal and Its Origins," 159, 163, 166, 225.

93. Theodore Marriner (Division of West European Affairs, State Department) to William T. Beck (White House staff), September 19, 1929, in Hoover MSS.

94. Memoranda on Shearer, Office of the Assistant to the Attorney General, September 14 and 20, 1929, Hoover MSS.

95. See Federal Bureau of Investigation report on Shearer links to NSL, September 10, 1929, and memoranda on Shearer, Office of the Assistant to the Attorney General, September 14 and 20, 1929, Hoover MSS.

96. Edwards, *Patriots in Pinstripe*, 136.

97. Report, "General History of Disarmament" (undated), CAB 4/19/ 998b; Roskill, *Naval Policy between the Wars*, 2; 45.

98. Leffler, *The Elusive Quest*, 221.

99. DeBenedetti, "American Peace Movement," 206-7.

6. The London Naval Conference

1. "Five Year Building Plan," General Board, September 27, 1927, GB 420-2, ser. 1358; Long memorandum, November 27, 1928, GB 420-8.

2. Report, "General Characteristics of Cruisers no. 37-41," by Director of Fleet Training, with attached conclusions of the General Board, December 11, 1929, GB 420-8, ser. 1455.

3. *Our Navy*, September 1929, in Bristol MSS.

4. Craig L. Symonds, "William Veazie Pratt," in *The Chiefs of Naval Operations*, ed. Robert W. Love, Jr. (Annapolis, Md., 1980), 73-74.

5. The admiral's position on the six-inch gun is interesting. He had not always supported such a gun and may have changed his mind during his tenure as commander of the fleet. He had always favored better protection and discounted the need for range, arguing that in the unlikely event of war with Britain many British bases would be captured, putting America on a par. Gerald E. Wheeler, *Admiral William Veazie Pratt*, 198, 238-39, 249, 296; Friedman, *U.S. Cruisers*, 165; Pratt to H.A. Wiley, Commander in Chief of the U.S. Fleet, October 17, 1928, William V. Pratt Papers (hereafter, Pratt MSS), Naval Historical Center, Washington Navy Yard, Washington, D.C., photocopy.

6. For more detail on the disagreements between the General Board and the bureau chiefs, see Philip T. Rosen, "The Treaty Navy, 1919-1937," in *In Peace and War: Interpretations of U.S. Naval History, 1775-1978*, ed. Kenneth J. Hagan (Westport, Conn., 1978), 221-36.

7. Charles G. Dawes, *Journal as Ambassador to Great Britain* (New York, 1939), 151.

8. Brief, Van Keuren remarks to delegates, January 28, 1930, GB 438-1; Van Keuren memorandum, February 1, 1930, in Pratt MSS.

9. Brief, Yarnell remarks to delegates, January 29, 1928, in Pratt MSS.

10. Harold E. Train, *Log of the London Naval Conference of 1930*, (hereafter, Train log, 1930) January 29, 1930, General Board Disarmament Conferences Records, series 9, National Archives, Washington, D.C.

11. Memorandum, Captain Smyth to Senator David Reed, February 3, 1930, in Pratt MSS; Train log, January 29, 1930.

12. Pratt memorandum, February 13, 1930, Pratt MSS. For more detail on Pratt's views vis-à-vis the General Board, also see Symonds, "William Veazie Pratt," 76-83.

13. William R. Braisted, "Charles Frederick Hughes," in *The Chiefs of Naval Operations*, ed. Love, 53-54, 62.

14. Wheeler, *Admiral William Veazie Pratt*, 296-98, 302-3, 308. Train noted that Pratt disapproved of a General Board and "campaigned actively" against it during the conference and in the months afterward. Train, "Reminiscences," 124.

15. For a fine general description of the training, experiences, and outlook of many of these senior officers, see Karsten, *The Naval Aristocracy*.

16. Dawes, *Journal*, 142; L. Ethan Ellis, *Republican Foreign Policy, 1921-1933* (New Brunswick, N.J., 1968), 169-70; Hall, *Britain, America, and Arms Control*, 92-94; Henry L. Stimson diary, February 24, 1930, Stimson MSS. Hoover wrote optimistically, if not accurately, in his memoirs: "Admirals Pratt, Hepburn, and Jones genuinely supported what we were trying to do." Herbert C. Hoover, *The Memoirs of Herbert Hoover*, vol. 2, *The Cabinet and the Presidency, 1920-1933* (New York, 1951-52), 341. About the Admiralty officers, he wrote: "They were naturally suspicious that the 'two welfare workers'—MacDonald and myself—were tangled up in a conspiracy to injure 'that greatest safeguard of world peace and world stability,' the British navy." Hoover to Roger Shaw, February 9, 1946, Herbert Hoover Miscellaneous Papers (hereafter, Hoover Misc. MSS), Hoover Institution on War, Revolution, and Peace, Stanford, Calif.

17. Train, *Reminiscences*, 193.

18. Report, "Comparison of two cruisers identical in size, protection, and speed, but with one armed with nine eight-inch guns and the other armed with twelve six-inch guns," by Lieutenant-Commander E.M. Williams for Rear Admiral Bristol, March 7, 1930, GB 420-8. In particular, Williams claimed that the six-inch gun lost its high rate of fire if mounted in gun houses, approaching that of the eight-inch gun.

19. For more on this, see Friedman, *U.S. Cruisers*, 184.

20. *New Statesman*, September 3, 1927, cited in Adelphia Dane Bowen, Jr., "The Disarmament Movement, 1918-1935" (Ph.D. diss., Columbia University, 1956), 142.

21. Madden cited in Roskill, *Naval Policy between the Wars*, 1: 546; Madden notes on Staff College report, May 17, 1928, ADM 1/8765/313.

22. Addendum, "Staff College Practice Results, 1922-1927"; Memorandum, "Small Cruiser Conclusions," by Sea Lords, September 27, 1929; Memorandum by Director of Plans, Roger Bellairs, November 14, 1928, all in ADM 1/8765/313. The Admiralty, as Madden conceded in early 1928, was under great pressure from the government to compromise on its stand at Geneva regarding limits on the eight-inch gun. Madden memorandum, May 17, 1928, ADM 1/8765/313.

23. Report, "Gun Armament and Protection of Small 8" Cruiser and Comparison with 6" Cruiser," December 4, 1928; Memorandum, B. Fairbairn, Director of Gunnery Development, December 4, 1928; Memorandum, Bellairs, July 28, 1929, all in ADM 1/8765/313.

24. Barry D. Hunt, *Sailor-Scholar: Admiral Sir Herbert Richmond, 1871-1946* (Waterloo, Ont., 1982), 189, 194, 198.

25. Chatfield memorandum, undated (early 1929), ADM 1/8765/313. Chatfield, however, could not carry other ranking officers with him.

26. Hansgeorg Jentschura, *Warships of the Imperial Japanese Navy* (London, 1977), 77-79.

27. Sadao Asada, "The Revolt against the Washington Treaty: The Imperial Japanese Navy and Naval Limitation, 1921-1927," *Naval War College Review* 46, no. 3 (Summer 1993): 92. Asada notes that in contrast to the more flexible top officers in the Ministry of the Marine, many officers of the Naval General Staff had advocated the 10-7 ration long before the Geneva Conference of 1927.

28. Dawes, *Journal*, 150; O'Connor, *Perilous Equilibrium*, 77, 80.

29. Stimson to Candace Stimson, February 22, 1930, Stimson MSS.

30. Stimson diary, February 3, 1930; CMD 3485.

31. Secretary Adams and Senator Robinson were the last to accept the lower figure. O'Connor, *Perilous Equilibrium*, 158 n. 44.

32. Stimson diary, February 2, 6, 1930; Dawes, *Journal*, 139; Stimson to Cotton, February 5, 1930, *FRUS, 1930*, 1: 18.

33. Arthur Henderson to Howard, February 11, 1930, *DBFP*, ser. 2, 1: 209; Stimson diary, February 11, 1930.

34. Notes from Delegates' Meeting, February 14, 1930, *DBFP*, ser. 2, 1: 218; Stimson to Cotton, February 28, 1930, *FRUS, 1930*, 1: 32; David Carlton, *MacDonald versus Henderson: The Foreign Policy of the Second Labour Government* (London, 1970), 124.

35. Harold G. Nicolson, *Dwight Morrow* (New York, 1935), 366.

36. O'Connor, *Perilous Equilibrium*, 88.

37. For background on the Franco-Italian naval rivalry in the 1920s, see Joel Blatt, "The Parity that Meant Superiority: French Naval Policy toward Italy at the Washington Conference, 1921-22," *French Historical Studies* (16) 1981: 223-48, and William Shorrock, "France, Italy, and the Eastern Mediterranean in the 1920s," *International History Review* 8 (1986): 70-82. Ironically, Briandistes in France had also talked periodically since 1922 of building relations with Italy to guarantee the independence of the East European states, as they distrusted British commitment to the Continent. See Piotr S. Wandycz, *The Twilight of French Eastern Alliances, 1928-1936* (Princeton, 1988), 254-55; Nicole Jordan, *The Popular Front and Central Europe: The Dilemmas of French Impotence, 1918-1940* (New York, 1992), 19.

38. Anthony Adamthwaite, *The Lost Peace: International Relations in Europe, 1918-1939* (London, 1980), 105; Leffler, *Elusive Quest*, 220-21.

39. Vaisse, *Sécurité D'abord*, 30.

40. Memo for Premier Tardieu, January 13, 1930, French foreign ministry archives, Tardieu Papers, vol. 41, cited in Adamthwaite, *The Lost Peace*, 109.

41. Walter E. Edge, *A Jerseyman's Journal: Fifty Years of American Business and Politics* (Princeton, 1948), 156-57.

42. Memo for Tardieu, January 13, 1930, cited in Adamthwaite, *The Lost Peace*, 110.

43. This paragrapah is based on Vaisse, *Sécurité D'abord*, 24-25.

44. Stimson to Hoover, February 17, 1930, Stimson to State Department, February 16, 1930, both in Stimson diary.

45. Navy League pamphlets, General Board Disarmament Conference Records, series 9, box 24; Memorandum on inaccuracies in Navy League pamphlets, West European Bureau, January 27, 1930, SD 500 A15 a3/630; Howard to Henderson, January 8, 1930, FO 371 14257 A588/1/45; W. Campbell to Henderson, March 19, 1930, FO 371 14260 A2095/1/45, "British Foreign Office, United States: Correspondence, 1930-1937," (Wilmington, Del., 1981). Microfilm.

46. Kathleen Courtney to Dorothy Detzer, December 16, 1929, WILPF MSS; *NYT*, January 15 and 21, 1930; Notes, delegates meeting, February 6, 1930, Stimson diary. The WILPF in the United States had organized an unsuccessful campaign supporting Jane Addams, its international president, as a delegate to London. Memorandum, SD 500 A15 a3 P43/73.

47. Morgan to Libby, February 6, 1930; Pamphlet, "What Has Happened at London?" NCPW MSS.

48. Dorothy Detzer, *Appointment on the Hill* (New York, 1948), 90; Prentiss Gilbert quoted in Detzer to Hull, February 12, 1930, Hull MSS.

49. Pamphlet, "London Naval Conference," GB Disarmament Confer ence Records, Series 9, Box 24.

50. Morgan to Libby, March 5, 1930, Libby to Morgan, March 6, 1930, NCPW MSS.

51. *NYT*, February 28, March 3, 1930; editorial, *The Christian Century*, February 26, 1930, in Balch MSS.

52. *NYT*, February 13, 1930.

53. Cotton to Stimson, March 3, 1930, and Stimson to Cotton, March 17, 1930, both in *FRUS, 1930*, 1: 40, 64. Stimson to Cotton, February 14, 1930, SD 500 A15 a3/695 1/2.

54. Hoover to Stimson, September 17, 1929, Hoover Miscellaneous MSS.

55. Hoover had conferred with British ambassador Howard with Kellogg's blessing and had proposed a joint Anglo-American publication of essays to "educate" the publics of both countries about what an Anglo-American war might entail if disarmament efforts did not succeed. Howard to Chamberlain, July 28, 1929, *DBFP*, ser. 1a, 3: 708-9; McKercher, *Second Baldwin Government*, 82-83.

56. Press clippings and analysis, British Library of Information, New York, February, 21, 1930, FO 371 A1706/1/45; *Japan Times*, March 2 and 5, 1930; Jahnke to Hoover, March 7, 1930, Hoover Misc. MSS.

57. Hoff-Wilson, *American Business and Foreign Policy*, 58-59; O'Connor, *Perilous Equilibrium*, 109; Costigliola, *Awkward Dominion*, 230.

58. Of course, Castle had been privy to little disarmament information before his arrival in Tokyo because Stimson disliked him. Castle to Gibson, January 29, 1930, Gibson MSS. For Castle's efforts in Washington to participate in disarmament, see Newton, "Anglo-American Relations," 188.

59. Castle to Cotton, March 7, 1930, SD 894.911/55.

60. For more on Reuters' control of international news in Japan, see Roger W. Purdy, "Nationalism and News: 'Information Imperialism' and Japan, 1910-1936," *Journal of American-East Asian Relations* 1 (fall 1992): 295-325.

61. Sterling Tatsuji Takeuchi, "Japan and the London Treaty," The Institute of Oriental Students 4 (1930), Univ. of Chicago, in Stanley K. Hornbeck Papers, Hoover Institution on War, Revolution, and Peace, Stanford, Calif.

62. Gregory T. Kasza, *The State and the Mass Media in Japan, 1918-1945* (Berkeley and Los Angeles, 1988), 35-36.

63. Harry Emerson Wildes, *Japan in Crisis* (New York, 1934), 192, 195; Ishida Takeshi, "Movements to Protect Constitutional Government—A Structural-Functional Analysis," in *Democracy in Prewar Japan: Groundwork or Facade?* ed. George O. Totten (Boston, 1965), 84. Kasza notes that interest groups in general were weaker in Japan than in the democracies of the West. Kasza, *State and Mass Media in Japan*, 106-7.

64. Cotton to Stimson, March 3, 1930, *FRUS, 1930*, 1: 40; Stimson diary, February 9 and 18, 1930. For more on British domestic developments in the late 1920s, see Philip Williamson, *National Crisis and National Government: British Politics, the Economy, and Empire, 1926-1932* (New York, 1992), chapter 1.

65. Stimson to Cotton, March 10, 1930, *FRUS, 1930*, 1: 55; Notes of delegates' meeting, March 12, 1930, *DBFP*, ser. 2, 1: 242; Walter Lippmann, "The London Naval Conference: An American View," *Foreign Affairs* 8 (1930): 513. Britons still opposed sanctions in 1935 according to a "peace ballot" sponsored by the League of Nations Union. Gordon A. Craig and Alexander L. George, *Force and Statecraft: Diplomatic Problems of Our Time* (New York, 1983), 63.

66. Stimson diary, March 21, 1930, and Stimson to Cotton, March 23, 1930, both in *FRUS, 1930*, 1: 55.

67. Stimson diary, March 22, 1930, O'Connor, *Perilous Equilibrium*, 96-100.

68. Libby to Morgan, March 21, 1930, NCPW MSS.

69. Cotton to Stimson, March 25, 1930, *FRUS, 1930*, 1: 81.

70. Lamont to Morrow, March 26, 1930, Thomas W. Lamont Papers, Baker Library, Harvard University, Cambridge, Mass.

71. *NYT*, April 1, 1930; Leffler, *Elusive Quest*, 224-25.

72. Stimson to Cotton, April 8, 1930, SD RG 43, E161, 200.5/5.

73. Crowley, *Japan's Quest for Autonomy*, 48-50.

74. Ibid., 46.

75. Ibid., 52, 55.

76. Stimson to Cotton, February 27, 1930, SD 500.A15 a3/716; Cotton to Castle, March 13, 1930, SD, "Confidential Diplomatic Post Reports, Japan, 1930-1935" (hereafter, CDPR) (Frederick, Md., 1982), microfilm; Henderson to Tilley, March 15, 1930, *DBFP*, ser. 2, 1: 249.

77. Quoted in Kobayashi, "London Naval Conference," 27.

78. O'Connor, *Perilous Equilibrium*, 83.

79. Castle to Cotton, March 19, 1930, CDPR.

80. Castle to Cotton, March 21, 1930, CDPR; Tilley to Henderson, March 19, 1930, FO 371 A2045/1/45. Before the Japanese responded, the French tried to persuade them to reject the proposal because of the submarine limits, and Stimson attempted to force acceptance by threatening Japan with foreclosure on a twenty-five year old loan. Stimson to Castle, March 29, 1930, SD 500.A15 a3/802.

81. *Japan Times*, March 21, 1930; Kobayashi, "London Naval Treaty," 35, 38.

82. Kobayashi, "London Naval Treaty," 31; Asada, "Revolt against the Washington Treaty," 91.

83. Crowley, *Japan's Quest for Autonomy*, 58-59, 64.

84. Ellis, *Frank Kellogg and American Foreign Relations*, 173-75. Ellis finds that George Rublee, an assistant to Morrow, came to favor a consultative pact and brought Stimson and Morrow around to this view.

85. Years later, Hoover wrote that he had considered French participation in a treaty secondary: "I instructed our delegation that we did not care whether the French limited their navy or not, and our major purpose of parity with Britain and the extension of the 5-3 ratio with Japan would be accomplished even if France and Italy stayed out of the agreement." Hoover to Roger Shaw, February 9, 1946, Hoover Miscellaneous MSS.

86. In addition, large cruisers performed poorly in the first important naval battle of the Second World War. In 1939, the German "pocket battleship," which was really a heavy cruiser, the *Graf Spee* (10,000 tons, eleven-inch guns), chanced upon three British cruisers, one with eight-inch, two with six-inch guns, off Montevideo. The Germans made a lucky hit on the firing mechanism of the slower heavy cruiser, but the light cruisers, darting about and peppering the larger ship with murderous fire, forced the *Graf Spee* into Montevideo harbor.

87. Train log, 1930, March 24, 1930; Wheeler, *Admiral William Veazie Pratt*, 309-10.

7. Disarmament in the Great Depression

1. Philip Jessup, *Elihu Root* (New York, 1938), 465-66; Richard Leopold, *Elihu Root and the Conservative Tradition* (Boston, 1954), 161.

2. O'Connor, *Perilous Equilibrium*, 109-10.

3. FCCCA *Information Service* newsletter, May 10, 1930, in Sayre file, Balch MSS.

4. A.G. Everett, "Navies, Taxes, and International Peace Insurance," *Journal of the American Bankers' Association* 23 (August 1930): 95.

5. "What the Naval Conference Means to Business," *Business Week* 20 (January 22, 1930): 5-6; president of the United States Chamber of Commerce to Hoover, July 1, 1930, Hoover MSS; Ernest T. Trigg, "Common Sense in National Defense," *Nation's Business* 18 (March 1930): 154-55.

6. *Commercial and Financial Chronicle* 131 (April 26, 1930).

7. Senate Committee on Foreign Relations (hereafter, CFR), *Hearings*

on the Treaty on the Limitation of Naval Armaments, 71st Cong., 2d sess., 1930 (Washington, 1930), 5.

8. Text, Stimson radio address, June 12, 1930, in Sayre file, Balch MSS; Jones memorandum, June 16, 1930, Jones MSS.

9. Johnson to his sons, May 17 and 24, 1930, *The Diary Letters of Hiram Johnson, 1917-1945,* vol. 5, ed. Robert E. Burke (New York, 1985), 5.

10. CFR, *Hearings on Treaty,* 359, 363.

11. Bristol to Hiram Johnson, June 13, 1930, Bristol to Arthur Ringland, September 25, 1930, Bristol MSS.

12. CFR, *Hearings on Treaty,* 241, 324; Admiral Jones expressed similar sentiments. Jones memorandum on London Treaty, undated, Jones MSS.

13. Sir Ronald Lindsay to Henderson, July 8, 1930, FO 371 A4645/1/45.

14. CFR, *Hearings on Treaty,* 285; H.W. Cook to William Beck, July 11, 1930, SD 500.A15a3/1010 1/2.

15. Robert Dean Pope, "Senatorial Baron: The Long Political Career of Kenneth D. McKellar" (Ph.D diss., Yale University, 1976), 193; Johnson to Hiram Johnson, Jr., May 30, 1930, *Diary Letters of Hiram Johnson, 5, 1928-1933;* Richard Lowitt, *George W. Norris: The Persistence of a Progressive, 1913-1933* (Urbana, 1971), 532; William R. Castle, Jr., diary, July 22 and 23, 1930, Castle MSS.

16. O'Connor, *Perilous Equilibrium,* 120; FCCCA *Information Service Newsletter,* May 10, 1930, in Sayre file, Balch MSS.

17. Cecil to Sir Maurice Hankey, October 28, 1933, Cecil MSS; O'Connor, *Perilous Equilibrium,* 120.

18. *Parl. Deb.,* (Commons), 5th ser., 239 (1929-30); 1791-94, 1901-3, 1909.

19. Tilley to Henderson, May 19, 1930, FO 371 A4229/1/45; O'Connor, *Perilous Equilibrium,* 82.

20. For press reaction, see Kobayashi, "London Naval Treaty," 57-58. Castle to Stimson, May 26, 1930, SD 500.A15 a3/969.

21. Tilley to Henderson, May 16, 1930, FO 371 A4229/1/45; Takeuchi, "Japan and the London Treaty," Hornbeck MSS; Kobayashi, "London Naval Conference," 59-117.

22. Tilley to Henderson, May 16, 1930, FO 371 A4257/1/45; Edwin L. Neville to Stimson, May 30, 1030, SD RG 43, E161 250/Japan/63; Tilley to Henderson, June 17, 1930, FO 371 A5132/1/45; Jansen, "Introduction to the Manchurian Incident," 130; Kobayashi, "London Naval Conference, 79-80, 93-94.

23. CFR, *Hearings on Treaty,* 302; Lindsay to Henderson, June 12, 1930, FO 371 A4337/1/45.

24. Stephen E. Pelz, *Race to Pearl Harbor: The Failure of the Second London Naval Conference and the Onset of World War II* (Cambridge, 1974), 78, 81-82.

25. Friedman, *U.S. Cruisers,* 130, 139.

26. Ibid., 197, 133; Director of Fleet Maintenance to CNO, September 22, 1936, U.S. Department of the Navy, Secret and Confidential Correspon-

dence of the Office of the Secretary of the Navy, 1927-1939, (hereafter, Sec-Navy) OP-12A-CTB, (SC)A1-3 D7014.

27. Alan D. Zimm, "The U.S.N.'s Flight Deck Cruiser," *Warship International* 16 (no. 3, 1979): 242, 232; General Board to Secretary of the Navy, December 18, 1930, GB 420-8, ser. 1515; Bristol to Secretary of the Navy, April 20, 1931, GB 420-8, ser. 1519.

28. Zimm, "The U.S.N.'s Flight Deck Cruiser," 243-44; Director of Fleet Maintenance to CNO, September 22, 1936, SecNavy OP-12A-CTB, (SC)A1-3 D7014.

29. Karsten, *Naval Aristocracy*, 360 n. 18; Weigley, *American Way of War*, 249-53.

30. Miller, *War Plan Orange*, 348. In contrast to Thomas C. Hone, M. Mandeles, Braisted, and Roskill, Miller argues that U.S. planners did appreciate carriers. He notes, however, that planners mistakenly saw carriers as auxiliaries to the battle line, rather than as leaders of strike forces. Ibid., 348-49.

31. Thomas C. Hone and M. Mandeles, "Managerial Style in the Interwar Navy: A Reappraisal," *Naval War College Review* 33 (September-October 1980): 91, 95-96.

32. Ibid.; Thomas H. Buckley and Edwin B. Strong, Jr., *American Foreign and National Security Policies, 1914-1945* (Knoxville, 1987), 104-5.

33. Buckley and Strong, *American Foreign and National Security*, chapter 5, 92-112; William R. Braisted, "On the American Red and Red-Orange Plans, 1919-1939," 178; Roskill, *Naval Policy between the Wars*, 1: 542-43. Mahan, of course, had argued in his widely read book *The Influence of Sea Power upon History* (1890) that modern navies must emphasize capital ships (i.e., the battleship) in their fleets to safeguard commercial routes. He had amplified these views in other books and articles since that time.

34. Report on Japanese strength, January 21 and 22, 1933, ADM 116/3116; Roskill, *Naval Policy Between the Wars*, 2; 289, 146-47; Jentschura, *Warships of the Imperial Japanese Navy*, 84-89.

35. Admiral Sir Herbert Richmond, who had publicly advocated fewer battleships and more cruisers and smaller ships, had had his views noticed by the government. But his criticism of the Labour plan for the London Naval Conference led to his retirement from the navy in 1931. Hunt, *Sailor-Scholar*, 189, 194.

36. Admiralty Board Minutes extract, October 9, 1933, ADM 1/9360. By early 1937, foreign building caused the British to build the *Southampton*-class cruisers with six-inch guns and displacements of 9,000 to 10,000 tons, far heavier than the British prototype favored a decade earlier at the Geneva Conference. Report, "Cruiser Building Policy," Plans Division, May 6, 1937, ADM 1/9427.

37. Roskill, *Naval Policy between the Wars*, 1: 536, 519-22.

38. Iriye, "Japan's Policies toward the United States," 445; Christopher Thorne, *The Limits of Foreign Policy: The West, the League, and the Far Eastern Crisis of 1931-1933* (London, 1972), 52-53.

39. "Bi-Weekly Intelligence Summary, Japan," August 17, 1933, C-10-e, 21201, Naval Attaché Reports, 1887-1939, ONI.

40. Asada, "The Japanese Navy and the United States," 226-28; Grew to Hull, September 15 and October 20, 1933, CDPR.

41. Grew to Hull, October 20, 1933, CDPR.

42. Pelz, *Race to Pearl Harbor*, 40.

43. Ibid.

44. Eric Lacroix, "The Development of the 'A Class' Cruisers in the Japanese Imperial Navy," *Warship International* 21, no. 3, (1984): 247, 255; Roskill, *Naval Policy Between the Wars*, 2: 148.

45. Roskill, *Naval Policy Between the Wars*, 1: 530; Thorne, *Limits of Foreign Policy*, 72.

46. Thorne, *Limits of Foreign Policy*, 80, 89.

47. Navy League press release, April 28, 1930, in William E. Borah Papers, Library of Congress, Washington, D.C.; Rappaport, *Navy League of the United States*, 135.

48. *Time*, November 9, 1931, in Hoover MSS; J. Edgar Hoover to Lawrence Richey (presidential secretary), October 31, 1931, Hoover MSS; J. Pierrepont Moffat diary, November 5, 1932, in Gibson MSS; White quote cited in Bowen, "The Disarmament Movement," 277.

49. Pamphlet, "The London Naval Conference: A Summary and an Interpretation," June 9, 1930, in Sayre file, Balch MSS; Morgan to Libby, May 20, 1930, NCPW MSS; Morley article, reprinted in *New York Herald-Tribune*, September 28, 1931, in Morley MSS.

50. Detzer to Hilda Clark, March 3, 1930, WILPF MSS.

51. Detzer to Kathleen Courtney, April 7, 1931, WILPF MSS; Chatfield, *For Peace and Justice*, 101.

52. Detzer quoted in Rosemary Rainbolt, "Women, War, and Resistance to War: A Transnational Perspective," paper read at American Historical Association meeting (December 1976), 7; Disarmament Committee of the Women's International Organizations *Newsletter*, (Autumn 1931), in Balch MSS; Minutes of Women's Peace Union meeting, October 1, 1931, Women's Peace Union Papers, Swarthmore College Peace Collection, Swarthmore, Pa.; Bristol to CNO, March 24, 1931, Bristol MSS.

53. Amy Woods to WILPF members, April 30, 1932, in Balch MSS. Kinkaid memorandum, September 26, 1932, in Jones MSS. Captain Dudley Knox, director of the Naval Historical Center, attacked the "arm chair pacifists" and argued that they failed to recognize that law was supported by force. Knox transcript, no date (circa 1932), Knox MSS.

54. Bowen, "The Disarmament Movement," 254-57.

55. Tano Jodai to Detzer, February 17, 1932, WILPF MSS.

56. Ransford S. Miller, State Department Division of Far Eastern Affairs, "The Japanese Situation," lecture to Naval War College, January 16, 1931, Hornbeck MSS; Sadako N. Ogata, *Defiance in Manchuria: The Making of Japanese Foreign Policy, 1931-1932* (Berkeley and Los Angeles, 1964), 29.

57. See, for example, League of Nations Association of Japan, *Supplement to the International Gleanings from Japan* (January 1931); Viscount

Ishii, "Manchukuo and the Manchurian Question," League of Nations Association pamphlet, October 20, 1932; Hornbeck MSS.

58. Gibson had feared that the isolationist Borah would be named and confided to Hugh Wilson that he was "burning candles to all the saints" that Borah would refuse to go if offered the job. Swerczeck, "The Diplomatic Career of Hugh Gibson," 269.

59. Gibson to William R. Castle, December 7, 1930, Gibson MSS.

60. Ibid.

61. Schulzinger, *Making of the Diplomatic Mind*, 138-39.

62. Stimson to Neville, May 31, 1932, SD 500.A15 a4/1048; Robert H. Ferrell, *American Diplomacy in the Great Depression: Hoover-Stimson Foreign Policy, 1929-1933* (New Haven, 1957), 98-99; Castle to Gibson, February 8, 1932, Gibson MSS.

63. Chamberlain to Cecil, January 20, 1932, Cecil MSS.

64. MacDonald to Cecil, August 13, 1930, Cecil MSS.

65. Wandycz, *Twilight of French Eastern Alliances*, 239-47; Vaisse, *Sécurité d'abord*, part 2.

66. Jordan, *Popular Front and Central Europe*, 20-21.

67. Memorandum, Director of Plans, "Number of Cruisers: Question of Cabinet Authority to working to the number 70," April 9, 1932, ADM 116/2827; "Notes for Naval Members of British Delegation," n.d., (circa 1932), ADM 116/2826.

68. Malcolm MacDonald to Cecil, n.d., (circa 1932), Cecil MSS.

69. This paragraph based on Hosoya, "Britain and the United States," 16.

70. Neville to Stimson, March 9, 1931, CDPR; Fujito Shin-Ichiro in *Gaiko Jiho* (Diplomatic Review), quoted in W. Cameron Forbes to Stimson, January 30, 1932, Ibid.

71. Hoover to Stimson, May 24, 1932, *FRUS, 1932*, 1: 180-82. Stimson strenuously disagreed with the president's approach. He wrote that although the proposal would publicize the conference, further concessions on the part of the U.S. Navy would not be popular in the United States except for a "few circles of organized pacifists." He concluded that "quiet diplomacy [is] better than publicity and bold strokes." Stimson memorandum, May 25, 1932, ibid., 182-85.

72. Jordan A. Schwartz, *The Speculator: Bernard M. Baruch in Washington, 1917-1965* (Chapel Hill, N.C., 1981), 260. Baruch swung back to a preparedness stance by 1935.

73. S.R. Vansittart to Sir John Simon, n.d., ADM 116/2827.

74. Gibson diary, Geneva Naval Disarmament Conference, June 27, 1932, Gibson MSS.

75. MacDonald to Baldwin, July 15, 1932, MacDonald MSS.

76. Pierrepont Moffat to Ferdinand Mayer, October 12, 1932, Ferdinand Mayer Papers, Herbert Hoover Presidential Library, West Branch, Iowa. Hugh Wilson to Norman Davis, December 14, 1932, Davis to Wilson, March 2, 1933, Wilson MSS; Kinkaid memorandum, September 26, 1932, in Jones MSS.

77. Josephine Young Case and Everett Needham Case, *Owen D. Young and American Enterprise* (Boston, 1982), 557, 630-32.

78. For assessments of Japanese politics in the 1930s, see Carol Gluck and Stephen R. Graubard, eds., *Showa: The Japan of Hirohito* (New York, 1992).

79. Chief of Staff to Henderson, March 14, 1934, FO 371 A2176/1/45.

80. Moffat to Mayer, September 27, 1933, Mayer MSS.

81. Quoted in Roskill, *Naval Policy between the Wars*, 2: 298.

82. Stanley Hornbeck memorandum of meeting in Executive Office, White House, November 19, 1935, Hornbeck MSS. Hornbeck, chief of the Division of Far Eastern Affairs, had considered disarmament dead by 1934 because of Japanese transgressions in China, which violated the Nine-Power Treaty. Memorandum, April 24, 1934, Hornbeck MSS.

83. Roskill, *Naval Policy between the Wars*, 2: 314.

84. The Americans would eventually engage in some cheating themselves—the carrier *Wasp*, laid down in January 1936 exceeded treaty limits on completion, as did the *New Orleans*-class cruisers. Roskill, *Naval Policy between the Wars*, 2: 177; Friedman, *U.S. Cruisers*, 155-57.

8. Conclusion

1. Levinson to Mrs. Jessie K. Jordan, October 21, 1930, David S. Jordan Papers, Herbert Hoover Institution, Stanford, California.

2. Stanley K. Hornbeck, memorandum of meetings at the White House, November 19 and 23, 1935, Hornbeck MSS.

3. Friedman, *U.S. Cruisers*, 323-24. For an example of how officers failed to notice the performance of eight-inch or six-inch guns, see U.S. Department of the Navy, ship logs, 1943, U.S.S. *Salt Lake City*, one of the first treaty cruisers.

4. Jaffe, "Abolishing War?," 49.

5. Ferdinand Mayer, report from Geneva Conference, no. 25, November 15, 1932, Mayer MSS.; Richard Dean Burns, "International Arms Inspection Policies between World Wars, 1919-1934," *Historian* 31, no. 4 (1969): 583-603.

SELECTED BIBLIOGRAPHY

Personal and Organizational Manuscripts

Balch, Emily Greene. Papers. Swarthmore College Peace Collection, Swarthmore, Pa.

Borah, William E. Papers. Library of Congress, Washington, D.C.

Bridgeman, William L., Viscount. Diary, Shropshire County Record Office, Shrewsbury, England.

Bristol, Mark L. Papers. Naval Historical Foundation Collection. Library of Congress, Washington, D.C.

Castle, William R. Diary. Houghton Library, Harvard University, Cambridge, Mass.

———. Papers. Herbert Hoover Presidential Library, West Branch, Iowa.

Cecil, Robert, Viscount of Chelwood. Papers. British Library, London.

Chamberlain, Sir Austen. Papers. In FO 800. Public Record Office, London.

Coolidge, Calvin. Papers. Library of Congress, Washington, D.C. Microfilm.

Dawes, Charles G. Papers. Northwestern University Library, Evanston, Ill.

Detzer, Dorothy. Papers. Swarthmore College Peace Collection, Swarthmore, Pa.

Gibson, Hugh S. Diaries, Letters, and Notes, 1922-1930. Herbert Hoover Presidential Library, West Branch, Iowa.

———. Papers. Hoover Institution on War, Revolution, and Peace, Stanford, Calif.

Hoover, Herbert C. Papers. Herbert Hoover Presidential Library, West Branch, Iowa.

———. Miscellaneous Papers. Hoover Institution on War, Revolution, and Peace, Stanford, Calif.

Hornbeck, Stanley K. Papers. Hoover Institution on War, Revolution, and Peace, Stanford, Calif.

Hull, Hannah Clothier. Papers. Swarthmore College Peace Collection, Swarthmore, Pa.

Jones, Hilary P. Papers. Naval Historical Foundation Collection. Library of Congress, Washington, D.C.

Jordan, David Starr. Papers. In John D. Crummy Peace Collection. Hoover Institution on War, Revolution, and Peace, Stanford, Calif.

Kellogg, Frank B. Papers. Minnesota Historical Society, St. Paul, Minn. Microfilm.

Knox, Dudley W. Papers. Naval Historical Foundation Collection. Library of Congress, Washington, D.C.

Lamont, Thomas W. Papers. Baker Library, Harvard University, Cambridge, Mass.

League of Nations Association. Papers. Swarthmore College Peace Collection, Swarthmore, Pa.

MacDonald, J. Ramsay. Papers. Public Record Office, London.

Mayer, Ferdinand. Papers. Herbert Hoover Presidential Library, West Branch, Iowa.

Morley, Felix M. Papers. Herbert Hoover Presidential Library, West Branch, Iowa.

National Committee on the Cause and Cure of War. Papers. Swarthmore College Peace Collection, Swarthmore, Pa.

National Council for the Prevention of War. Papers. Swarthmore College Peace Collection, Swarthmore, Pa.

Pratt, William V. Papers. Naval Historical Center, Washington Navy Yard, Washington, D.C. Photocopy.

Roosevelt, Theodore, Jr. Papers. Library of Congress, Washington, D.C.

Schofield, Frank H. Diary, the Geneva Naval Conference of 1927. Naval Historical Center, Washington Navy Yard, Washington, D.C.

Stimson, Henry L. Diary and Papers. Yale University Library, New Haven, Conn. Microfilm.

Train, Harold C. Log of the London Naval Conference of 1930. General Board Disarmament Conference Records. Series 9. National Archives, Washington, D.C.

———. Log of the Third Session of the Preparatory Commission for the Reduction and Limitation of Armaments. General Board Disarmament Conference Records. Series 5. National Archives, Washington, D.C.

———. "Reminiscences." Columbia University Oral History Project. Annapolis, 1965-66. Library of Congress, Washington, D.C. Microfilm.

Van Keuren, Alexander. Papers. Hoover Institution on War, Revolution, and Peace, Stanford, Calif.

Wilbur, Curtis D. Papers. Library of Congress, Washington, D.C.

Wilson, Hugh R. Papers. Herbert Hoover Presidential Library, West Branch, Iowa.

Women's International League for Peace and Freedom. Papers. Swarthmore College Peace Collection, Swarthmore, Pa.

Women's Peace Union. Papers. Swarthmore College Peace Collection, Swarthmore, Pa. Microfilm.

Yarnell, Harry E. Papers. Naval Historical Center, Washington Navy Yard, Washington, D.C.

———. Papers (after 1937). Naval Historical Foundation Collection, Library of Congress, Washington, D.C.

Government Manuscripts

U.K. Admiralty. Files, ADM 1, ADM 116, ADM 167. Public Record Office, London.

U.K. Cabinet. Papers, CAB 2, CAB 4, CAB 23, CAB 24, CAB 29. Public Record Office, London.

U.K. Foreign Office. Files, FO 371, FO 800, FO 412, Public Record Office, London.

————. FO 371. British Foreign Office, United States: Correspondence, 1930-1937. Wilmington, Del., 1981. Microfilm.

U.K. Parliament. Command Papers. Public Record Office, London. Microprint.

U.S. Department of State. Confidential Diplomatic Post Reports, Japan, 1930-1935. RG 43, Frederick, Md., 1982. Microfilm.

————. General Records. RG 59. Decimal Files. National Archives, Washington, D.C.

U.S. Department of the Navy. General Records of the Joint Army and Navy Board, 1903-1947. National Archives, Washington, D.C.

————. General Board Disarmament Conference Records, Series 5, 9 National Archives, Washington, D.C.

————. Office of Naval Intelligence Files, RG 39, Naval Attaché Reports, Tokyo, 1887-1939. National Archives, Washington, D.C.

————. General Records of the Navy General Board, 1926-1936. National Archives, Washington, D.C.

————. Secret and Confidential Correspondence between the Office of the Chief of Naval Operations and the Secretary of the Navy, 1919-1927. National Archives, Washington, D.C. Microfilm.

————. Secret and Confidential Correspondence of the Office of the Secretary of the Navy, 1927-1939. National Archives, Washington, D.C.

————. Ship Logs, 1943, U.S.S. *Salt Lake City*, U.S.S. *Pensacola*. Naval Historical Center, Washington Navy Yard, Washington, D.C.

Government and Organizational Documents

Congressional Record. 1922-1930. Washington, D.C.

Documents on British Foreign Policy, 1919-1939. Edited by W.L. Medlicott et al. Series 1a, 2. London, 1966-1984.

France. Ministère des affaires étrangères. *Limitation des armements navals: Trente-cinq pieces relative aux travaux préparatoires du désarmement et à la limitation des armements navals, 21 mars 1927-6 octobre 1928.* Paris, 1928.

League of Nations. Documents of the Preparatory Commission for the Disarmament Conference. Series 2.

————. *Records of the Conference for the Limitation of Naval Armament, Held at Geneva from June 20th to August 4th, 1927.* Geneva, 1927.

League of Nations Union. *Annual Report.* London, 1927-1930.

Papers Relating to the Foreign Relations of the United States, 1921-1936. Washington, D.C., 1936-54.

U.K. *Parliamentary Debates*, Commons. 5th series (1909-).
U.K. *Parliamentary Debates*, House of Lords. 5th series (1909-).
U.S. Congress. Senate. *Records of the Geneva Conference for the Limitation of Naval Armament*. 70th Cong., 1st sess., 1928. S. Doc. 55.
U.S. Congress. Senate. Committee on Foreign Relations. *Hearings on the Treaty on the Limitation of Naval Armaments*. 71st Cong., 2d sess., 1930.
U.S. Congress. Senate. Committee on Naval Affairs. *Alleged Activities at the Geneva Conference*. 71st Cong., 1st sess., 1930.
————. *Hearings before the Senate Committee on Naval Affairs on the London Naval Treaty of 1930*. 71st Cong., 2d sess., 1930.

Books

Adamthwaite, Anthony. *The Long Peace: International Relations in Europe, 1918-1939*. London, 1980.
Adler, Selig. *The Isolationist Impulse: Its Twentieth Century Reaction*. New York, 1957.
Allen, Frederick Lewis. *Only Yesterday: An Informal History of the 1920s*. New York, 1932.
Almond, Gabriel. *The American People and Foreign Policy*. New York, 1960.
Bacon, Sir Reginald H.S. *The Life of John Rushmore Earl Jellicoe*. London, 1936.
Ball, Stuart. *Baldwin and the Conservative Party: The Crisis of 1929-1931*. New Haven, Conn., 1988.
Bamba, Nobuya. *Japanese Diplomacy in a Dilemma: New Light on Japan's China Policy, 1924-1929*. Vancouver, B.C., 1972.
————, and John F. Howes. *Pacifism in Japan: The Christian and Socialist Tradition*. Kyoto, 1978.
Bariety, Jacques. *Les relations franco-allemandes après la première guerre mondiale*. Paris, 1976.
Beasley, W.G. *Japanese Imperialism, 1894-1945*. New York, 1987.
Birn, Donald S. *The League of Nations Union, 1918-1945*. New York, 1981.
Borg, Dorothy, and Shumpei Okamoto, eds. *Pearl Harbor as History: Japanese-American Relations, 1931-1941*. New York, 1973.
Braisted, William R. *The United States Navy in the Pacific, 1909-1922*. Austin, Tex., 1971.
Bridgeman, William. *The Modernisation of Conservative Politics: The Diaries and Letters of William Bridgeman, 1904-1935*. Edited by Philip Williamson. London, 1988.
Brune, Lester A. *The Origins of American National Security: Sea Power, Air Power, and Foreign Policy, 1900-1941*. Manhattan, Kans., 1981.
Bryn-Jones, David. *Frank B. Kellogg: A Biography*. New York, 1937.
Buckley, Thomas H. *The United States and the Washington Conference, 1921-1922*. Knoxville, Tenn., 1970.
————, and Edwin B. Strong, Jr. *American Foreign and National Security Policies, 1914-1945*. Knoxville, Tenn., 1987.

Burner, David. *Herbert Hoover: A Public Life.* New York, 1979.

Burns, Richard Dean. *Guide to American Foreign Relations since 1700. For the Society for Historians of American Foreign Relations.* Santa Barbara, Calif., 1983.

Butler, Nicholas Murray. *Across the Busy Years: Recollections and Reflections.* 2 vols. New York, 1940.

Bywater, Hector C. *Navies and Nations.* Boston and New York, 1927.

———. *Seapower in the Pacific: A Study of the American-Japanese Problem.* Boston and New York, 1921.

Carlton, David. *MacDonald versus Henderson: The Foreign Policy of the Second Labour Government.* London, 1970.

Case, Josephine Young, and Everett Needham Case. *Owen D. Young and American Enterprise.* Boston, 1982.

Ceadel, Martin. *Pacifism in Britain, 1914-1941: The Defining of a Faith.* New York, 1980.

Cecil, Robert, Viscount of Chelwood. *A Great Experiment: An Autobiography.* New York, 1941.

Chalmers, W.S. *The Life and Letters of David, Earl of Beatty.* London, 1951.

Chamberlain, Sir Austen. *Down the Years.* London, 1935.

Chaput, Rolland A. *Disarmament in British Foreign Policy.* London, 1935.

Chatfield, Charles. *For Peace and Justice: Pacifism in America, 1914-1941.* Knoxville, Tenn., 1971.

Churchill, Sir Winston S. *The Gathering Storm.* Boston, 1948.

Cohen, Bernard. *The Public's Impact on Foreign Policy.* Boston, 1973.

Cohen, Warren. *Chinese Connection: Roger S. Greene, Thomas W. Lamont, George E. Sokolsky and American-East Asian Relations.* New York, 1978.

Coletta, Paolo E., ed. *American Secretaries of the Navy,* vol. 2, *1913-1972.* Annapolis, Md., 1980.

Coolidge, Calvin. *The Autobiography of Calvin Coolidge.* New York, 1929.

Costigliola, Frank. *Awkward Dominion: American Political, Economic, and Cultural Relations with Europe, 1919-1933.* Ithaca, N.Y., 1984.

Craig, Gordon A., and Felix Gilbert, eds. *The Diplomats, 1919-1939.* Princeton, 1953.

Craig, Gordon A., and Alexander L. George. *Force and Statecraft: Diplomatic Problems of Our Time.* New York, 1983.

Crowley, James B. *Japan's Quest for Autonomy: National Security and Foreign Policy, 1930-1938.* Princeton, 1966.

Current, Richard N. *Secretary Stimson: A Study in Statecraft.* New Brunswick, N.J., 1954.

Curti, Merle E. *Peace or War: The American Struggle, 1636-1936.* New York, 1936.

Dallek, Robert. *The American Style of Foreign Policy: Cultural Politics and Foreign Affairs.* New York, 1983.

Danelski, David, and Joseph Tulchin, eds. *The Autobiographical Notes of Charles Evans Hughes.* Cambridge, 1973.

Davis, George T. *A Navy Second to None.* New York, 1940.

Dawes, Charles G. *Journal as Ambassador to Great Britain*. New York, 1939.
DeBenedetti, Charles. *Origins of the Modern American Peace Movement, 1915-1929*. Millwood, N.Y., 1978.
DeConde, Alexander, ed. *Isolation and Security*. Durham, N.C., 1957.
Detzer, Dorothy. *Appointment on the Hill*. New York, 1948.
Dictionary of American Naval Fighting Ships. Washington, D.C.: 1959-1981.
Dingman, Roger. *Power in the Pacific: The Origins of Naval Arms Limitation, 1914-1922*. Chicago, 1976.
Duus, Peter. *Party Rivalry and Political Change in Taisho Japan*. Cambridge, 1968.
Edge, Walter E. *A Jerseyman's Journal: Fifty Years of American Business and Politics*. Princeton, 1948.
Edwards, John Carver. *Patriots in Pinstripe: Men of the National Security League*. Lanham, Md., 1982.
Ellis, L. Ethan. *Frank B. Kellogg and American Foreign Relations, 1925-1929*. New Brunswick, N.J., 1961.
———. *Republican Foreign Policy, 1921-1933*. New Brunswick, N.J., 1968.
Engely, Giovanni. *The Politics of Naval Disarmament*. London, 1932.
Feis, Herbert. *The Diplomacy of the Dollar: First Era, 1919-1932*. Baltimore, 1950.
Ferrell, Robert H. *American Diplomacy in the Great Depression: Hoover-Stimson Foreign Policy, 1929-1933*. New Haven, Conn., 1957.
———. *Frank B. Kellogg and Henry L. Stimson*. Vol. 11 of *American Secretaries of State and Their Diplomacy*. New York, 1962.
———. *Peace in Their Time: The Origins of the Kellogg-Briand Pact*. New Haven, Conn., 1952.
———, and Howard H. Quint, eds. *The Talkative President: The Off-the-Record Press Conferences of Calvin Coolidge*. Amherst, Mass., 1964.
Ferris, John Robert. *The Evolution of British Strategic Policy, 1919-1926*. New York, 1989.
Friedman, Norman. *U.S. Cruisers: An Illustrated Design History*. Annapolis, 1984.
Fuess, Claude M. *Calvin Coolidge: The Man from Vermont*. Boston, 1940.
Gamson, William. *The Strategy of Social Protest*. 2d ed. Belmont, Calif., 1992.
Glad, Betty. *Charles Evans Hughes and the Illusions of Innocence: A Study in American Diplomacy*. Urbana, Ill., 1966.
Gluck, Carol, and Stephen R. Graubard, eds. *Showa: The Japan of Hirohito*. New York, 1992.
Grew, Joseph C. *Ten Years in Japan, 1932-1942*. New York, 1944.
———. *Turbulent Era*. 2 vols. Boston, 1952.
Hall, Christopher. *Britain, America, and Arms Control, 1921-37*. New York, 1987.
Heinrichs, Waldo H., Jr. *American Ambassador: Joseph C. Grew and the Development of the United States Diplomatic Tradition*. Boston, 1966.
Herman, Sondra. *Eleven against War: Studies in Amrican Internationalist Thought, 1898-1921*. Stanford, 1969.

Higham, Robin. *Armed Forces in Peacetime: Britain, 1918-1940, A Case Study.* London, 1962.

Hilderbrand, Robert C. *Power and the People: Executive Management of Public Opinion in Foreign Affairs, 1897-1921.* Chapel Hill, N.C., 1981.

Hoag, C. Leonard. *Preface to Preparedness: The Washington Disarmament Conference and Public Opinion.* Washington, D.C., 1941.

Hoff-Wilson, Joan. *American Business and Foreign Policy, 1920-1933.* Lexington, Ky., 1971.

———. *Herbert Hoover: Forgotten Progressive.* Boston, 1975.

Hooker, Nancy H., ed. *The Moffat Papers: Selections from the Diplomatic Journals of Jay Pierrepont Moffat, 1919-1943.* Cambridge, 1956.

Hoover, Herbert C. *The Memoirs of Herbert Hoover.* Vol. 2, *The Cabinet and the Presidency, 1920-1933.* New York, 1952.

———, and Hugh S. Gibson. *The Problems of Lasting Peace.* New York, 1942.

Howard, Esme. *Theatre of Life.* 2 vols. Boston, 1935-36.

Howland, Charles P. *Survey of American Foreign Relations: 1928.* New Haven, Conn., 1928.

Hughes, Barry. *The Domestic Context of American Foreign Policy.* San Francisco, 1979.

Hunt, Barry D. *Sailor-Scholar: Admiral Sir Herbert Richmond, 1871-1946.* Waterloo, Ont., 1982.

Iriye, Akira. *After Imperialism: The Search for a New Order in the Far East, 1921-1931.* New York, 1973.

Ishii, Kikujiro. *Diplomatic Commentaries.* Baltimore, 1936.

Jacobson, Jon. *Locarno Dipomacy: Germany and the West, 1925-1929.* Princeton, 1972.

Jane's Fighting Ships. 1924-36. London, 1939.

Jones, Thomas. *Whitehall Diary.* 2 vols. Edited by Keith Middlemas. London, 1969.

Jellicoe, Admiral Earl John. *The Grand Fleet, 1914-1916: Its Creation, Development, and Work.* New York, 1919.

Jentschura, Hansgeorg, et al. *Warships of the Imperial Japanese Navy.* London, 1977.

Jessup, Philip. *Elihu Root.* New York, 1938.

Johnson, Hiram. *The Diary Letters of Hiram Johnson, 1917-1945.* 7 vols. Edited by Robert E. Burke. New York, 1983.

Jordan, Nicole. *The Popular Front and Central Europe: The Dilemmas of French Impotence, 1918-1940.* New York, 1992.

Josephson, Harold. *James T. Shotwell and the Rise of Internationalism in America.* Cranbury, N.J., 1974.

Juergens, George I. *News from the White House: The Presidential Press Relationship in the Progressive Era.* Chicago, 1981.

Karsten, Peter. *The Naval Aristocracy: The Golden Age of Annapolis and the Emergence of Modern American Navalism.* New York, 1972.

Kasza, Gregory, T. *The State and the Mass Media in Japan, 1918-1945.* Berkeley, 1988.

Kennedy, Malcolm D. *The Estrangement of Great Britain and Japan: 1917-35.* Los Angeles, 1969.

Kenworthy, J.M. *Peace or War?* New York, 1927.

Knox, Dudley W. *The Eclipse of American Sea Power.* New York, 1922.

Latimer, Hugh. *Naval Disarmament.* London, 1930.

Leffler, Melvyn P. *The Elusive Quest: America's Pursuit of European Stability and French Security, 1919-1933.* Chapel Hill, N.C., 1979.

Leopold, Richard. *Elihu Root and the Conservative Tradition.* Boston, 1954.

Levering, Ralph. *The Public and American Foreign Policy, 1918-1978.* New York, 1978.

Love, Robert W., Jr., ed. *The Chiefs of Naval Operations.* Annapolis, Md., 1980.

Lowitt, Richard. *George W. Norris: The Persistance of a Progressive, 1913-1933.* Urbana, Ill., 1971.

Marquand, David. *Ramsay MacDonald.* London, 1977.

McCoy, Donald R. *Calvin Coolidge: The Quiet President.* New York, 1967.

McIntyre, W. David. *The Rise and Fall of the Singapore Naval Base, 1919-1942.* London, 1979.

McKercher, B.J.C. *The Second Baldwin Government and the United States, 1924-1929.* New York, 1984.

———, ed. *Arms Limitation and Disarmament: Restraints on War, 1899-1939.* New York, 1992.

Marks, Sally. *The Illusion of Peace: International Relations in Europe, 1918-1933.* New York, 1976.

Meyer, David S. *A Winter of Discontent: The Nuclear Freeze and American Politics.* New York, 1990.

Middlemas, Keith, and John Barnes. *Baldwin: A Biography.* London, 1969.

Miller, Edward S. *War Plan Orange: The U.S. Strategy to Defeat Japan, 1897-1945.* Annapolis, Md., 1991.

Morison, Elting E. *Turmoil and Tradition: A Study of the Life and Times of Henry L. Stimson.* Boston, 1960.

Morley, James W., ed. *Dilemmas of Growth in Prewar Japan.* Princeton, 1971.

———, ed. *Japan Erupts: The London Naval Conference and the Manchurian Incident, 1928-1932.* New York, 1984.

Neidpath, James. *The Singapore Naval Base and the Defence of Britain's Eastern Empire, 1919-1941.* London, 1981.

Neuman, R.W. *The Paradox of Mass Politics: Knowledge and Opinion in the American Electorate.* Cambridge, Mass., 1986.

Nicolson, Harold G. *Dwight Morrow.* New York, 1935.

Nish, Ian H. *Alliance in Decline: A Study in Anglo-Japanese Relations, 1908-1923.* London, 1972.

———. *Japanese Foreign Policy, 1869-1942: Kasumigaseki to Miyakezaka.* London, 1977.

———, ed. *Anglo-Japanese Alienation, 1919-1952: Papers of the Anglo-Japanese Conference on the History of the Second World War.* New York, 1982.

Noel-Baker, P.J. *Disarmament and the Coolidge Conference.* London, 1927.

O'Connor, Raymond G. *Perilous Equilibrium: The United States and the London Naval Conference of 1930.* Lawrence, Kans., 1962.

Ogata, Sadako N. *Defiance in Manchuria: The Making of Japanese Foreign Policy, 1931-1932.* Berkeley and Los Angeles, 1964.

Ostrower, Gary B. *Collective Insecurity: The United States and the League of Nations during the Early Thirties.* Cranbury, N.J., 1979.

Pelz, Stephen E. *Race to Pearl Harbor: The Failure of the Second London Naval Conference and the Onset of World War II.* Cambridge, 1974.

Pencak, William. *For God and Country: The American Legion, 1919-1941.* Boston, 1989.

Petrie, Sir Charles. *The Life and Letters of the Right Hon. Sir Austen Chamberlain.* 2 vols. London, 1940.

Pusey, Merlo J. *Charles Evans Hughes.* New York, 1952.

Rappaport, Armin. *The Navy League of the United States.* Detroit, 1962.

Reynolds, Clark G. *The Fast Carriers: The Forging of an Air Navy.* New York, 1968.

Richardson, Dick. *The Evolution of British Disarmament Policy in the 1920s.* New York, 1989.

Rose, Kenneth. *The Later Cecils.* London, 1975.

Rosenau, James N. *Public Opinion and Foreign Policy: An Operational Formulation.* New York, 1961.

Roskill, Stephen W. *Churchill and the Admirals.* London, 1977.

———. *Hankey, Man of Secrets.* Vol. 2, *1919-1931.* London, 1977.

———. *Naval Policy between the Wars.* Vol. 1, *The Period of Anglo-American Antagonism, 1919-1929.* London, 1968. Vol. 2, *The Period of Reluctant Rearmament, 1930-1939.* London, 1976.

Russett, Bruce. *Controlling the Sword.* Cambridge, Mass., 1990.

Schulzinger, Robert D. *The Making of the Diplomatic Mind: The Training, Outlook, and Style of United States Foreign Service Officers, 1908-1931.* Middletown, Conn., 1975.

———. *The Wise Men of Foreign Affairs: The History of the Council on Foreign Relations.* New York, 1984.

Schwartz, Jordan A. *The Speculator: Bernard M. Baruch in Washington, 1917-1965.* Chapel Hill, N.C., 1981.

Sherry, Michael S. *The Rise of American Air Power: The Creation of Armageddon.* New Haven, Conn., 1987.

Small, Melvin. *Johnson, Nixon, and the Doves.* New Brunswick, N.J., 1988.

Sprout, Harold, and Margaret Sprout. *Toward a New Order of Sea Power.* Princeton, 1943.

Stimson, Henry L., and McGeorge Bundy. *On Active Service in Peace and War.* New York, 1947.

Takeuchi, Tatsuji. *War and Diplomacy in the Japanese Empire.* Chicago, 1935.

Tarrow, Sidney. *Struggling to Reform: Social Movements and Change: Policy Change during Cycles of Protest.* Ithaca, N.Y., 1983.

Tate, Merze. *The United States and Armaments.* Cambridge, 1948.

Taylor, Sandra C. *Advocate of Understanding: Sidney Gulick and the Search for Peace with Japan.* Kent, Ohio, 1984.

Temperley, A.C. *The Whispering Gallery of Europe.* London, 1938.

Thorne, Christopher. *The Limits of Foreign Policy: The West, the League, and the Far Eastern Crisis of 1931-1933.* London, 1972.

Tilley, Sir John. *From London to Tokyo.* London, 1942.

Toynbee, Arnold J. *Survey of International Relations: 1927; 1928; 1929; 1930.* Under the auspices of the Royal Institute of International Affairs. London, 1929-1932.

Vaisse, Maurice. *Sécurité D'Abord: La politique française en matière de désarmement, 9 décembre 1930-17 avril 1934.* Paris, 1981.

Vansittart, Sir Robert. *The Mist Procession: The Autobiography of Lord Vansittart.* London, 1958.

Van Voris, Jacqueline. *Carrie Chapman Catt: A Public Life.* New York, 1987.

Villard, Oswald. *Prophets True and False.* New York, 1928.

Vinson, John Chalmers. *The Parchment Peace: The United States Senate and the Washington Conference, 1921-1922.* Athens, Ga., 1955.

Wandycz, Piotr S. *The Twilight of French Eastern Allinces, 1928-1936.* Princeton, 1988.

Weigley, Russell F. *The American Way of War: A History of United States Military Strategy and Policy.* Bloomington, Ind., 1973.

Werner, Morris Robert. *Privileged Characters.* New York, 1935.

Wheeler, Gerald E. *Admiral William Veazie Pratt, U.S. Navy: A Sailor's Life.* Annapolis, Md., 1974.

———. *Prelude to Pearl Harbor: The United States Navy and the Far East, 1921-1931.* Columbia, Mo., 1963.

Wheeler-Bennett, John W. *Disarmament and Security since Locarno, 1925-1931.* London, 1932.

White, William Allen. *A Puritan in Babylon.* New York, 1938.

Wildes, Harry Emerson. *Japan in Crisis.* New York, 1934.

Williams, Benjamin H. *The United States and Disarmament.* New York, 1931.

Williamson, Philip. *National Crisis and National Government: British Politics, the Economy, and the Empire, 1926-1932.* New York, 1992.

Wilson, Hugh R. *Diplomat between the Wars.* New York, 1941.

Wittkopf, Eugene R. *Faces of Internationalism: Public Opinion and American Foreign Policy.* Durham, N.C., 1990.

Wittner, Lawrence S. *Rebels against the Cause: The American Peace Movement, 1933-1983.* Philadelphia, 1984.

Young, Kenneth. *Stanley Baldwin.* London, 1976.

Articles

Andrade, Ernest, Jr. "The Cruiser Controversy in Naval Limitations Negotiations, 1922-1936." *Military Affairs* 48 (1984): 113-20.

———. "The United States Navy and the Washington Conference." *Historian* 31 (May 1969): 346-50.

Asada, Sadao. "The Japanese Navy and the United States." In *Pearl Harbor as History, Japanese-American Relations, 1931-1941*, edited by Dorothy Borg and Shumpei Okamoto, 225-60. New York, 1973.

———. "The Revolt against the Washington Treaty: The Imperial Japanese Navy and Naval Limitation, 1921-1927." *Naval War College Review* 46, no. 3 (Summer 1993): 82-97.

Baker, Arthur Davidson III. "Japanese Naval Construction, 1915-1945: An Introductory Essay." *Warship International* 24, no. 1 (1987): 45-68.

Berg, Meredith William. "Admiral William H. Standley and the Second London Naval Treaty, 1934-36." *Historian* 33, no. 2 (1971): 215-36.

Blatt, Joel. "The Parity that Meant Superiority: French Naval Policy toward Italy at the Washington Conference, 1921-22." *French Historical Studies* 16 (1981): 223-48.

Braeman, John. "Power and Diplomacy: The 1920s Reappraised." *Review of Politics* 44 (July 1982), 342-69.

Braisted, William R. "Charles Frederick Hughes, 14 November 1927-17 September 1930." In *The Chiefs of Naval Operations*, edited by Robert William Love, Jr., 49-66. Annapolis, Md., 1980.

——— "On the American Red and Red-Orange Plans, 1919-1939." In *Naval Warfare in the Twentieth Century, 1900-1945: Essays in Honor of Arthur J. Marder*, edited by Gerald Jordan, 175-99. New York, 1977.

Burns, Richard Dean. "International Arms Inspection Policies between World Wars, 1919-1934." *Historian* 31, no. 4 (1969): 583-603.

Bywater, Hector C. "The Treaty Cruiser—Is It Worthwhile?" *Scientific American* 135 (November 1926): 326-28.

Carlton, David. "The Anglo-French Compromise on Arms Limitation, 1928." *Journal of British Studies* 8 (1969): 141-62.

———. "Great Britain and the Coolidge Naval Disarmament Conference of 1927." *Political Science Quarterly* 82 (1968): 573-99.

Converse, Philip E. "The Nature of Belief Systems in Mass Publics." In *Ideology and Discontent*, edited by D.E. Apter, 206-61. New York, 1964.

Coolidge, Calvin, "Promoting Peace through Limitations of Armaments." *Ladies Home Journal* 48 (May 1929): 3-4, 93.

———. "Promoting Peace through Preparation of Defense." *Ladies Home Journal* 48 (April 1929): 3-4, 65.

———. "Promoting Peace through Renunciation of War." *Ladies Home Journal* 48 (June 1929): 60, 160-61.

DeBenedetti, Charles. "Alternative Strategies in the American Peace Movement in the 1920's." *American Studies* 13 (Spring 1972): 69-81.

———. "The American Peace Movement and the State Department in the Age of Locarno." In *Doves and Diplomats: Foreign Offices and Peace Movements in Europe and America in the Twentieth Century*, edited by Solomon Wank, 202-16. Westport, Conn., 1978.

Dulles, Allen W. "The Threat of Anglo-American Naval Rivalry." *Foreign Affairs* 7 (1928-29): 173-83.

Eisinger, Peter K. "The Conditions of Protest Behavior in American Cities," *American Political Science Review* 67 (1973): 11-28.

Epstein, Marc. "The Historians and the Geneva Naval Conference." In *Arms Limitation and Disarmament: Restraints on War, 1899-1939*, edited by B.J.C. McKercher, 129-48. New York, 1992.

Everett, A.G. "Navies, Taxes, and International Peace Insurance." *Journal of the American Bankers' Association* 23 (August 1930): 94-95, 142.

Fagan, George V. "Edward Price Bell: the Journalist as Diplomat." *Newberry Library Bulletin* 4 (November 1955): 24-27.

Fanning, Richard W. "The Coolidge Conference of 1927: Disarmament in Disarray." In *Arms Limitation and Disarmament: Restraints on War, 1899-1939*, edited by B.J.C. McKercher, 105-28. New York, 1992.

———. "Peace Groups and the Campaign for Naval Disarmament, 1927-1936." *Peace and Change* 15, no. 1 (January 1990): 26-45.

Ferguson, Thomas. "The Right Consensus: Holsti and Rosenau's New Foreign Policy Surveys." *International Studies Quarterly* 30 (1986): 411-23.

George, Alexander L. "Case Studies and Theory Development: The Method of Structured, Focused Comparison." In *Diplomacy: New Approaches in History, Theory, and Policy*, edited by Paul Gordon Lauren, 43-68. New York, 1979.

Heinrichs, Waldo H., Jr. "The Role of the U.S. Navy." In *Pearl Harbor as History, Japanese-American Relations, 1931-1941*, edited by Dorothy Borg and Shumpei Okamoto, 197-223. New York, 1973.

Heller, Roger K. "Curtis Dwight Wilbur, 19 March 1924-4 March 1929." In *American Secretaries of the Navy*, vol. 2, *1913-1972*, edited by Paolo E. Coletta, 605-630. Annapolis, 1980.

Holsti, Ole, and James N. Rosenau. "The Domestic and Foreign Policy Beliefs of American Leaders." *Journal of Conflict Resolution* 32, no. 2 (June 1988): 248-94.

Hone, Thomas C. "The Effectiveness of the 'Washington Treaty' Navy." *Naval War College Review* 32 (November-December 1979): 35-59.

———, and M. Mandeles. "Managerial Style in the Interwar Navy: A Reappraisal." *Naval War College Review* 33 (September-October 1980): 88-101.

Hosoya, Chichiro. "Britain and the United States in Japan's View of the International System, 1919-1937." In *Anglo-Japanese Alienation, 1919-1952: Papers of the Anglo-Japanese Conference on the History of the Second World War*, edited by Ian Nish. New York, 1982.

Houghton, Alanson B. "Disarmament and Depression." *Nation* 133 (December 23, 1931): 695.

Iriye, Akira. "Japan's Policies Toward the United States." In *Japan's Foreign Policy, 1868-1941: A Research Guide*, edited by James W. Morley, 407-59. New York, 1974.

Ishida, Takeshi. "Movements to Protect Constitutional Government—A Structural-Functional Analysis." In *Democracy in Prewar Japan: Groundwork or Facade?* edited by George O. Totten, 82-95. Boston, 1965.

Jaffe, Lorna S. "Abolishing War? Military Disarmament at the Paris Peace Conference, 1919." In *Arms Limitation and Disarmament: Restraints on War, 1899-1939*, edited by B.J.C. McKercher, 43-60. New York, 1992.

Josephson, Harold. "The Search for Lasting Peace: Internationalism and American Foreign Policy, 1920-1950." In *Peace Movements and Political Cultures*, edited by Charles Chatfield and Peter van den Dungen. Knoxville, Tenn., 1988.

Kitschelt, Herbert P. "Political Opportunity Structures and Political Protest: Anti-Nuclear Movements in Four Democracies." *British Journal of Political Science* 16 (January 1986): 57-85.

Kobayashi, Tatsuo. "The London Naval Treaty, 1930." In *Japan Erupts: The London Naval Conference and the Manchurian Incident, 1928-1932*, edited by James William Morley. New York, 1984.

Lacroix, Eric. "The Development of the 'A Class' Cruisers in the Japanese Imperial Navy." Parts 3, 4, and 7, *Warship International* 16, no. 3 (1979): 329-61; 18, no. 1 (1981): 40-76; 21, no. 3 (1984): 246-305.

Lamont, Thomas W. "What Will Europe Renewed Mean to the United States?" *Nations' Business* 125 (May 20, 1927): 17.

Lippmann, Walter. "The London Naval Conference: An American View." *Foreign Affairs* 8 (1930): 499-518.

———. "Public Opinion and the Renunciation of War." *Academy of Political Science Proceedings* 13 (January 1929): 243-47.

Lynch, Cecelia. "A Matter of Controversy: The Peace Movement and British Arms Policy." In *Arms Limitation and Disarmament: Restraints on War, 1899-1939*, edited by B.J.C. McKercher, 61-82. New York, 1992.

May, Ernest R. "The Development of Political-Military Consultation in the United States." *Political Science Quarterly* 70 (1955): 161-80.

Miller, Ransford S. State Department Division of Far Eastern Affairs, "The Japanese Situation." Lecture to Naval War College, January 16, 1931. Found in Stanley K. Hornbeck MSS.

Morton, Louis. "War Plan Orange: Evolution of a Strategy." *World Politics* 11 (1959): 221-50.

O'Connor, Raymond G. "The 'Yardstick' and Naval Disarmament in the 1920s." *Mississippi Valley Historical Review* 45 (1958-59): 441-63.

Ogata, Sadako. "The Role of Liberal Nongovernmental Organizations in Japan." In *Pearl Harbor as History, Japanese-American Relations, 1931-1941*, edited by Dorothy Borg and Shumpei Okamoto, 459-86. New York, 1973.

Page, Benjamin I., and Robert Y. Shapiro, "Effects of Public Opinion on Policy." *American Political Science Review* 77 (1983): 175-90.

Perkins, Dexter. "The Department of State and American Public Opinion." In *The Diplomats, 1919-1939*, edited by Gordon A. Craig and Felix Gilbert, 282-308. Princeton, N.J., 1953.

Purdy, Roger W. "Nationalism and News: 'Information Imperialism' and Japan, 1910-1936." *Journal of American-East Asian Relations* 1 (Fall 1992): 295-325.

Rainbolt, Rosemary. "Women, War, and Resistance to War: A Transnational Perspective." Paper presented at the annual meeting of the American Historical Association, December 1976.

Risse-Kappen, Thomas. "Public Opinion, Domestic Structure, and Foreign

Policy in Liberal Democracies." *World Politics* 43 (July 1991): 479-512.

Rosen, Philip T. "The Treaty Navy, 1919-1937." In *Peace and War: Interpretations of U.S. Naval History, 1775-1978,* edited by Kenneth J. Hagan, 221-36. Westport, Conn., 1978.

Shorrock, William. "France, Italy, and the Eastern Mediterranean in the 1920s." *International History Review* 8 (1986): 70-82.

Small, Melvin. "Public Opinion." In *Explaining the History of American Foreign Relations,* edited by Michael J. Hogan and Thomas G. Paterson. New York, 1991.

Symonds, Craig L. "William Veazie Pratt." In *The Chiefs of Naval Operations,* edited by Robert W. Love, Jr., 69-86. Annapolis, Md., 1980.

Takeuchi, Sterling Tatsuji. "Japan and the London Treaty." The Institute of Oriental Students, 4 (1930). University of Chicago.

Trigg, Ernest T. "Common Sense in National Defense." *Nation's Business* 18 (March 1930): 154-55.

"What the Naval Conference Means to Business." *Business Week* 20 (January 22, 1930): 5-6.

Wheeler, Gerald E. "Isolated Japan: Anglo-American Diplomatic Co-operation, 1924-36." *Pacific Historical Review* 30 (1961): 165-78.

Zimm, Alan D. "The U.S.N.'s Flight Deck Cruiser." *Warship International* 16, no. 3 (1979): 216-46.

Dissertations and Theses

Abbott, Frank. "The Foreign Policy Association." Ph.D. diss., Texas Tech University, 1972.

Andrade, Ernest, Jr. "United States Naval Policy in the Disarmament Era, 1921-1937." Ph.D. diss., Michigan State University, 1966.

Bowen, Adelphia Dane, Jr. "The Disarmament Movement, 1918-1935." Ph.D. diss., Columbia University, 1956.

Clemenson, Adolph Berle. "The Geneva Tripartite Conference of 1927 in Japanese-American Relations." Ph.D. diss., University of Arizona, 1975.

Fagan, George V. "Anglo-American Naval Relations, 1927-1937." Ph.D. diss., University of Pennsylvania, 1954.

Kitchens, Joseph H. Jr. "The Shearer Scandal and Its Origins: Big Navy Politics and Diplomacy in the 1920s." Ph.D. diss., University of Georgia, 1968.

Mannock, James H. "Anglo-American Relations, 1921-1928." Ph.D. diss., Princeton University, 1962.

Newton, Christina "Anglo-American Relations and Bureaucratic Rivalry, 1927-1930." Ph.D. diss., University of Illinois, 1975.

Pope, Robert Dean. "Senatorial Baron: The Long Political Career of Kenneth D. McKellar." Ph.D. diss., Yale University, 1976.

Swerczeck, Ronald E. "The Diplomatic Career of Hugh Gibson, 1908-1938." Ph.D. diss., University of Iowa, 1972.

Trimble, William F. "The United States Navy and the Geneva Conference for the Limitation of Naval Armament, 1927." Ph.D. diss., University of Colorado, 1974.

West, Michael Allen. "Laying the Foundation: The House Naval Affairs Committee and the Construction of the Treaty Navy, 1926-1934." Ph.D. diss., Ohio State University, 1980.

Newspapers and Periodicals

Headway: A Monthly Review of the League of Nations. League of Nations Union. London. 1925-1931.

Japan Times. Tokyo. 1922-1933

Literary Digest. New York. 1922-1934.

Nation. New York. 1926-1932.

New York Times. New York. 1921-1933.

Times. London. 1922-1934.

U.S. Naval Institute *Proceedings.* Annapolis, Md. 1918-1935.

INDEX